STARTING YOUR OWN BUSINESS

STARTING YOUR OWN BUSINESS: NO MONEY DOWN

M. JOHN STOREY

JOHN WILEY & SONS
New York / Chichester / Brisbane / Toronto / Singapore

Library of Congress Cataloging in Publication Data:

Storey, M. John.
    Starting your own business.

    Bibliography: p.
    1. New business enterprises.   I. Title.

HD62.5.S76   1987   658.1′141   87-2051
ISBN 0-471-85769-6
ISBN 0-471-63839-0 (paperback)

Printed in the United States of America

10   9   8   7   6   5   4

To Matthew J. Storey, for his continuing inspiration to communicate well, and to Helen Frances Storey, without whose energy and sense of optimism this and most other challenges would never have been undertaken.

Preface

One of the best things that ever happened to me was my growing up in suburban middle class New Jersey in the 1950s. In that post-World War II America, there was a sense that things could be done, possibilities existed, opportunities were just around the corner.

My mother was an athlete and optimist, who made the 1928 Olympic team as a high jumper only to be bumped when she got water on the knee. It didn't slow her down, which impressed me not a little when I first heard the story. My father, who was born poor, worked in a western Pennsylvania glass factory when he was 10, beat the odds by getting a scholarship to the University of Pennsylvania, and eventually a job with Western Electric. When the Depression came, he went from five days a week to two, but he was never fired. This impressed me, too.

We weren't at the top of the heap economically, but we were far from the bottom. I always looked forward to having a little "walking around money." Consequently, I became an entrepreneur at the age of eight, when I sold all my toys, and I've been one for more than 30 years. As a kid, I learned that selling Kool-Aid and lemonade was relatively easy on a hot August afternoon, and that the neighbors were delighted to have their lawns mowed, leaves raked and snow plowed as the different seasons rolled by. Later I found lots of ways to earn a better income—working at the Little League field, serving as batboy on the Chatham varsity baseball team and generally keeping my eyes open for money-making opportunities.

It wasn't until I became an official representative of the Packard Shirt Company, selling custom-tailored shirts to my friends at summer camp, that I realized I would need to have capital to expand my business. That was a shock—actually having to put out money in order to be able to carry on a business. But I learned then that there is always money available for a sound business proposition. It's still true.

Later, as I began a corporate career, my itch to be an entrepreneur inevitably led to moonlighting as a consultant and copywriter, my credentials being my reputation as a bright young trainee at the Time-Life organization. This activity led to various local exurban small-scale clients, all of them undercapitalized, and to another fundamental discovery: It's not a bad idea to ask for money up front— or at least for half of it. My early collection rate was not high; I was getting a fast early education in credit and collection.

Consulting assignments were okay, and I was feeling successful until Dick Jordan, one of my early mentors, said to me, "You're not creating a flywheel."

"What happens if you wake up in the morning and you feel terrible?" he asked. "Wouldn't it be better to have something that goes on day after day, whether you feel great or not?"

So I began to search for the flywheel. My first attempt in pursuit of it was called Venture Marketing. I had looked around for a low barrier-to-entry business and found that the one with just about the lowest is newsletter publishing. It's a place where anyone with a good idea and a few bucks can get going easily, so the less-than-well-known *Practical Gardener's Newsletter* came into being. That was in 1973. Operating from our kitchen table in Ridgefield, Connecticut, we attracted 1,000 subscribers at $12 apiece and discovered the ecstasy of $12,000 cash rolling in, to be matched only by the agony of $25,000 worth of suppliers' bills arriving shortly thereafter. But I did get a taste of what the flywheel could be like. I learned how favorable the margins are on paper and ink products, and I found that one entrepreneurial project leads inexorably to the next. In my case, the "next" was a wonderful eight-year relationship with what was at the time the most entrepreneurial company in mail-order America: Garden Way, Incorporated.

There I met one of the great entrepreneurs of the twentieth century, Lyman Wood, who had parlayed a $500 ad in *Organic Gardening Magazine* in 1966 into a $125 million enterprise a mere 15 years later. Wood was a true entrepreneur, a veritable direct marketing swashbuckler. His skills were mathematical and propositional, a "knock-em dead" combination in the mail-order game.

Money was almost never discussed in the Garden Way organization. I remember my first job review; I had carefully prepared for it, assembling all of the justification I could to prove why a substantial salary increase was in order. I met with Wood at his log cabin perched above Lake Champlain. We sat together, talking, and I could never quite work around to the question of money. Finally, as I left, I screwed up my courage and awkwardly said to him, "Lyman, would it be possible to get a salary increase for next year?" He looked at me in amazement and said, "Sure. How much do you want?" I was so floored that I asked for considerably less than I now know he was prepared to pay.

Wood surrounded himself with equally venturesome friends. There was Ed Robinson, for one, who created the "Have More Plan," a booklet published for G.I.s returning from World War II. It sold a half million copies and we keep it in print today. There were people like Cecil Hoge, a 70-year-old entrepreneur whose belief is that every failure leads to a success—and that the idea is simply to make more money on your successes than you lose on your failures.

I also noticed that these men rarely worried about where the money was going to come from—and were certainly never paralyzed by the problem. They each said it a bit differently, but the message that came through was: "There will always be more money out there than there are good ideas."

I am grateful to these entrepreneurs, and to the mail-order world that I have been a part of for the last 20 years, for showing me that there are very few obstacles that can't be overcome through effective problem solving—good thinking, good copy, good product, good offer, and dependable customer service. While we will talk about many different kinds of businesses in this guide to low-cost entrepreneurship, great fortunes are still being made in the world I know most intimately—direct marketing. I hope it continues.

M. JOHN STOREY

Pownal, Vermont
March 1987

Acknowledgments

I would like to acknowledge the support and skill of many other people who have made my 30-year journey as an entrepreneur, from my first tentative venture in the newsletter field to my present four-year-old Vermont-based publishing corporation—and now, this book. To Martha Storey, without whose partnership and support this venture could not have taken place; to my family, Jennifer, Jessica, and Matthew, the best pool of labor any entrepreneur could hope to have, who consistently have helped me to keep the overhead low and whatever spare cash we have all in the family. To my lawyer Don Dubendorf, whose legal counsel has been a continuing source of vitality and creativity. To the accountants, bankers, and friends, all of whom have helped. To Kate Stovel, for her research assistance; to Cyndi Garrison, Patti Loncto, and Jessica Storey for their help in manuscript preparation; and to Jim Knox, Rollie Stichweh, and Prescott Kelley, whose early willingness to serve as directors of this venture was priceless. All of these people have shown me that any obstacle is temporary, and that great success can frequently come from apparent failure.

M.J.S.

Acknowledgments

Contents

Contents

1

Why Now Is The Best Time To Start Your Own Business

What we are going to show you in this book is how to become the owner of your own business with virtually no investment of your own money, whether you start it or whether you buy it from someone. Impossible? Magical? It's neither. Read on.

Based on my experience and the experience of many entrepreneurial friends, this book will show you how you can begin to develop a profitable business with positive cash flow using the basic concept of leverage. It will yield money, compensation to you, and financial security to your family. Very simply, you're going to own your own business by using other people's money.

If you've ever borrowed money in order to buy a car, a boat, a house, you've already made the basic move. All you'll do is apply the same principle to buy something considerably larger than before. The boat, the car, or the house became collateral for your banker or lender; now you're going to buy a business and the business's assets are going to become the collateral for your banker or the seller.

This book will teach you a system and techniques that are far more dramatic than putting aside 10 percent of each paycheck in the (un-

1

realistic) hope of amassing the money necessary to buy a business. Business leverage operates dynamically, allowing you to use the existing assets, profit, and cash that's flowing through the business to pay the lender, over a period of time, whether it be banker or seller.

According to the latest figures from the U.S. Department of Commerce, there are approximately four million businesses defined as small, or "mid-market"—doing between $500,000 and $10 million a year. The Department estimates that nearly 200,000 of these businesses are sold every year. We know that somewhere between 600,000 and 700,000 small businesses are started each year, and a large number liquidated annually as well. The liquidation on these is based on anything from .10 to .50 cents on the dollar, primarily because the seller, or liquidator, doesn't know how to go about finding a buyer. These businesses represent opportunities for you as an entrepreneur, and we want to position you to be able to take advantage of them, to be prepared for the chances that present themselves.

This chance may come when you least expect it. In my case I was able to leverage a business investment of $2,500 into a line of credit of nearly $1 million in just a few years. You can, too! There has never been a better time to buy a business—and dozens of bankers and venture capitalists out there agree. It will get you ahead of the game, improve your business situation, better your salary, perks, and net worth.

So why not get going? I'll not only show you how to acquire or start your business, but how to get additional people, suppliers, customers, even employees, to participate in this process with you. You'll also learn some basic tax strategies and get some operating tips that may come in handy in your new entrepreneurial situation. I'll show you how to determine whether you're cut out for the business of entrepreneurship, how to take stock of your assets and your liabilities, and, with the help of a lawyer and an accountant, how to identify and create or locate the business you want. How to finance it. How to make the first important decisions administratively and operationally. How to get tremendous value from low-cost marketing programs. How to reduce costs dramatically within your business. And finally, how to meet the risks and savor the rewards that are awaiting you. As you read this book, you'll learn negotiation, finance, and how to structure your deal. You'll see how your value and your net worth can grow, and you'll learn how to project the lessons in the book into a solid, meaningful, long-term business.

DON'T UNDERESTIMATE YOUR POTENTIAL

I was able to leverage a personal investment of just $2,500 into a business that is now doing $4 million a year. But there is nothing particularly special about me. I'm part of a growing group of entrepreneurs intent on breaking the myth that it is impossible to succeed in your own small business. I left the security of corporate life some four years ago, against the advice of many; and the fact that our fledgling business is still operating would suggest that the initial judgment, at least, was accurate. The jury is certainly still out on long-term moneymaking, but I *was* able to leave a corporate situation that was giving me less daily inspiration than I wanted, and to discover the exhilaration of being on my own. It would not have happened without considerable financial leveraging.

WHAT DO WE MEAN BY LEVERAGING?

The word comes from the lever, one of the first tools that man discovered, thousands of years ago. With it, he found that he could move enormously heavier weights than he could hope to by using just his muscles.

In the business world, it's the same: You can lift considerably more weight off the ground with a lever than you can by scrimping and saving from your personal earnings. The kind of capital required for your business venture could take a lifetime to save putting 5 percent of every paycheck into a savings account.

On the other hand, if you can convince others that you have the character, contacts, background, experience, and skill to make your new business work, and that you can create cash flow, you'll find that you can use that background and ability to leverage loans of $25,000, then $50,000, $250,000, and even $1 million or more in a short period of time.

And you can do it "with no money down." I mean it.

Well, almost. You had to buy this book, and that meant shelling out a little bit of money (and a royalty for me).

But, do we really mean *no money down*? I am in the process of launching a new corporation, and it is going to cost me $500 in legal and accounting fees. Author T. Nicholas Peterson, of Delaware, sells a book (*How To Form Your Own Corporation Without A Lawyer For Under $50,* New York, Enterprise Publishing) that has been enormously popular, showing how to incorporate yourself for under $50. So if you are adventurous, and have only $50, shun the standard $500 start-up in favor of a $50 investment and try it yourself.

YOU HAVE MORE ASSETS THAN YOU KNOW

You have many assets that will be more valuable than cash. The trick is to understand and leverage those assets into borrowing capacity that will start that flywheel turning. Once momentum develops, the small business train will be under way. So, think constantly about leveraging those personal experiences, contacts, initiative, ideas, creativity, abilities, and modest assets. Convince others, be they bankers, investors, venture capitalists, in-laws, or former employers that if they don't get on board with you they are missing a million dollar sure thing!

What about your unique skills? Linda Wells of New York, a writer, started free-lancing 15 years ago because she was so broke "I didn't know where my next typewriter ribbon was coming from." Now she has 3 word processors and over 100 copytest winners. She earns conservatively, well, as much as she wants to earn.

Less obvious assets might be things such as experience, contacts (use your Rolodex as a daily action device), your ideas, and your persuasiveness.

Look at yourself. Do you have a strong sense of drive? Do you get satisfaction from doing things yourself? Would you rather take equity than a certain amount of compensation per hour? Are you able to recognize and take risks? Do you enjoy working on your own? Are you action oriented?

Certainly age has little to do with it. People like Lyman Wood and Cecil Hoge, both in their late-70s, wake up every day thinking about what new business they can start.

What assets do typical entrepreneurs have? Personal savings? Doug Flynn, of Flynn Direct Response, Inc., Trumbull, Connecticut, took $56,250 of long-time savings, plus a bank credit line of $125,000, and after one year, employed 5 salespeople, a support staff of 10, and generated annual sales of almost $5 million.

Equity? Consider taking the equity that you've developed in your employer's corporation in the form of pension, profit sharing, or stock, and translating that into a new equity position in a new company. There may even be a tax-advantageous way to do that. I sold Venture Marketing to Garden Way Inc., acquired stock over a five-year period, and rolled all of that accumulated equity into 100 percent ownership of Storey Communications.

Victor Kiam, in his recent book, *Going For It*, talks about how he came up with $750,000 and became the owner of a $25 million enterprise. In the pages ahead, we'll go into all of the detail about how you, too, can take a modest amount of assets and leverage, leverage, leverage, far beyond what you now think is possible.

Your trick, as an entrepreneur, is to gamble your time, not your money. My own leveragable assets, for instance, include 20 years of corporate publishing and direct marketing experience, an entrepreneurial past, good solid references, the building of modest equity in a previous corporation, good contacts, a high energy level, and an industrious family.

Everybody in my family has been on the payroll of Storey Communications at one time or another. Martha, who had previous design and production experience, became the production manager, and now three years later handles all operations for the company. Jennifer, age 20, started with clerical chores and most recently sold advertising space for the *Gardeners' Marketplace*. Jessica, age 17, is perhaps the best word processor that we have, operating at odd hours from a home terminal tied in by modem with our CPU. Matthew, age 13, is learning about picking, packing, shipping, and other warehousing chores. This arrangement, of course, puts money in their pockets, and keeps it "all in the family." The cost of hiring that kind of talent would have easily been $50,000 a year. So the family becomes an asset.

I have also had a 20-year period of learning from experience with winners and losers, both in the divisions I have operated and in the small businesses I have started. I learned the importance of "the package." A book published as *The Squash Cookbook* went nowhere; renamed *The Zucchini Cookbook* it has sold over 400,000 copies. In 1967, the belief at Time-Life was that the maximum amount of money people would spend for a mail-order sale was $50 to $100. But Lyman Wood sold a Troy-Bilt Rototiller for $1,500 and a Sun Room Solar Greenhouse for $15,000, with 20 percent down payments.

Additional valuable experience came from actually negotiating an "insider buyout" of Garden Way Publishing from Garden Way Inc. Potential backers were not unimpressed with my ability to make that happen.

From all of this, I learned two basic rules that have helped me in my money-raising efforts:

On the revenue side, nothing happens until you sell something.

On the cost side, don't buy anything until someone is screaming for it.

SOME OTHERS WHO HAVE DONE IT

I am certainly not the only one trying it with "no money down." John Fabian, president of Fabian and Behm, a San Francisco advertising agency, left his management supervisor's job with Ogilvy and Mather Direct and started his own direct response advertising agency in March 1985 with zero capitalization. Within 6 weeks he had four clients and monthly billings of over $20,000. Now, three years later, he is grossing over $1 million.

Dave Schaefer, of Burlington, Vermont, started in the public relations and television production business in 1984 with no money down. His first TV production won an award, and is now being distributed to 100 overseas outlets in videocassettes by the U.S. Information Agency.

Then there's Morris Dees, of Birmingham, Alabama, who started with seed capital of less than $500 and an original idea of selling birthday cakes to the parents of college students who were away from family and friends on their birthdays. He did this so well that Fuller and Dees, now a full-range direct marketing company, later grew to $100 million a year in annual revenues.

Take the experience of Harold and Lu Ester Mertz, who started with an unusual way of selling magazines from their basement, later becoming the world's largest mail-order subscription service for magazines, Publisher's Clearing House on Long Island, now doing well over $100 million a year.

Or, Michael Lerner, who, at age 32, thought that a humorous little "Baby on Board" sign for the back window of automobiles might be a hit with all of those new parents, and quickly developed more than $2 million in sales.

More and more niches need filling. Nancy Franks, who went searching for a natural baby food and couldn't find one, took a $10,000 personal loan, lined up a whopping $650,000 privately for product development, market research, and promotion, and then built a business that expects to ship 800,000 cases of Baby's Garden baby food in 1985 for $6.3 million in revenues—all in just five years.[1]

New Yorker Sally Reich started her own executive recruiting firm with no seed money, from the dining room of her apartment, using her home phone, an old portable electric typewriter, and just relying on friends to get going. This was in 1982. Today, Sally has offices in Chicago and Los Angeles, four full-time consultants, a full-time secretary, and her firm is housed in a beautiful brownstone in Manhattan with clients across the country. Why? She filled a niche with talent and service.

THE ADVANTAGES OF ENTREPRENEURSHIP

Why are so many Americans turning to entrepreneurship and small business? Why are they leaving the corporations in droves?

The statistics would suggest it is primarily because of a new desire for self-sufficiency in the 1980s. A study by Laventhol and Horwath in *USA Today* (February 10, 1986) shows that 86 percent of small business owners cite "personal independence" as the chief attraction.[2]

Over the years, corporations have evolved into highly mechanized and efficient, but frequently dull, uninspiring places to be. As a result, corporation employment is shrinking. Virtually all new jobs cre-

---

[1]Sid Kane, "Natural baby food," *Venture*, August 1985, p. 9.

[2]Laventhol and Horwath, "Special focus on small business" *USA Today*, February 10, 1986.

ated in the United States during the past decade came from small businesses, those with fewer than 100 employees. For the first time in U.S. history, more than half of the nation's workers are on the payroll of businesses with fewer than 100 employees, according to the U.S. Bureau of Labor Statistics.[3]

David Birch, who has become a leading expert on small business growth within America at the Massachusetts Institute of Technology (MIT) has shown that the labor forces of the nation's 500 largest companies dropped by 2.2 million people between 1980 and 1985.

Small business, entrepreneurship, by its very nature, is innovative. It can move considerably more quickly than the large corporation ever can. Hence, small business reacts more quickly to information, events, problems and failures. The small business owner who walks through his or her plant every day is likely to notice something that might go unnoticed in a larger corporation, literally for years. The 669,000 new business incorporations in America in 1985, up 26 percent from 530,000 in 1980, show that more than a few people believe that the odds aren't too discouraging for starting their own business. That, of course, is the thesis of this book. And my fundamental business belief.

Look at the evidence:

The economy is ripe for small business. In 1985, the White House Conference on Small Business recognized that the role of small business in the U.S. economy in the last 10 years has been greater than ever before. And the Small Business Administration (SBA) won't be eliminated.

Inflation rates have been low. They may not be for long, they certainly won't be forever, but when the major car companies announce 0 to 3 percent financing, you know that you are looking at unusually low and stable interest rates.

There has been a strong and steady growth in consumer spending.

Many people live in two-income households, and have more disposable income and a higher net worth than ever before. Use a portion of this to get going.

There are more opportunities to buy pieces of corporations than

[3]"The shift to smaller employers," *Wall Street Journal*, July 23, 1986, p. 23.

ever before, as strategic planning has led to corporate divestiture of problem divisions.

There's a rising number of jobs in small business, and dramatic growth in the service and high-tech areas.

More and more people are working at home. The 1980 census shows 2 million, according to the Bureau of Labor Statistics, but AT&T statistics, which should be even more reliable, show a figure of 10 to 12 million. The atmosphere has never been better for working at home.

There is a favorable tax situation and legitimate writeoffs. And even with the changes in income tax regulations, small business should continue to benefit.

WHAT IS THE RISK OF FAILING?

As I look at my own situation, I know we still have a very long way to go; but according to annual figures from Dun & Bradstreet (D&B) about business failures, I have already passed a critical point. Interestingly, from the first year to the second to the third, the odds of failure go up; then they begin to go down. So in the fourth through the tenth year, the odds slide over more to your favor.

Every year, D&B tracks business failures and publishes the grimy statistics in their annual *Business Failure Record*. You can learn from it, for instance, fascinating facts such as your chances of failure are much higher in the mountain states than they are in New England, or that failure in infants' and children's wear is eight times that of the drugstore or department store business.

The D&B statistics will also tell you that the larger the amount of liabilities you have, the greater your chance of failure. For instance, those who have under $5,000 in liabilities failed at a 3.4 percent rate; $5,000 to $25,000 at a 13.3 percent rate; $25,000 to $100,000 at a 33 percent rate; and $100,000 to $1 million at a 44.2 percent rate.

Gordon Baty, author of *Entrepreneurship: Playing to Win* (1974) is not impressed with failure rates, pointing out that your odds improve dramatically when you do your business homework. In his book, he shows that those companies that have developed full-blown business plans, and gotten financing off the ground, move onto a different plane where very few actually fail completely—that is, go out of business with a loss to creditors. The average in this category is not 80 percent, but less than 1 percent.

He acknowledges that business closures are much more typical: one-third within the first year, half within two years, and two-thirds within four years. But the important point he makes is that rates can be dramatically reduced through careful planning and early management. Professor Edward Robert, of MIT, further points out that only 20 percent of MIT spin-offs ever fail completely. This is still a reasonably high failure rate but nothing like the 80 percent that you might conclude by reading the D&B figures.[4]

I read Dale Carnegie's classic *How To Win Friends and Influence People* a long time ago and he talked about fear. The one idea I remember from that book is Carnegie saying, "When you're up against fear, ask yourself 'What's the worst thing that could happen to me?'" I have asked myself that simple nine-word question many times in the last several years. It's amazing, but it will allow you to overcome paralysis, and deal logically and realistically with your situation. What's the worst thing that could happen to you? Will you die? Will you lose all of your assets? Your house? Your car? Unlikely. Might you have to start over again? Possibly, but that's not the worst thing in the world. Are you employable? Quite probably.

And on the flip side, what if, just what if, you turn out to be successful? There's certainly a lot in your background and experience to suggest success as the more likely result. You've been successful before. Are things suddenly going to change now? What might happen if this success transfers to your independent business? Your life will be changed—for the better.

HELP WHEN YOU NEED IT

Don't think you are wandering into this alone. There is plenty of help out there. The SBA, whose demise, like that of Mark Twain, was greatly exaggerated, will be very much back in business again, and it can help you. The banks want to help you. Your family and friends will certainly want to help you. Your old employer(s) might be help-

[4]Gordon Baty, *Entrepreneurship: Playing to Win*. (Reston, Virginia: Reston, 1974), pp. 9–10.

ful. You'll even find a handful of people from your previous corporate life who will want to help you. You'll find that Uncle Sam has some lovely tax advantages for you. You'll also discover that you have inner resources that you don't know about until you push yourself beyond some of your traditional limits. Just like the Outward Bound program, which forces you to take on more, push harder, and ultimately discover more about yourself, entrepreneurship will bring all of your senses to life. So ask yourself, "Do I have what it takes? Am I excited about finding out?" And just because you don't have lots of money, don't be discouraged.

The list of those who successfully took that first small step of faith ranges from Sears and Roebuck, who launched the first catalog operation in the late nineteenth century, to L. L. Bean, who discovered that a pair of rubber boots could build a business worth $300 million. Where will the next "California Cooler" or "Baby on Board" idea come from? Maybe from you!

GO WITH IT!

I'm certain you have dreamed of quitting the rat race, of working for yourself, of ending the twice-daily commute, of living where you choose. Join the club. A recent survey of corporate middle managers suggested that as many as 80 percent are unhappy with their jobs.

So how do you go about putting together the plans, the early preparedness, and most important, the capital to succeed? That's what this book is all about. I would hope that by reading it, you will become one of the more than 600,000 new entrepreneurs in the United States who will take the leap into their own business next year. More important, this book is aimed at helping you go on with confidence to succeed at what you're sure you can do, by showing you how to avoid undercapitalization and by reaching into many pockets of opportunity.

So before corporate ossification sets in, make a pledge to yourself. Pledge that you'll do something about it now! The signs, the times, have never been better. Whether you're thinking about moonlighting on the side (a great idea!) or starting a new business on your own, now is a great time for action. The odds are increasingly in your favor, so act!

2

Your Personal
Balance Sheet:
What Are Your Assets?
Your Liabilities?

So the idea of starting your own business appeals to you? Terrific! There is excitement in the prospect. Your entrepreneurial gleam might turn out to be a sensation—anything from an Apple Computer to a Xerox Corporation—both of which started as good ideas in search of money. Remember that every Fortune 500 corporation, every "big board" company that you take for granted today had to start as a small idea in the back of some zealot's head . . . *Time* and *Life* magazines in the back of Henry Luce's head, Genentech Corp. in the back of gene-splicer Herbert Boyer's head, Sears and Roebuck as a catalog idea in the back of Richard W. Sears' head. Just because they are mammoth and highly established companies doesn't mean that they weren't small potatoes at some point.

While it is okay to dream of making *Inc.* magazine's 100 Fastest Growing Companies list, *now* is the time to be sure, to take off the rose-colored glasses, to stop being a Polyanna. It's the moment to make a very serious assessment of whether entrepreneurship is for you, and you for it.

In this chapter we will talk about the central personal and business decisions that you are facing; but, perhaps most importantly, also about your personal characteristics and qualities, so as to create your own personal asset and liability sheet that will reveal your entrepreneurial net worth before you become the owner of your own business.

Of equal importance, we will try to lay the groundwork and ask the questions which will enable you successfully to find, and secure, the financing that you will need to launch your venture.

For many, finding money becomes *the* insuperable hurdle, *the* psychological wall, the impossible request to make. I mean, just try asking out loud, right now, "May I have $500,000?" Does it sound ridiculous? Improbable? Unconvincing?

At the time of our insider buyout of the Garden Way Publishing Company from Garden Way Inc., I remember Carl Grimm, a 75-year-old member of the Garden Way board of directors looking at me squarely and asking very soberly, "Got your financing lined up?" I didn't, but I got under way very quickly, getting business plans into the hands of 5 bankers within 10 days, and receiving commitments from 4 of the 5 within 3 weeks. I'll always thank Carl for sticking the initial needle in my rear end.

More than anything else, he forced me from theory to action, from corporate executive to aggressive small business hustler, and did I ever look at myself carefully! Self-assessment is not easy, and you are better served if you have a very close friend, honest partner, or frank spouse, who will be willing to critique you in a constructive fashion. Face it, we all see in ourselves what we like to see, concentrating on the positive and ignoring many of the things that aren't so pretty. Our friends, partners, and mates provide an advantage in being willing to take those blinders off.

GOAL DEVELOPMENT

Begin by taking a crack at it yourself. What are your goals? Are they financial? Do you have a certain amount of money? One of my friends has a lifetime goal of amassing $1 million in assets and retiring at the age of 50. Entrepreneurship may be the worst way for him to do it. In my best year in corporate life, I earned nearly $300,000. When I put my business plan together, I hoped that the business could pay me about one-third of that. I was wrong! It turned out that I could comfortably take out only one-sixth of that best year's compensation. So, ask yourself, soberly, if the goal of making a lot of money is your objective, will you be able realistically to achieve that in the first few years of a startup business situation? Some have, but most are building future equity value rather than maximizing current income.

Cecil Hoge will tell you that the less money you can pull out of your new corporation in the first few years for yourself personally, the better for everyone. The banker will be impressed, and the employees will feel a sense of fair play. The point of entrepreneurship is to build equity, to build true asset value in your corporation. To do this, you must be willing to scrimp, to defer expenses, to reduce personal costs to a point where the asset value of your new entity can begin to grow at a rate that will attract outside bankers, investors, and supporters and assure long-term stability. Obviously, the more you pull out of your venture, the harder it will be for real asset value to develop.

Perhaps your goals are different. Do you want to be personally independent? And is that independence *for* yourself, or *from* your previous boss and your previous corporate world? If it is the latter, be prepared to meet your new bosses in the form of investors, joint venture partners, suppliers, and bankers. Don't fool yourself into thinking for a minute that by cutting the strings with your previous corporation you will never have anyone to report to again. That's a dangerous fallacy.

Perhaps your goal is to create a different lifestyle for yourself. This is reasonable. You may have become entirely exhausted from 15 years of commuting 3 hours a day into midtown Manhattan, or battling the freeway traffic in Southern California. Perhaps you have established a part-time or summer location in exurban New England, where life is simpler and costs are lower. It may be reasonable to think that this part-time situation can become full-time; but be realistic, and put a dollar value on both your earnings potential and the reduced cost of your new lifestyle. Frank Kirkpatrick, a Madison Avenue graduate who left Young and Rubicam for a general store in

Peru, Vermont (pop. 311), suggests some humorous realities in the chart titled "How Long Have You Been in the Country?". Don't be too hard on yourself, however. If your goal is financial improvement, for example, you may find that less actually can be more. Sounds like you're going in the wrong direction? How can less be more? you ask. Well, if your income is lower, your taxes are certainly going to go down; and if you have intelligently created a new corporation for yourself, you will find many new advantages that were not previously available to you. These might include your entire family being on your payroll, travel that is supported by the business, and your own company car. All of these may have been impossible in your old corporate situation.

Remember, also, as you pursue greater independence, that you may find a flip side, called loneliness. Believe me, there are days when the phone doesn't ring and the mail is light. Are you prepared for

---

How Long Have You Been in the Country?
(Look at strangers, and you can tell by these signs)

The Signs	Just Arrived	1-2 Years	5 or more years
Shoes	$200 hiking boots	L. L. Bean boots	Workshoes
Trousers	Designer jeans	Jeans (worn)	Surplus pants
Winter coat	Fur-trimmed parka	Ski jacket	Hunting coat
Hat	Irish fishing hat	Ski cap	Flourescent hunting cap
Car	New station wagon	4-wheel drive pickup	1972 Chevy
Favorite sport (summer and fall)	Tennis	Jogging	Deer-hunting
Favorite sport (winter)	Downhill skiing	Cross-country skiing	Snowmobiling
Serves when entertaining	Smoked salmon, white wine	Homemade bread, home-raised vegetables, home-pressed wine	Six-pack
Favorite topic of conversation	Beauty of country	Improvements needed	Neighbors (not there)
Favorite political cause	Stricter zoning	Improving roads	Cutting taxes
Summer activity	Entertaining friends from city	Vegetable gardening	Sitting
Livestock	Two Lab. Retrievers	Two goats	14 cats
Landscaping at home	Evergreens	Edible plants	Tire with pansies
Person you'd like to be like	Thomas Jefferson	Robert Rodale	Your plumber
Financial Aim	$1 million by age 50	Enough to Retire by 65	This month's mortgage payment

this? Can you do without the enjoyable conversation with colleagues in your current corporate hallways? Lunch at the University Club? Sales meetings, with golf and tennis tourneys, at Marco Island?

Your desired lifestyle may become the most important question. If you have sat back and said you can easily do without many of the aspects of your corporate life, and you are completely committed to improving the quality of your life, your leisure time, your family relationships, you can achieve this through entrepreneurship. Convert your three hours of commuting to 10 minutes each way, bid farewell to the thousands of dollars worth of suits, shirts and shoes that you needed in the city, eat at home more often and out less, use two cars instead of three, spend time working with each member of your family rather than sitting in front of the TV—in short, welcome the simpler lifestyle.

However, you must ask yourself realistically, and now, if you can make these adjustments. What are you really like? It is far easier to change your financial situation than to change your personality type. Will you be able to live this way? What are your peculiar assets and your peculiar liabilities?

In my own case, I knew that my assets did not include large cash accounts. On the other hand, I had always been strong on ideas, contagious concepts, enthusiasm, and energy. I had also worked hard to develop and maintain friendships within the industries in which I operated—contacts. My answers lay in putting my idea-generating ability, publishing background, direct marketing experience, and contacts together with my money, liabilities, or absence of either. Once that was simple and clear in my head, I went about doing it, and making it happen.

In short, the trick is to match up your weaknesses with other people's strengths to create formidable teamwork. Ever notice how some teams, clearly outgunned on a one-to-one basis can run a no-star zone defense and shut out their opponents? It's the same here. Ask yourself how versatile you really are. Are you a triple threat—marketing, finance, production? Will you be able to handle everything that goes along with owning your own business?

In its most recent assessment of business failures, D&B indicated that in nearly 25 percent of all cases, failure came from "unbalanced experience." This means that the owners experience was not well rounded in sales, finance, purchasing, and production in proprietorships, or in the case of two or more partners or officers constituting a management unit. Is it possible that you might sell brilliantly, but be a disaster at financial management? Make sure you answer these questions in advance, and support yourself in areas of acknowledged liability.

A tremendous number of studies have been done on entrepreneurial characteristics. The Stanford University Graduate School of Business spends time each summer focusing on this. One of the outstanding, and now famous, lecturers within Stanford's School of Management is Tom Peters, who, with Robert H. Waterman, wrote a book which he thought would sell about 300 copies ("to all my relatives"). It has now sold millions, and its title is familiar worldwide: *In Search of Excellence: Lessons From America's Best Run Companies* (New York, Harper and Row, 1982). Following is Peters' asset chart, containing his eight attributes of excellence, which suggests how to be an effective business person, whether entrepreneur on your own or entrepreneur within a corporation.

1. A bias for action
2. A closeness to the customer
3. Autonomy and entrepreneurship—latitude and flexibility
4. A belief in productivity through people
5. A hands-on, value driven operation
6. A tendency to stick to the knitting—don't overdiversify
7. A simple form and a lean staff
8. Simultaneous loose—tight properties, which inspire the average employee to give his or her best, will create the informal, innovative, entrepreneur of the 1980s.[1]

Warren Avis, who built Avis Corp. into an empire, puts it differently: "The entrepreneur loves business first, has a one-track mind, has great stamina, good judgment about people, and high energy levels, nurtured by periods of relaxation."[2] These assets are important

[1]Tom Peters' keynote presentation at *The Challenge of Growth: The Fourth Annual Conference on Entrepreneurship*, May 18, 1985, Stanford Center for Entrepreneurship, Stanford California.
[2]Tim Metz, "The Betty Crocker of the venture capital set," *Wall Street Journal*, June 23, 1986, p. 19.

to try to identify within oneself. Are they there? How can you find them if they're not?

Stanford's 1985 Conference on Entrepreneurship concluded that a "dedication to excellence and performance" is central to entrepreneurial success. This is probably obvious. Not so obvious were additional entrepreneurial characteristics identified: "frequently ego-driven, impatient, reluctant to delegate, very high energy-level, thrives on stress, works and plays hard, unusually demanding of subordinates, has a sense of the core of a problem, often has a mentor, and often had an uncomfortable or not particularly well adjusted childhood orr homelife."

In fact, no group, not even Stanford, will ever completely catalog what makes for successful entrepreneurs. One might just as easily ask what makes for successful book titles. A few, out of the 50,000 published each year, become best sellers.

But pull out a sheet of paper and ask yourself the following questions, and try to be as specific as you can be in answering them:

1. What functions (not titles) have you been doing for the past 5, 10, 20 years?
2. What's the relevance of these skills to your new business idea?
3. Are you active, a doer, an initiator, or more of an administrator?
4. Are you able to deal with adversity? Fail, and start over?
5. What are your hobbies, your passions? (Dick Denholtz, a former company colleague, turned his passion for rare coin collecting into a numismatic business that has taken off like a rocket).
6. Are you direct?
7. Are you aggressive?
8. Can you be flexible in the face of unforeseen circumstances? Do you roll with the punches?
9. Are you analytical? Are you able to get to the root of a problem? Then solve it?
10. Are you a salesperson? Have you *ever* sold *anything* before? Are you willing to go door-to-door to try? (Ariane Daguin and George Faison believed so firmly in their *fois gras* and im-

ported New Zealand venison, that they put $15,000 into a cart full of products which they rolled door-to-door to get their first accounts in 1984. Now, they have above $500,000 in sales![3]

11. Are you willing to sacrifice personally for the sake of your new firm? Almost certainly, there will be a week when you will not be able to meet the payroll. This is not the worst thing in the world, it just means that you may have to grit your teeth and pull $5,000 from an already modest bank account in order to cover it and get back into business on Monday.

12. Are you creative? An idea person? Can you spot niches? Norman W. Edmund did, way back in 1942, when, as an amateur photographer, he needed a special lens which stores didn't carry. He had to buy a whole set from the manufacturer in order to get the one he needed. He launched the *Edmund Scientific Catalog*, which now, 45 years later, is a major corporation.

13. Are you willing to do any task that comes along? You'd better. The advantage is that you'll learn more about your own business. But, can you get beyond the ego and mental block of always having had someone else to do it for you? Tom Davidson, president of Cambridge Tile Manufacturing in Cincinnati, put it this way: "At Procter & Gamble, you have a myriad of resources that you can call on for everything from a new ad to a sales letter. At a small company you don't have that. You are doing a lot more of the things you once had done for you."[4]

14. How do you handle failure? Not just setbacks, but real failure? Can you rise from the adversity, find a silver lining in the failure, and convert it into your next marketing success? Recently we were asked by WBZ-TV in Boston to do a 12-minute stint on our newest hot-selling book title, *The Cat Lover's Cookbook*. We went out and spent 75 dollars on aprons and chef's hats, thinking this would be a cute way to get people's

[3]"As American as homemade foie gras," *Venture*, August 1985, p. 8.
[4]Steven P. Galente, "Corporate executives quitting to buy rust belt businesses," *Wall Street Journal*, April 28, 1986, p. 27.

attention. The day before the presentation, the executive producer called and said we were off. Bumped! Rather than licking our wounds, we looked at the beautiful aprons with silkscreened cats that we had created for the TV show, and decided we had a unique merchandise item which is now one of our strongest sellers. Are you prepared to look for silverlinings in black clouds?

15. Finally, are you persistent? Do you keep coming back again and again? My friend Harold Schwartz, direct marketing entrepreneur once called me a "palooka bag." "Remember the old blow-up punching bags that we got when we were kids?" asked Harold, "You'd knock them down only to have them pop back at you! That's you," Harold said. Do you have that kind of resilience?

The following section can help you to rate yourself. Where are you strongest? Where are you weakest? Can you support yourself in those areas of weakness? And put time, energy, and money into your strength?

PREPAREDNESS FOR YOUR NEW VENTURE

Now you must ask yourself, is this *the best time* for your particular venture? Do you have—now—the leveraged assets which will help you find more money, perhaps a great deal of money, and make a go of it? Do you have the specific and peculiar experience that will allow you to be taken seriously and prepare you for success in a business of your own? Sounds dumb, but ask yourself whether you have actually worked in this business before. Do you know the tasks which have to be performed? Do you have a unique marketing plan for success? For many years at Time-Life, we were told that our skills were transferable from one function to another. This was a great early confidence launcher. So regularly, the comptroller of Time, Inc., for instance, would be rotated into the *Fortune* magazine publisher's position or the group vice president magazines would swap with the group vice president books. This cross-training was believed to be in everybody's interest. However, when someone from the magazine division was brought in to run our book clubs, it was a disaster. He "didn't know the territory." This is the time *not* to fool yourself, and not to jump into an industry area, or channel of distribution that you know nothing about. Remember that education can be a very expensive proposition, and in this case you'll be paying personally. Also ask yourself: Do you have the contacts, within the industry, the potential clients in this channel of distribution to really make things work? Make a list of who your clients will be. Rate them in terms of the sales potential and the dollar value that you can reasonably expect to collect from them in year one.

Bankers love contacts that are certain, contracts that are rock hard. A part of our contractual launch of Storey Communications was a three year book packaging contract, worth approximately $300,000, that we could leverage in terms of bank financing.

Other examples abound. Peter Pollack knew the computer business. He worked for IBM until he decided to form a partnership providing temporary help to the EDP industry. As an IBM sales representative, he had developed wonderful relationships with many business clients, which he is now serving to the tune of $15 million per year.

Perhaps you are particularly knowledgeable about dealing with the government. The federal government loves to award contracts to small business. *Venture* magazine recently cited a company, Adams Marketing Associates, which sells office supplies *only* to the federal government. They're now doing $3 million in sales with a pretax profit of $100,000.

Ask yourself: Is one of my assets endurance? Is my new venture something that I am genuinely interested in, not just for a short time, but for the long haul? Many people succeed at their own business by turning their hobbies into avocations and their avocations into vocations. Bob Bennett, a rabbit breeder in Burlington, Vermont, launched his *Rabbit Breeders Newsletter* and a book that sold 130,000 copies! If you have a deep-seated interest in your subject matter, you are more likely to be successful. And certainly more convincing when you are trying to raise capital.

Ask yourself: Do I have inside information, patents, trademarks, lists, that will help my new business grow? In the case of Storey

Communications, we started with one million names on a master mailing list. Those names produced $50,000 in list rental income and $250,000 in sales—residual, "hidden" benefits—during the first 12 months of our enterprise. This money was critical in keeping us going early on.

Ask yourself whether there is a seasonality factor in your business, and whether you are headed into a strong or a weak seasonal period at the moment you launch. Frequently businesses will enter the market just before their weakest selling time, just after their best collection period. And bankers will pull the plug on a marginal business at the same time. Think very carefully about the seasonality factor involved. Are the three months ahead strong or weak? Determine the trend of the industry, the company, or the product lines that you are involved in. In the case of Garden Way Publishing, we had everything from a hot cooking line to a dead line of energy books. To be sure, other things have heated up and cooled down in the meantime; but you must know the relative vitality of the product lines that you are involved in, and their likelihood to prosper and grow.

Ask yourself finally: What are your other financial obligations. Are things stable for you currently? Or are you already deeply in debt? Is it reasonable for you to take on new debt at this particular time? Or should you clean up, and consolidate, your old debts first prior to embarking on something new? Successes are few and far between when someone is desperately rolling the dice to cover previous mistakes.

While you must be realistic about your dream, you can't be discouraged just because you don't seem to have huge financial assets. There are ways to turn the assets and the *understood* liabilities that you have personally into equity. Also, so much of your financial self-assessment is psychological. If you are pessimistic and believe that you can't possibly start your own business because you have a mortgage and two kids in college, you may be shown up by the person who looks at that same situation and recognizes that she has $150,000 in home equity and a relatively cheap source of labor—her kids.

YOUR FINANCIAL ASSETS

We will discuss assessing and arranging financing in considerably more detail later, including how to turn your personal equity into usable cash, and how to secure external sources of money and credit. But it is a good idea to have a crystal clear picture as to what you can contribute to your venture personally. And, understand early on that no banker or venture capitalist will be interested in investing in you unless there is a big piece of you and your equity in the project.

So let's take a look at what you have in terms of financial assets. Let's divide them into three categories:

1. *Liquid.* Cash in your pocket, personal savings, checking accounts, and money market funds.
2. *Less Liquid.* Things that require some paperwork. Conversions, with or without penalties, of stocks, which might have been purchased at a high price, bonds, treasury bills, municipal funds, or life insurance.
3. *Least Liquid.* Big decisions. Your house, vacation cabin, land, your car, your furnishings, or your art collection.

Many of your liquid assets can be put directly into the venture, but first think about using your less liquid and your least liquid assets as unconverted assets or collateral. These can be borrowed against so you needn't cash them in prematurely, or at an unfortunate time from the point of view of original or eventual value. The banker will look for at least 50 percent of your own personal assets in the venture, a venture capitalist less, but there are many cases where less than that has gone in.

Assess yourself, recognizing where you are strong and where you are weak, but most importantly to "unfreeze" yourself and then your assets. Think about supporting yourself in your areas of weakness, taking on a partner whose assets might complement your own, balancing the financial resources that you lack with your contacts in business or your good management skills.

Let's say you are looking for $50,000. Here is how you might do it:

EXAMPLE ONE: EQUITY RAISING

January 1, 1987
Total Assets—$5,000 in savings accounts.
$1,000 in checking account.
Living in a rental apartment.

Borrow $20,000 from your in-laws at a set interest rate. Combine with your $5,000. Approach a banker to finance your buying as good a house as you can find in a fast-growing neighborhood. Look to spend $75,000 for the house, which will be financed with $25,000 of your money and $50,000 worth of bank mortgage. Improve the house through sweat equity. Sell it in two years for a compounded growth rate of 20 percent per year, or $112,500. Pay your $50,000 bank loan and $10,000 of your personal loan and you've got $62,500 in equity. Magic? No, it is what every solid real estate market in America has been doing in the last 20 years. You can continue buying houses, restoring them, and selling them indefinitely, which intelligent real estate investors have done for years; or you can pull money out of the equity by using it as collateral against a new business venture, which might grow at an even faster rate than real estate, and will almost certainly be a lot more interesting for a lot longer time.

See the point? You are putting money to work that you don't really have. You are borrowing now to increase your eventual stake in a sound property, and getting bankers to go along with you. This process is continuous, never ending, and can be applied successfully time after time.

In my own case, I was able to go from $2,500 of lifetime savings in 1967 to a line of credit of nearly $1 million in 1986, just 20 years later. This is no big deal. Many other people have done it much faster, and more adeptly.

If you're an average, hard working, alert person, you can easily do the same.

ASSESSING YOURSELF

What types of people shouldn't get into business for themselves? Here is my list:

1. *Lazy People.* You'll put in a minimum of 60 hours a week and more like 80. You'll forget about the distinction between weekdays and weekends. Prepared for that?

2. *Compliant People.* Suppliers, clients, investors, and even bankers will sometimes push you around. If you are too accepting you are not likely to get very far. You'll get hurt.

3. *People Who Accept Failure.* You'll lose.

4. *Pessimists.* People who look at a situation and automatically see the worst in it. You must be able to see silver linings.

5. *Poor Judges of Character.* You'll eventually have to be hiring people, and depending on them. In order to do that, you have to be a reasonably good judge of character.

Once you have successfully passed this entrepreneurial personality test, you must figure out how to use your assets to get some money and to get going. Maybe you know just exactly what you want, and you have actually laid out a time line for yourself to make it happen. You want to be the manager of your corporate program within 2 years, look for an available radio station property to buy into within 5, and own it within 10. Or, maybe you are patiently waiting for something specific to happen within your own corporation. Either you are going to become the executive vice president or you are not. Either the division that you are running is going to achieve corporate return on investment objectives or it's going to be lopped off. This is what happened in my case and I was prepared when it did.

Maybe your business plan is completely done, and you are just waiting for appropriate timing to do it—for high interest rates to come down, or investment optimism to come back. My initial draft of a new business prospectus was completed in the summer before my opportunity arose. It was for something called the New England Communications Group, a newsletter and consulting business specializing in publishing and direct marketing, . . . based on the assets I identified in myself. I know two people who work on their business plan every day while commuting to New York. They're waiting for their moment and they'll be ready when it comes.

BUSINESS OPTIONS

There are certainly many ways to go about becoming a business owner, and finding the one that is right for you is a matter of weighing risks and rewards. You can start from scratch. This is the purest way to begin, but it is also the riskiest, with the highest failure rate. You are building something from square one, often with no customers, no trade credit, no employees, no product, no revenues, and no well defined markets. It is certainly possible to succeed this way and there are many who have done it.

Richard Thalheimer, president and owner of the Sharper Image, started his company by selling a running watch for joggers. He had a product, a little money, and an ad. It worked, and his growth rate has been phenomenal. His business grosses well over $100 million a year. Sharper Image is now in the process of going public.

Understand, however, that every ad shot is not going to result in a Sharper Image. The early risks and costs tend to be high, and these are the hardest of new ventures to launch with conventional financing.

When I launched the *Practical Gardener's Newsletter* in 1975, I spent $250 in the *New York Times* Sunday gardening section and got enough orders to pay for another Ad ($1,000) in *Organic Gardening* magazine. Results here were encouraging enough to plan a 50,000 piece direct mail test at $300 per 1,000. I couldn't find any bankers venturesome enough to lend me the $15,000 required, so I found three partners with $5,000 each and off we went!

Another method is to buy something that already exists. The risks here are lower, generally, and there is no reason that you can't quickly maximize the returns on existing assets by reducing overheads and achieving positive cash flow. You're in a real fast race here, once you've plunked your down payment on the table, to stem whatever bleeding may be going on. The whole process is much faster, and you have instant credibility.

In our own case, people would say, "Oh yes! Garden Way Publishing. I've heard of that." It became easier to describe, and certainly easier to finance because of an established product line, established channels of distribution, even though it was extensively unprofitable. The banker depended in large part on promise to reduce overhead dramatically (we eliminated $750,000 on the first day) and to deliver positive cash streams in the future.

You may ask, reasonably, "How do I go about finding a business that is both available and that I can afford?" It is really no different from buying a house. Like real estate, there are many businesses for sale in the $150,000 to $1 million price range. You know what kind of house you can afford even with little realty experience. Why shouldn't you know exactly what kind of "business house" you can afford, given your years of business experience?

FINDING YOUR BUSINESS

A good way to get going on the search is to check regularly the business opportunity pages of the *Wall Street Journal* as well as your own trade magazines. By doing this, you can become extremely familiar with the business investment market in a short period of time, acquaint yourself with hundreds of particular businesses that are available, and begin to assess your own likelihood of success. I recommend writing to those that interest you and request their business plans, which will range from a scrap of paper to a full blown, 50-page bound book. This will give you a great deal of information about their history, products, markets, image, and quality. For the cost of a stamp, or a phone call, you can become specifically familiar, over a comfortable period of time, with the market values and asking prices of hundreds of companies. I did this for three years, accumulating over 100 plans, and considered it a form of simple market research. It cost me $25, less than a six-month subscription to the *Wall Street Journal*, which I found at the local library, a tremendous source of information.

Be aware of local opportunities as well. Believe it or not there are probably businesses that are very suitable to your interests and background right within your own hometown. I chuckle at myself over a business in my own field that was sold to someone else locally because I wasn't aware of the fact that it existed or was for sale. Check in with local real estate agents, letting them know the business area you are interested in, and ask them to keep you in mind as things come along. They'll all put you on their mailing list and send you information regularly.

You should be discreet, but not furtive about your objectives. I think it's a good practice to be totally up front with your current employer while this process is under way. I'd tell my employer over lunch someday that, "I would really like to own my own business, just like you do." He will be complimented and regard this as a sign of ambition and personal drive. It's also good preventive insurance— far better than being caught with a piece of mail or a phone call at a later point that causes him to wonder about your loyalty. At the very least, be prepared with an answer if you are caught while involved in such communication. The consequences of not being prepared can be severe. Two friends of mine were fired on the spot when their respective stories about a planned new venture did not match up when their employer questioned them individually on it. This can be tough medicine.

Once you have begun your research, and see something that you like, make a phone call to the owner and ask specific questions, such as;

1. What are you selling? Be careful here. It can be anything from the entire corporation with both assets and liabilities, to just the assets. Be careful that this is specifically spelled out. Are you buying the debts? Are you buying the accounts receivable? The inventory? Be prepared. My entire deal hinged on the acquisition of $500,000 in accounts receivable, which were thrown in at the eleventh hour. We were able to swing it, only because we had prepared for this "outside chance."

2. What is the asking price? How was it arrived at? What does it represent?

3. What are the primary product lines? The market? What are the trends? How have the product lines developed over the past several years? Which are rising, and which sagging?

4. Are you selling your name and image? Or just products?

5. What about the inventory? What is the turnover rate? Has slow moving stuff been written down and off?

6. What other assets are there? What is their value? Are their invisible assets?

7. Why is it for sale? Will I be able to remedy existing problems quickly?

8. What kind of management is in place? How is the labor force?

9. What does the financial history look like? What has its track record been? What return on investment do you, the owner, predict?

10. Are you hoping to sell the corporation or just the assets of the corporation?

11. What will it take to make it a great success? Will you help me? Specifically, will you take part of the financing in exchange for future gains personally, from future payouts from future earnings?

12. What is wrong with it today? What will we fix tomorrow morning?

13. What are your future plans? Will you sign a noncompete agreement?

If all of these phone conversation items are satisfactory, make a date and say, "May I come see it? I'd like to walk through with you." You can see an incredible amount in a personal tour of the operation. Its location, how the employees are functioning, what condition the inventory is in. Whether it is a humming, busy office, or whether it is dead.

After gathering all of that information, you must ask yourself whether it fits well with your plans. Is it the particular kind of business that will help you attain your goals or not? Does it look feasible, financially at this early stage? Remember, you will probably not have to pay for the whole thing out of your personal savings. How much will it take under the best and worst of cases to make it work? And finally, can you afford it?

Recently I had a call to look at a mail-order gardening catalog. It had lost heavily in the prior year, and was on the market for nearly $500,000, which seemed like a lot, and which I didn't have. But hard asset value (property, plant equipment, inventory, receivables) was $380,000, and bankers would lend $300,000 on that. If we had pushed, I think we could have gotten it for $50,000 down, a bank note of $100,000 and a promise to pay the owner another $100,000 out of future savings. You must ask yourself, "Can this business work? Will I be able to fix what's wrong with it, and how will that all happen?" In this case, the owner had lost $750,000 on $1 million in sales the year before, so the question was critical. The match up of their assets and ours was not really good one, and another successful mail-order gardening tool catalog company picked it up and will do extremely well with it.

CONSTRUCTING AN OFFER

So now that you have identified the business that you want to buy, what do you do now? How do you structure an offer? The obvious place to start is by asking the asking price. Then begin the process, very diplomatically, of going back and forth with the owner, or with the business broker handling the sale, and carefully point out your thoughts about the business. The best place to start, without embarrassing anyone, is to say, "Your asking price is $500,000, but what would the value of this be if the assets were broken up and sold piece by piece?" So-called salvage value has certainly gone through the mind of the owner and through the mind of the business broker, so establishing that salvage value is important.

You might say, "While you are asking $500,000 for the business, I can only find $250,000 in hard assets. Can you help me understand the difference between the hard assets in inventory and receivables, and the $500,000 that you are seeking?" Your objective, obviously, is to probe, keeping the conversation going. You will also get a good sense as to how hungry the seller really is. He will probably come back and say, "Well, you are right, we have $250,000 in hard assets, but $250,000 in goodwill." Now goodwill is a term that the accountants use to demonstrate the years of time, effort and money that people have put into things without profit. They are not definable assets. And it's hard to borrow on them.

Your response might be, "I appreciate the goodwill, but is it fair to equate the hard asset value to the good will? Perhaps it is, but my banker is only prepared to cover the hard assets. Do you think you could adjust your asking price?" Then wait to see what the new asking price is. Perhaps it will come down to $400,000, at which point you are $150,000 apart. A good counter on your part at this time is to say, "You may be right, it may be worth that, so why don't we construct the offer this way? I'll pay you $250,000 for the hard assets and $150,000 out of future earnings, over a 10-year period. No argument about price. Just give me some time to pay it out. Will that be satisfactory?"

When trying to discern the true value of the hard assets, go to the professionals. Pay (if you have to) to get a fair opinion from an appraiser, from a banker, or from somebody who might even be able to help you convert the assets into hard cash. In our case, the nearly $600,000 in receivables from Garden Way Inc. was acquired for 75 percent of face value, or $420,000. I went to the best collection person I could find in the publishing business, solicited his advice, ("Don't pay a penny over 75 percent") and paid him $30,000 to collect nearly $600,000. Not a bad way to start a business.

The banker should be willing to give you 80 percent on receivables, 60 percent on inventory, and perhaps 50 percent of other identifiable assets. So look at it through the banker's eyes as you are trying to construct an offer to the seller of the business. Understand also

CALCULATING YOUR PRICE

1. Amount of money you can raise:
   - Bank accounts $ _____
   - Investment, securities _____
   - Equity house _____
   - Other sources _____
   - Total available $ _____
2. Less 30% (reserve) _____
3. Amount for business purchase $ _____
4. Amount you can borrow
   (70 percent of total cost, or 2.333 times item 3) $ _____
5. Total price for business*
   (Total of items 3 and 4) $ _____
6. 20 percent of item 5 (asking price likely to be more
   than final selling price) $ _____
7. Your price range (add items 5 and 6) $ _____

*Everything except inventory. That will be calculated and financed later.
Source: Frank Kirkpatrick, How to Run a Country Store, © Storey Communications Inc. Pownal Vermont, 1986, p. 24.

Figure 2-1. Calculating Your Price.

A SHORT FORM FOR VALUATION

1. **Sales**, estimated for 12-month future period.   _____

2. **Operating expense**, stabilized as outlined in article to eliminate all anomalies. include cost of goods and operating labor.   _____

3. **Administrative expense**, to be prepared after close examination of normal expenses required that are not included in Line 2. Do not include owner's salary, depreciation, or interest expenses.   _____

4. **Owner's salary**. Should be what would be paid for competent hired manager.   _____

5. **Replacement fund**. This is a "sinking fund" that replaces the book depreciation expense. It is "charged" to earnings so that funds will be available to replace assets as they wear out.   _____

6. **"Stabilized" earnings** (Line 1 less Lines 2 through 5).   _____

7. **Value of assets plus necessary working capital**.
   A. Land   _____
   B. Buildings   _____
      Inventory:
         Raw   _____
         Work in process   _____
         Finished   _____
         Resale inventory   _____
   C. Total Inventory   _____
   D. Equipment   _____
   E. Furnishings & fixtures   _____
   F. Other tangible asset value   _____
   G. Total tangible asset value (A through F)   _____
   H. Working capital needed   _____
   I. Tangible assets & working capital (G & H)   _____

8. **"Underlying" interest rate** (use current inflation rate + 4 points).   _____

9. **"Cost of money"**
   A. Reenter tangible asset value + working capital from Line 7-1.   _____
   B. Reenter underlying interest rate from Line 8 (use decimal.)   _____
   C. Multiply 9-A by 9-B.   _____

10. **"Excess Earnings"**
    A. Reenter stabilized earnings (Line 6).   _____
    B. Reenter "cost of money" (Line 9-C).   _____
    C. Excess earnings (Line 10-A less 10-B).   _____

11. **Calculate multiple** (Ratings are 0-6).
    A. Risk   _____
    B. Competitive   _____
    C. Industry   _____

D. Company   _____

E. Growth   _____

F. Desirability   _____

G. Total   _____

H. Total ÷ 6   _____

12. **Value of excess earnings**

A. Reenter excess earnings (Line 10-C).   _____

B. Reenter multiple (Line 11-H).   _____

C. Value of "excess earnings" (Line 12-A × 12-B).   _____

13. **Total business value:**

A. Reenter asset value (Line 7-G).   _____

B. Reenter value of "excess earnings" (Line 12-C).   _____

C. Total business value (13-A + 13-B).   _____

*If this figure is used by a purchaser, he or she will have to provide any extra working capital to operate the business. The total business value as shown here includes inventory. This figure does not apply to a stock purchase. The stock purchase value will be this figure (13-C) less total liabilities to be assumed. In addition, other adjustments may need to be made in the event of a stock sale if tax benefits are lost as a result by the buyer.

Source: "What's It Worth To You?" Jim Howard. Inc. Magazine, July, 1982. Reprinted with permission, Inc. Magazine, July, 1982 Copyright © 1982, by Inc. Publishing Company, 38 Commercial Wharf, Boston, MA. 02110.

Figure 2-2. Short Form for Valuation*

that valuation is not a sure science. Many hobby businesses, hi-tech businesses, pure communications businesses, or start-ups are extremely hard to value. Perhaps the only way in these cases is to look at earnings potential and see how likely those are to develop over a five-year period, and the personal assets you bring to the party.

This should be easier now that you have identified your strengths and weaknesses, and have put a needs list together to make it happen. You have looked at your own peculiar strengths and at others' balance sheets to find a match. You're really ready to go.

On pages 32–34 are two helpful charts: "Calculating Your Price" (Figure 2-1) and "A Short Form For Valuation" (Figure 2-2). Try • them as you look at various businesses.

3

Your Dream
for Tomorrow:
Today's Strategy,
Tactics, and Plan

You have decided to go for it. You have looked carefully at your personal assets and your liabilities. Now is the time to get down to the hard planning. This chapter will show you how to think about the all-important business plan—how to organize it, how to execute it, and how to present it.

It will include the actual business plan that I utilized to raise $600,000 in initial capitalization, on a revolving credit basis, in spring 1983, and which I was able to expand a year later while eliminating all personal guarantees.

I include the plan not so much as a masterpiece of business planning, but to demonstrate how a corporate manager (myself) with about 15 years of corporate business skills, could relatively easily translate that experience into the most single important document of his lifetime.

Dreaming, by the way, is healthy.

There is nothing wrong with continuing to nurture your dream. Share it with your family, or close friends. Surprisingly they'll take you seriously. Dreams are the stuff that great business successes come from. Victor Kiam talks about painting the big picture—"paint the landscape." You should never lose the dream of entrepreneurship that you have been living with; rather, you should consciously cultivate it.

One of my earliest dreams as an eight-year-old little league baseball player was that somehow I would bump into my big league idol, Mickey Mantle, on a street corner. I got into the habit of looking for him, everywhere. One day when I was 10, my dad told me I'd be missing school the next day because he wanted me to have a chance to meet Mickey Mantle in person. I couldn't believe my ears. My dream had been so vivid that I couldn't tell the difference between reality and illusion. But sure enough, the next day when I awoke my Mom drove to Pleasantville, New York, rather than to school, and my dream began to come true. Thanks to General Foods, with whom my Dad did some business, I was able not only to see Mickey at an exhibition, but then to ride with him from Pleasantville, New York, all the way into Yankee Stadium. (As a sidenote, Mickey had an upset stomach for the entire trip, and I got the mumps the next day, causing me to check the headlines daily to see whether he too had contracted "my" mumps.) The dream persisted through junior high and high school, driving me to be a great athlete. I'll always remember how sustaining a dream can be.

During his rookie year, Eric Hipple, quarterback of the Detroit Lions, was asked to stop in at a cancer hospital and see a 10-year-old boy who was not doing well. When he arrived, he told the boy that he wanted to share a secret with him. The boy listened carefully. "Tomorrow, when you watch me in the game, I'm going to throw a touchdown pass just for you, Bobby," said Hipple. "So when you watch the game, make sure that you see it, and after it happens, I'm going to hold up my hand like this." Hipple showed him the "V" for victory sign. "That means you're going to be a winner, Bobby."

Sure enough, the next day, in front of 60 million television viewers, Eric Hipple was called into the game, and threw a touchdown pass. After congratulating the receiver, Hipple stood dead still in the end zone and held his hand up with the characteristic "V". Even Howard Cosell asked, "What is Hipple doing?" Only two out of 60 million people knew. One was Bobby, and that dream sustained Bobby for many months to come.

You can never lose your business dream. If you do, your whole venture will begin to turn as flat as yesterday's seltzer water. Nurture it, encourage it, and dream it every day. It is critical to your vitality, emotions, optimism, and ultimately to your success in your new venture.

There will be many times when you will feel broke and lonely, and will have to dig deeper into your inner resources. The strength that you'll need to pull your venture through can be rekindled by that early dream.

A BUSINESS PLAN GUARANTEED TO GET YOU THE MONEY YOU NEED

Realistically, you'll have to balance your dreaming with hard research, hard planning, and hard execution. Bankers, accountants, and venture capitalists are not likely to take easily to "dreamers." They'll want a business plan. So let's get very sober at this point, because you have a big job to do. There does not have to be a high cost to it. If you want, you can leverage your time (125 hours in my case) rather than money. You are the best one to do it. This is something that you cannot hire accountants to do, although they can be helpful with projections. But you are the right one to form the assumption and draft the big ideas behind your plan. Why? Because it is a reflection of you, your vision, your commitment, your personality that must come through in this most important selling document. You also have skills you need, honed by 5, 10, 15, 20 years of company experience.

What you have to do is translate all that business time, experience, and skill into numbers, figures, data, dollars, digits, and so on. It may be hard going, but just remember: These are the things that the *banker* dreams about, these are the things the *accountant* dreams about. So play ball, and get ready to quantify every single idea, comment, observation, and concept in your plan.

Ask yourself, "What are we really trying to do with the business plan?" You are simply trying to answer some very fundamental questions, and doing it so well, you'll get an A +. Questions like how are you going to achieve profitability in your venture? When will you achieve positive cash flow? What kinds of assets are going to be created as the basis for substantiating (collateralizing) the amount that you wish to borrow.

All of these questions assume a familiarity with numbers. I had the opportunity of growing up in a corporate training program at Time, Inc. where every department—circulation, advertising, production—were numbers driven. My first three bosses were people who lived by the numbers.

I am assuming that you have had some similar exposure. If you haven't, it is important you get yourself to the nearest library and digest several books on financial statements, profit and loss, asset and liability, and cash flow. There are probably 10 with the title "How to Read a Financial Statement." Another good one is *Accounting for Non-Accountants*.[1] If not, call up brokerage houses and ask them what brochures and pamphlets they are available to help read profit-and-loss and asset-and-liability statements. It is critical that you get up to speed in this area, both for the business plan and, as importantly, for running your new business.

There are also numerous seminars and courses that are available on this subject. It might not be a bad idea, even while you are still an employee, to suggest to your employer that kind of course would be beneficial to you. Find a good one, sign up for it, and strengthen your own ability to deal with numbers.

In the end, what you are trying to understand is simply the way a profit-and-loss statement is constructed, what an asset-and-liability sheet reflects, and how cash flows work. All of this will lead to an understanding of what kind of return you will get on business assets under your management, the crux of the issue as seen by a banker or investor.

You know what kind of return you expect when you put money in the bank. It's not different here.

For example, an inventory asset of $100,000 is a hard asset, with value, and may even allow you to borrow $60,000 in cash to carry it until you sell it. If you turn that inventory over six times a year, you will have a much more interested banker/investor/partner than if you

---

[1] John N. Myer, *Accounting For Non Accountants* (New York: Dutton, 1979).

turn it over only once. By increasing inventory turnover you'll accelerate cash flow.

There are times when business pressures may tempt you to take the $100,000 inventory asset and sell it for $75,000. The result of this would be a $25,000 loss on your profit-and-loss statement, (difference between inventory carrying cost and realization) but it might also be the difference between your staying in business and not.

On the flip side of that coin, there are times when opportunistic purchasing may stand to your advantage. Garden Way Inc. had a $200,000 inventory of slow moving mini-books that I was able to purchase for $100,000. The sellers were delighted to get the cash, which I produced through financing, so they didn't worry about their initial higher investment. Over a two-year period, we found the secret of moving that inventory (primarily through mail order) and at the same time were able to increase our margin in that part of the business from 5 times cost to 10 times cost because of the favorable buy. In short, I had been able to acquire "distressed" inventory that was twice as valuable as if I had had to produce it myself. Whole businesses have been built on this concept. COMB, a Minneapolis-based vendor of close-out merchandise, has had sales skyrocket recently with its direct-to-consumer TV marketing under its president, Ted Deikel.

You will quickly learn that cash is king. There are many businesses that have failed in their first year of operation, even while making a paper profit, because of no cash—due to inability to collect on receivables, convert inventories, generate sales. What your business plan should do is to provide you with a road map, not just in terms of the profit-and-loss statements that you recognize from your corporate experience, but in terms of how the cash will come in and flow out for the first three years of your venture. This is critical.

The end result of all of this effort is going to be a 50-to-75 page document that will be *the* most professional thing you ever created. It will cause people to take you very seriously. But more importantly, it will answer, if you've done the detail work properly, every imaginable question that could be raised about your business.

Entire books, manuals, and seminars have been created on the "business plan." There are many good ones, and I recommend in particular Joseph Mancuso's *How To Write A Winning Business*

Plan.[2] I can't devote the entire book to this; but, by passing along key principles, and analysis of my own business plan, I believe you will turn the last page of this chapter with confidence, and with the familiarity you need in order to begin the business planning process.

You must keep in mind that no matter how compelling your dream is, if you approach bankers and potential investors without a thorough and well-thought-out business plan, you will come away with your dream intact, but no money.

As one Boston banker candidly put it, "I'm not in the business of bankrolling dreams. I finance inventory, receivables, and income streams." Or, as my accountant put it, "Every request for more than $50,000 needs a business plan. These are the guys with the black hats and the hard noses. The realists." The nice ones may say, "I love your idea. Show me how I'm going to get my money back."

YOUR AUDIENCE

So let's take the first concrete step toward turning your dream into a reality. You might still ask, "Who's the business plan really for? Why do I have to spend all that time and effort preparing one? Can't I get money without it? Five good reasons:

1. *It is for yourself.* It will test your idea. It will answer convincingly the questions: Will the business work? Are you prepared? Have you covered all your bases? As importantly, it will give you an operating plan for the first three years of your business.

You do the plan for yourself, among other things, as an exercise in self-discipline, an organizational effort forcing you to define your goals and locate your strengths and weaknesses. The business plan will allow you to test how successful your business might be. And if there are holes in the plan, isn't it better to fail with your plan on paper than in the marketplace? Christopher Whipple, *Esquire* magazine entrepreneur, once commented, "Publishing a new magazine is essentially an embarassing process." Why not embarass yourself in private?

[2]*How To Write A Winning Business Plan.* Joseph Mancuso, Englewood Cliffs, NJ: Prentice-Hall, 1985).

2. *It is for your investors.* It will show each of your potential investors how they are going to earn a return on their investment. Investors could range from your grandfather, to a business colleague, to a venture capital firm. In many cases, the business plan is the only thing that the ten or twenty investors have in common! Craig C. Taylor, president of Asset Management Company of Palo Alto, California, spoke at Stanford University's 1985 Conference on Entrepreneurship about the components that investors are seeking in an effective business plan. In each of the last five years, his company has started one new high-tech company from scratch. Companies that Asset Management has played a major role in launching are California Microwave, Teradyne, Coherent, Applied Molecular Genetics, Boole and Babadge, Tandem Computers, Applied Biosystems, and Archive. Last year, the partners in Asset Management read more than 400 business plans in depth, and invested their funds in eight new ventures.

According to Taylor, the questions that an effective business plan should answer are: (1) What is the company going to do? (2) Why is it worth doing? (3) How are you going to do it? (4) Who is going to prevent you from doing it? (5) What does it take to do it and why will it work well? (6) What are the rewards? In drafting the effective business plan, Taylor advocates seven major components as follows: (1) The Executive Summary, (2) the Company, (3) the Product, (4) the Market, (5) Technology and Risks, (6) an Operations Plan, (7) the Financial Plan.

If all of these questions are answered succinctly and well, the plan will clearly show the potential investor the importance and financial attractiveness of your idea.

3. *It is for your banker.* Your banker is going to want extensive financial data from you. You cannot possibly give him too much! The business plan will outline in detail those financial plans so that you can easily translate your ideas, assumptions, strategies and tactics into profit and loss, assets and liabilities, and most importantly, flows of money.

It will show the banker how he'll get paid back. John Hannon was formerly the president of Bankers Trust Company in New York. When I met with him at a meeting, he was interested in my new venture. He looked me squarely in the eye and said, "You want to get money from a banker? You have to do just one thing. Show him how he's going to get his money back."

If every business plan does nothing more than show a banker how he is going to get his money back, it will have done its job.

Bankers, as previously discussed, want very much to avoid significant risk, but at the same time, they are looking for new business growth for their bank. This is perhaps one of the great built-in contradictions of all time, but it is a fact—growth without risk, lending to people who don't need it. To be sure, your banker will turn your business plan over to a credit analyst, so do make sure all of your numbers add up. If they don't, you'll hear about it and perhaps receive demerits.

4. *It is for trade suppliers.* You will have many new suppliers and vendors after you get going, who will *want* to believe very much in your credit worthiness, but who will need convincing. The complete business plan, together with a D&B listing, will be extremely helpful to you in arranging for trade credit. Without trade credit, you'll have to dig into your own pockets considerably deeper.

In our own case, our most important suppliers when we launched the business were two people with whom we would be doing approximately $150,000 to $200,000 a year in volume. This was not gigantic business for either the Westvaco Paper Company, or for Spencer Press, but both of these suppliers, one of paper, one of printing, were critical to our early plans. We sat down at a formal luncheon with the president, sales representative, and credit manager from Spencer Press, showed them our complete business plan and how cash flows would develop. They saw both our historical experience and our plans for new advertiser support, and at the end of the meeting the president shook hands and said, "Well, we're with you," climbed back on his private jet at the local airport, and flew back to Boston. I picked up the tab (which always surprises a supplier) figuring that the $150,000 in trade credit for $100 worth of steak and pasta was a pretty good return on investment.

In the case of our paper suppliers we fared less well. Westvaco, notoriously tough on credit for new accounts, looked at our plan, and despite the best efforts of the sales department, turned it over to the credit and collection department. The answer came back, "We'll be happy to do business with you. Just provide 100 percent payment for your paper up front."

Gulp! Cash. 100 percent. Up front. Not words that were music to my ears at that moment.

Unfortunately we had no alternatives. We had not had adequate time to line up competitive paper suppliers and could not risk an untested paper on this complicated and critical printing. Even those we were able to contact could not guarantee us that their paper would run with the same quality and absorbency that we needed. We were in a bind.

The answer was to go back, once again, with business plan in hand, to the friendly banker, and say that our assumptions in terms of trade credit had not materialized to the degree that we had planned, and while there was nothing fundamentally wrong with our assumptions, we would have to advance approximately $100,000 which we had expected to draw in September, to early June. The banker complied, thank God!

Interestingly, in the first 30 days following bank acceptance of our plans, we went back twice with major changes. The banker dealt with each on the logic and merits of the case, and went along with us.

During the course of the next year, we experimented with three alternative paper suppliers, each of whom was delighted to supply us with test rolls of paper to run against the Westvaco paper. By year two, we had outgrown our dependency on Westvaco and were enjoying a brand new competitive supply relationship among three paper producers. By year three we had been able to change the terms of paper supply from 100 percent cash up front to 100 percent 30 days after delivery. We were even getting an incentive for prompt (10 day) payment.

5. *It is for potential employees.* The final group of people who will be interested in your business plan are potential employees. It is critical to assemble a management team during the early days of your venture, one capable of covering those areas which you have already identified in your personal asset-and-liability sheet as your weaknesses. In my own case, there were several weaknesses, and I approached four key employees and asked them to join up with me in this brand new high risk venture.

You can understand their reluctance to leave what they were doing to join me in what I had already described to them as a very well-thought-through, but speculative, venture. I believe that without the thorough and professional business plan, which showed losses in year one, break-even in year two, and profit in year three, none of the four people would have joined me. Each of them did, one by one, and I was able to assemble a solid management team that not only impressed the bankers at the outset, but even more importantly helped our business take its first, tentative steps in the summer 1983.

I hope I have conveyed my very strong belief that the business plan, rather than being simply a dry-as-dust accounting document, can be an extremely dynamic selling tool for bankers, investors, trade suppliers, employees, and most importantly, for yourself.

One of the very best ways to become savvy about effective business planning is to become familiar with the business plans of others. You should read lots of them. I actually collected them for three years before I launched my business. There are several ways to do this:

1. Let people know that you are an investor. This is a surefire way to get pitched on various proposals that are chasing money. In my own small town, Williamstown, Massachusetts, I received a business plan almost every quarter from people who were looking to launch new businesses. By reading them carefully and asking questions of the entrepreneur, I was able to determine the strengths and weaknesses of their business plans without investing large amounts of money.

2. Of course, as an investor in any American corporation, you will receive an annual report and quarterly updates from the management. This is another easy way to become familiar with financial statements, from some of the major corporations in America. You can get dozens of reports by owning one share of stock in each of a number of different companies. While you won't make a lot of friends in the brokerage community, it is completely legal and practical.

3. You can send for business plans from people who are advertising the sale of their business. As mentioned earlier, the *Wall Street Journal* "Business Opportunity" section, as well as your own trade press, (*Publisher's Weekly, Advertising Age*, and *Direct Marketing* in my case) carry business opportunities every week. It is very easy, for the price of a stamp or a phone call, to accumulate 25, 50, or 100 different financial plans and business statements at a leisurely pace; and within a very short period of time, you will became pretty expert at reading them.

Like resumes, there is no "perfect" format for financial statements. What matters is what is between the lines. Each paragraph should have key facts and should sell. But in the process of noticing what makes some good, some bad, some unique, and some ho-hum, you can also become extremely familiar with financial statements. You will learn how to read them, you will learn to spot strengths and hidden weaknesses.

ELEMENTS OF A PROFESSIONAL BUSINESS PLAN

I'd like to share with you at this point our successful "Storey Communications Business Prospectus" (Figure 3-1), the product of approximately 125 hours of labor, calling attention to some of the strengths and weaknesses of it. This plan resulted in four bank acceptances, and an initial line of $600,000. I believe that in this hands-on, case-study way, we can walk through the step-by-step elements and assembly.

So you have provided a brief business description, a sense of management resources, staff and organization, market anlaysis, strategic plans, start-up timetables, start-up finance plans, financial statements for five years showing where the earnings are going to come from and what it all amounts to, pro forma financials on each part of the business, and appendixes. The appendix is a good place to take both hard and soft information and show it to your potential lender. By hard information I mean definites, such as contracts. (If you have them in place, list them.) By soft information I mean your pontential (note in particular in Figure 3-1 the letter from the Computer Directions Corporation regarding the potential of the mailing list, an asset which does not show up on the balance sheet). Our appendix included a primary publishing asset, not on the balance sheet of more than 200 author/publisher agreements, the equivalent of contracts, that had been acquired.

Don't underestimate the importance of references—at the highest possible level. When my current banker assessed our total situation, he saw both the risks and the potential rewards of the venture. To get additional perspective, he called one of my five references, Gilbert C. Maurer, president of Hearst Magazines, for whom I had worked 10 years earlier. In a 45-minute conversation with Maurer he became

BUSINESS AND FINANCIAL PLANS

Select a solid, bold, confident type face

FOR

STOREY COMMUNICATIONS, INC.

MAY, 1983

No specific day. "May" gives you a 4 week headstart, which may be helpful later.

This Table of Contents provides 15 "chapters" and 5 "appendices". Your own might have specialized features such as "Technology" or "Patents"

STOREY COMMUNICATIONS, INC.

A critical picture of your plans. Really serves as an "Executive" Summary

1. Brief Business Description
2. Background
3. Business Divisions
4. Timing — You've Told People why... Now Tell Them Why Now!
5. Organization
6. Financial
7. Key Assumptions

These will be the first commitments to be achieved. Make sure you can deliver

8. Startup Schedule
9. References — Don't ignore this! Pick the 5-10 best you can and talk to them in advance.
10. Marketing Opportunities
11. Review Process
12. Location
13. Ownership — Be prepared to discuss your approach and philosophy on this in detail. A banker will want to see a number of investors; you'll probably want as few as possible.
14. Potential
15. Philosophical Background

Appendix A and E, first and last, cover "hard" assets. B, C, and D "romance" a bit with "softer" assets.

Appendix A - Assets of SCI
Appendix B - Editorial Program
Appendix C - Key Management
Appendix D - Publicity
Appendix E - Financial Plans

47

STOREY COMMUNICATIONS, INC.

Here are 51 factors in a business start-up that you're saying "I've thought about." Tho only 1 or 2 lines each, they provide a feeling of industry competence and thoroughness

BRIEF BUSINESS (DESCRIPTION)

PRODUCTS: Garden Way's Quality Trade Paperback Books Line, Hardcover Books, Bulletins, and Advertising Card "Marketplaces".

SERVICES: Supplies Editorial Packaging to Garden Way Under Contract.

EMPLOYEES: 14

LOCATION: Publishing and Editorial Offices, Bennington, Vermont. Customer Service, Warehousing and Distribution, Charlotte, Vermont.

PRODUCTION: Subcontracted to major printers.

DISTRIBUTION: Direct to the Consumer by Mail Order; Indirectly, to the Trade and Special Markets, through Commissioned Sales Representatives.

Acknowledge right away that all is not perfect, or easy.

STRENGTHS: Name, Image, Lists, Editorial Niche, Advertising Sales Capacity, with 12 Year History and roots going back 40 years. Quality product, high degree of Customer satisfaction, Experienced Management.

(WEAKNESSES:) Transitional situation, product packaging.

STRATEGY: Growth in, and into, high potential publishing areas.

OWNERSHIP: M. John and Martha M. Storey - 95%. Key Employees - 5%.

SCOPE: Producing and selling editorial material to numerous consumer markets.

KEY STATISTICS: Revenues $3MM, Profit $(30M), Assets $450M. Anticipate $3.9MM in 1984 revenues, with profitability.

INDUSTRY DEFINITION: Publishing, through Mail Order, Trade and Special Channels.

CUSTOMER GROUP: "Country Living" readers and consumers, affluent and exurban.

NEED SERVED: Do-it-yourself information, plans and dreams for country life.

TECHNOLOGY: Printing and Paper

48

INDUSTRY SIZE: Multi-segmented $7.6 billion. Quality Trade Segment $350 million. Growth anticipated in latter segment at above average levels between 1984-86.

FACTORS AFFECTING GROWTH: Disposable Income up, Population shifts to country up, Housing starts up, Growth in gardening and self sufficiency, Do-it-yourself interest up.

PRODUCT VULNERABILITY: Cheaper books, Data base publishing, T.V. and Home Entertainment.

PRODUCT BREADTH: Extensive. 150 titles. 5 major subject categories.

BARRIERS TO ENTRY: Capital and development of Image, Name, List.

TECHNOLOGY: None currently. Will look to electronic and data base publishing as those industries emerge.

INTEGRATION: Limited. Will explore greater control of editorial production, and eventually printing.

PRINTING: All subcontracted, avoiding large investments in plant and equipment at this time.

PROFITABILITY: Modest currently. 8% by 1986. Objective 10%+.

CHANNELS OF DISTRIBUTION: Mail, Trade, Special, Foreign, Premium.

PRICES: Average $8.95. Increasing.

TERMS - CONDITIONS: Trade and Special 60-90 days. Varies by segment.

IMPORTS: Non competitive. Source of raw product.

SEASONALITY: Spring, Fall strength.

COMPETITORS: Lane (Sunset), H.P. Books, Ortho, Rodale.

[handwritten margin notes:]

Continue the "good news/bad news" approach throughout the plan. Providing a balanced view gives you great credibility.

This is what the whole business plan is really about. Here you're saying "And here's what I'd like to talk with you about."

give an early sense of prudent risk taking and your business orientation.

Background

Backers will be looking immediately for uniqueness. Tell them promptly what yours is.

This prospectus outlines an unusual business opportunity created by the divestiture of a publishing division by a major corporation to its key executive. The new organization will focus on opportunities currently being missed by publishers and direct marketers.

The prospectus describes a new publishing entity, called Storey Communications, Inc., (hereafter referred to as SCI), which will operate three distinct, but integrated divisions; Garden Way Publishing, the Gardener's Marketplace, and Country Book Producers. SCI will be a private, profit oriented company.

give the impression right up front that "this train is moving." Time to get aboard.

SCI was formed in May, 1983 in Williamstown, Massachusetts, prompted by the divestiture of the 12 year old Garden Way Publishing Company, formerly an operating division of Garden Way, Inc. All of the assets, and none of the liabilities of the division were acquired. Those assets are outlined in Appendix A.

Segments of the $7.6 billion U.S. book publishing industry have been depressed during the past two years, but far from representing an unattractive investment, certain segments represent a significant opportunity for those who have publishing experience who are used to working with low overheads, and who understand the new technologies. *You are establishing your credentials early.*

Industry market research can be compelling and is difficult to challenge. Gives a sense of attractive future opportunity.

The quality trade paperback segment, as well as non fiction do-it-yourself lines, have outstripped growth of other industry segments consistently during the past several years, and projections suggest similar potential in the days ahead. Now (1982) at $350 million, growth to $700 million is expected by 1986.

Direct marketing, for its part, has grown from $12 billion in 1975 revenues to over $100 billion in 1982. Projections by the Direct Marketing Association, suggest $250 billion by 1990.

Failure in publishing has resulted from a lack of distinct image, poor distribution and excessive costs, all symptomatic of major corporate acquisitions of small, "cottage industry" publishing operations during the 1960's and 1970's. A reverse trend is now underway, with numerous divestments afoot.

High corporate costs also help to explain why a fledgling "Book Producing", or "Packaging" industry has emerged, where entrepreneurs are producing faster and lower overhead books for considerably larger publishers and marketers. Today, book packaging with word processing and electronic "interconnect" capacities, are increasingly decentralizing the book publishing world, while reducing publisher's high operating costs and dependence on metropolitan (New York, Boston) locations.

"Niche" definition which says "I'm opportunistic and I've spotted something."

50

First statement of strategy.
How you're going to take a problem and fix it.

SCI (aims) to overcome already identified publishing problems inherent in Garden Way's corporate setting with extraordinarily low overheads, a "confederacy" of highly experienced management professionals, and a wide-reaching linkage with outstanding free lancers, offering specialized services on a fee basis.

It is expected that within 5 years, SCI will be a leader in the publishing field, if not in size, then in quality of product and service, as well as quality of working life. We anticipate that this new venture will benefit directly from the strong growth of consumer interest in country living, and comfort with direct response marketing and distribution methods.

Finally, we feel that launching this company (at this time,) as the consumer economy begins to turn around, with measurable increases in customer confidence, will lead to a fast start, and a solid foundation for future growth.

Again you've thought about the "Why Now"

Business Divisions

The first, and primary division, of SCI is Garden Way Publishing. We believe that the entry into this field of "country publishing", detailed recently by Country Journal as one of the fastest growth segments of publishing nationwide, will be accelerated through the acquisition of all assets of the Garden Way Publishing Company. Rather than launching a new publishing business, with heavy startup costs, Storey proposed to Garden Way's Management the divestiture of this 12 year old business, which has been generating $3-$4 million in annual paperback revenues and has developed a very favorable reputation and image in its markets.

You're saying "This is what I want to do and here's why it makes sense"

The objective of this new division of SCI, which will sell Quality Paperback Books through Trade, (Book Store) Special and Mail Order channels, will be to achieve breakeven within the first 6 months of new operation, then to grow modestly in volume, but strongly in profitability in 1984, 1985, and 1986. We believe this can be accomplished through greatly reduced overheads, more aggressive salesmanship and distribution, powerful editorial and graphic presentation, and professional, heavily experienced publishing management.

"And here's how"

An (unusual) aspect of the acquisition was the agreement on Garden Way's part to license the name "Garden Way" to Storey for 5 years. Garden Way, established in 1965, has sold approximately $1 billion worth of merchandise under that name with advertising expenditures of approximately $150 million. The use of the Garden Way Publishing name will be extremely helpful to the launch and early success of this business, with decreased emphasis in time as new imprints are established.

Again "here's what's unique"

51

The decision to license also reflects GWI management's confidence in SCI. New titles will be introduced semi-annually on subjects of "country living" interest, including gardening, do-it-yourself, country land and business opportunities, home construction, maintenance, and repair, and cooking and preserving. A listing of the 1983-85 book lists are attached as Appendix B, and the current Trade Catalog is enclosed.

Longer term, the publishing group will launch a newsletter program. The explosion of available information in the business, tax, career planning, health and retirement fields will continue. The proliferation of data will be confusing and frustrating. SCI's planned newsletters and in-depth analyses should help to crystallize opportunities and provide specific steps for readers and planners who want to change their lives.

This publishing group would aim to become the publishing arm of not just SCI, but also of client firms who have an urge to "get a newsletter going" but don't know how exactly to go about it.

For instance, a tax advisory firm tries to stay in touch with its clients by sending out a monthly letter. It's loaded with the kind of tax wisdom that could easily launch a new publication and profit center. SCI would help.

Editorial coverage would extend to areas of fast change, providing specific answers to questions such as:

1. Where shall I live?

2. At what should I work?

3. How can I change jobs?

4. How can I acquire a small business?

5. How can I keep more of what I have?

The attempt would be to provide difficult-to-find information in readable, helpfully consultative fashion. The detail, or "specific gravity" of the subject matter would be high enough to dictate an attractive subscription price, of perhaps $24-$48 per year, with very attractive (cash advance/deferred subscriber liability) business dynamics.

A second major division of SCI will be the Gardener's Marketplace, a 10 year old Garden Way business that sells advertising units in card type publications, generating $1 million in annual revenues. The new company acquired trademarks to the Gardeners Marketplace, the Energy Savers Marketplace and the Farmer's Marketplace. Additional Marketplaces are planned, focusing on "Country Living". It is anticipated that this arm of the new company, already a positive cash producer, will grow

This is like money in the bank. You're saying we're already going and have major client recognition and support.

rapidly, and achieve a pre-tax profit in 1984. The Marketplace Division has extensive contacts in the Direct Marketing Industry, 2,000 active accounts, strong advertising sales capacity and experienced management.

The third major activity of SCI will be a book packaging service for Garden Way and other publishers and marketers. In this regard, a 5 year, $300,000 contract has been entered into with Garden Way. As editorial, research and design overheads have escalated in the publishing business, a brand new industry has emerged, referred to as packaging, producing, or co-publishing. Fundamentally, publishing services are sold to larger organizations by smaller editorial and production units, who can turn out skillfully researched, designed and packaged editorial product, generally at half the cost, and twice the speed of traditional publishers. *Music to the bankers' ears.*

Shows in a paragraph, your knowledge of the business and sense of opportunity.

A recent example is Garden Way's Joy of Gardening, a 384 page, 4-color book which required 3 years and $350M in investment before reaching the printing press. Its sequel, Garden Way's Joy Of Gardening Cookbook will be completed under the packaging agreement in 12 months, for about $200M, a 40%+ cost reduction even with a 30% margin built in for the producers. A part of this packaging program will be a unique pre-screening market research device, geared to improving the odds of product launch for the marketer.

First discussion of what some of the bankers money is going into.

SCI will have book producing capacity which it will market to a target client list in both the publishing and direct marketing fields. Prospects are strong for a fast growth business, based on the Garden Way contract, the track record of the packaging team, and the sales results of "Joy" (200,000 copies in print) and anticipated first printing target of 100,000 copies for the Joy of Gardening Cookbook. Startup requirements are modest, including a word processing system, typesetting and composition system, and stat camera, each of which has been identified, and can qualify for investment tax credit.

Timing

The launch of SCI in May, 1983 is not coincidental. We believe that Spring 1983 represents a rare conjunction, where the needs, and opportunities, of the publishing industry have never been greater and where the consumer economy is turning around.

Income growth, combined with the lowest inflation rate in 10 years, is boosting consumer buying power. Consumer confidence

53

rose 10 points in March, the largest monthly gain in a decade. Consumer wealth is at an all time high.

This ironically, almost caused the buyout deal to evaporate. After months of sluggish performance we have 2 great months in a row!

The Publishing industry, traditionally an harbinger of things to come, completed a first quarter with earnings 11% above 1982 while the Wall Street Journal index of all industries dropped 8%. Garden Way Publishing has just completed the two strongest months, back to back, in its history. This adds up to excellent timing for the launch of SCI as the recession ends, consumers have additional discretionary income and the confidence to spend it, interest rates continue down to a point where debt financing should be more moderate, and where venture capital availability, if necessary, has increased to its highest point in 5 years.

But primarily, 1983 also represents a year in which Garden Way, Inc., the parent company of Garden Way Publishing, has come to grips with its own publishing future, with the divestiture of a division, that did not "fit" its strategic plan for the future. As a result, we believe the asset value of the division will prove to be significantly greater than the leveraged buyout purchase price. *Critical for the banker to realize that we're not just inheriting someone elses mistake.*

Additionally, prior commitments on the part of the other key professionals, all with major New York corporate publishing experience, have kept them from coming together until this time. The group has agreed to a July 1 commencement date for publishing operations in the Bennington, Vermont area, allowing the group to maintain the quality Vermont image, while locating it just 30 minutes away from its primary client, Garden Way, Inc., of Troy, New York.

Important to pick a very specific date and "make it happen"

Organization

The company will be simply organized, with the parent company, SCI, owning the operating divisions. Key managers coming into the organization will be offered equity arrangements so as to achieve a management totally involved in the success of the company from the outset. Initially, this may represent 5% of equity in the corporation.

And in that regard, very important to make your financing request in person and together.

M. John Storey in his 17th year in the publishing and communications industry, will be Chairman and President of the Corporation, and Martha M. Storey his wife, will serve as a Vice President. A Board of Directors will be formed, with key professionals from various fields serving as a strong working board.

Three key publishing partners have been identified and will join the organization at the outset. The organization will remain streamlined so as to maximize speed and minimize overheads as the business develops as below:

SCI

| Garden Way Publishing Division | Marketplace Division | Book Producing Division |

A total of fourteen people, and target payroll not to exceed $350M will be assembled prior to June 30.

Shows you're consulted with professionals lawyers and accountants

The venture is being organized as a (subchapter S) corporation offering significant tax advantages to the participants. Additional tax benefits would arise when the proposed newsletter publications are launched due to the sheltering aspects of unfulfilled subscription income.

without you're yet having said so.

A primary purpose of the corporation is to allow the participants to build assets at a rate faster than that which could be anticipated in a traditional corporation. It is expected that SCI will attract key direct marketing and publishing professionals with significant track records, interested in an atmosphere of creative freedom.

Each division will be run as an entrepreneurial business, geared to high levels of performance in measurable results. Each will have a carefully selected principal or managing partner, and the entire group will operate as an alliance, rather than a hierarchy, a professional firm rather than a tight corporation.

Financial

Fundamental, and critical - to - achieve strategy. You must do this immediately.

We expect the company to transition quickly from corporate to independent, and to grow moderately in volume, but attractively in profits in the period between 1984 and 1986. This transition, and the planned relocation to Bennington, will allow the new company to (shed enormous corporate overheads) that have built up over a decade while the division's output was being viewed as "marketing communications" in support of the corporation's other product lines, rather than published products for profit. Without these overheads, we have a substantial, going business (instantly viable) well established and regarded in its field, and managed by heavily experienced publishing professionals. (see Appendix B.)

You are using selling words here and throughout

(Specifically,) the changes already underway include the following:

- Staff. Reduced from 40 to 14.

OK, Let's roll up the sleeves and get going. Here's steps 1, 2, 3, 4, 5 and 6

- Payroll. Reduced from $750,000 to $350,000.

(handwritten left margin: Bonker will have quickly calculated. over a million $ savings. Don't tell him... let him have some fun.)

- Inventory. Reduced from $700,000 to $300,000.

- Corporate Advertising Fees. Reduced from $600,000 to $100,000.

- Finance and Administration Expenses. Reduced from $400,000 to $200,000.

- Facilities Rental. Reduced from $7.50 psf to $3 psf, with only 3,000 square feet initially required.

And this process will continue. As we take full respon- sibility for our own customer service, warehousing, distribution, and fulfillment (no later than January 1, 1984), additional savings will accrue.

We feel these targeted cost reductions are conservative, based on the fact that the continuing management, all equity participants, know exactly where these reductions are to be found, and have a tremendous incentive to eliminate them.

(handwritten left margin: Again, here's what's unique fellas!)

While significant infusion of working capital will be required in June-July 1983, to handle seasonal demands for paper, printing, postage and lettershop services, the actual acquisition of Garden Way Publishing by SCI was significant in terms of a pure asset buyout, without either liabilities or long term indebtedness. It is anticipated that a combination of bank loans (90%) and equity investment (10%) will produce the $350M level of funding required for working capital. *(handwritten: Had to be doubled because of the last minute addition of the Accounts Receivable to the deal.)*

A full financial package is attached, as Appendix E, detail- ing profit and loss estimates, asset and liability projections, as well as cash flows for the period July 1983 - December 1986. Additionally, performance estimates for each of the three major business areas are included. The initial capitalization of $350M will be obtained prior to the launch of the business on July 1, 1983. Secondary financing of $1,000,000 will be iden- tified at the outset, so as to allow rapid expansion as addition- al high return activities, (newsletter and periodical) are identified and tested. It is anticipated that the $1,000,000 would be the maximum capital infusion required for successful working capital and expansion of SCI during the 1983-1986 period.

(handwritten left margin: Shows you're planning to be in business for awhile and are already thinking ahead.)

These estimates will be continuously updated so as to monitor operating results closely, and to maximize communications with partners and financiers.

Finally, we feel the initial asset valuation of $450,000 will grow to $1,000,000 in 1984, as the publishing assets under management are brought quickly to their full potential (see "list" valuation, attached).

Key Assumptions

This venture is built on the premise that the powerfully entrepreneurial direct response industry, now approaching $100 billion in sales volume, will continue to prosper in the next 25 years and that the demand for services, information and people will be great.

It also anticipates continuing growth and a continued high quality of life in the New England region. The 1970's represented the first decade where more people moved to rural than urban areas, reversing a 150-year trend. Even now there are some 200 direct response firms operating in New England, with new firms moving into towns like Peterboro, New Hampshire, and Manchester, Vermont, regularly. Our location, while close to airports and attractive urban centers, will allow significantly lower cost operations.

It is mandatory that you set up a schedule here that you can hit or surpass. This will be your first opportunity to show your banker just exactly what you can do... and that you can deliver on what you promise.

Startup Schedule

A tight schedule has been developed, but with assurance of adequacy in planning, Bennington area site selection and financing. Its key dates are as follows:

1.	Negotiation of Investment with Garden Way	By May 1
2.	Business Plan and Financial Projections	By May 15
3.	Agreements with Principals and Legal Organization	By May 30
4.	Site Selection	By June 1
5.	Financing Arrangements	By June 15
6.	Launch	July 1

We believe that this schedule represents adequate time to cover planning and startup arrangements. More detailed schedules exist for each part of the operation. While additional lead time would have been desirable, divestitures and leveraged buyout opportunities rarely develop, and when they do the need for fast action is essential. This prospectus should, at the same time, demonstrate the degree of attention to detail that has been invested in this business exploration.

Here's where you can help, dear banker!

57

References

Lending institutions understandably may desire a more specific idea of Storey's background and career experience, and credit worthiness. References can readily be secured from industry leaders.

2 from previous corporation

Edward Scofield	EVP - Marketing	Garden Way, Inc. (518) 235-6010
Jairo Estrada	EVP - Chief Financial Officer	Garden Way, Inc. (518) 235-6010

2 high level references from mega-corporations

Gilbert C. Maurer	President	(Hearst) Magazines (212) 262-5700
Joan D. Manley	Group V.P.	(Time Inc) Books Group (212) 586-1212
Peter Willmott	President	(Carson Pirie Scott) (312) 744-2000 *unrelated to anything in particular*

2 from industry you're a part of

Rose Harper	Chairman	Direct Marketing Association (212) 599-4140
Nat Ross	President	DMIX (212) 889-8647

These people have (not been specifically contacted) but would be pleased to discuss Storey's background and business experience in detail.

in fact, they should be. You do not, however, want to give the impression of a "staged scene."

Marketing Opportunities

The growth in country living has been at the heart of SCI's launch. Following 7 years of city living, the principals left New York, and have lived for over a decade in exurban or "country" New England. (Storey has been involved) in country publishing since 1973...initially with Time-Life's Encyclopedia of Gardening (James Crockett), then with Hearst's "Do It Yourself" Encyclopedia, followed by their own publishing venture, the "Practical Gardener's Newsletter" and finally with publishing and communications activities as Vice President of Garden Way Incorporated, the leading U.S. company in the direct marketing sale of country products, services and publications. Storey also served as Garden Way's President of Research, Publishing and Solar Greenhouse Divisions.

specifically related experience

58

Blair and Ketchum's <u>Country Journal</u>, perhaps the healthiest new magazine launched in a decade, recognizes and represents key facts that are auspicious in terms of SCI launch:

[handwritten left margin: This is "soft" market research but all contributes (facts) to your increasingly strong "case". It also provides pace, and interesting balance to your presentation.]

o   The dramatic decentralization in population in the '70's and early 80's and '90's, reversing a 150 year trend.

o   The nationwide, non-regional, nature of the trend.

o   The fact that this is primarily an educated, "upscale" shift.

o   The expanded need for "how to" and country living information.

In short, analysis of the latest census figures indicates that metropolitan areas are in decline, while small towns and the countryside are growing, perhaps epitomized by "Up Country" New England.

There are numerous successful competitors in this field, (Rodale, Sunset, HP Books, Ortho) but each has inherent limitations. Competition has been studied from a strategic point of view and both strengths and weaknesses assessed.

The primary strengths of SCI will be its fundamental concept, its diversified and yet integrated management, and its ability to move quickly as opportunity presents itself.

Review Process

[handwritten: Important to form, early, an impressive "Board." The most critical phase of Board of Directors' activity may well be before you launch anything!]

A number of executives experienced in legal, financial and organizational matters, have been involved in reviewing the investment opportunity and the formation of the Storey organization. Initially their help in strengthening the business plan and start-up assumptions was sought. Now, as partners or participants in the Board of Directors, their direct input will be sought. This list includes the following:

James Edgar	Partner (Consultant)	Edgar, Dunn, Conover Assoc. San Francisco, California
Roland Stichweh	Partner (Consultant)	Towers, Perrin, Forster, Crosby Boston, Massachusetts

Don Dubendorf	Attorney	Grinnell & Dubendorf Williamstown, Massachusetts
Charles Saunders	Accountant	Saunders & Associates Greenfield, Massachusetts
Rick Sommer	Consultant	New Canaan, Connecticut

Location

SCI will be based in the Bennington, Vermont area, a small country college town one-half hour east of Troy, New York, and 45 minutes from the Albany airport. Customer service, warehousing and distribution activities will take place in Charlotte, Vermont under contract with Garden Way, just south of Burlington, through December 31, 1983.

Traditionally, publishing companies have required access to "big city" services and skills. Today with word processing and data processing interconnects, as well as a decentralized professional work force, this is no longer necessary.

Bennington was selected because of its true country feel, its access to research facilities, its easy accessibility to the Albany airport, to Boston (2½ hours), and New York City (3½ hours). Office possibilities are being finalized now so as to provide 3500 square feet as a launch point for July 1 occupancy, with growth plans under review with both Bennington and Vermont Industrial Development officers. It is anticipated that on additional 10-15,000 square feet of space will be required in January, 1984 to allow customer service and warehousing facilities.

We believe that location should reflect an organization's purpose, and with traditional industry moving to Vermont, high technology showing interest in Troy and Bennington, quality of living unsurpassed, and increasing early retirement bringing larger numbers to the area, Bennington represents an ideal location for SCI.

Ownership

M. John and Martha Storey, who have developed the concept, research, business planning and financing for SCI will retain 95% of ownership. Five percent will be made available to key managers at the outset. The balance of initial financing is expected to come from debt arranged with lending institutions.

SCI will be organized so as to maximize personal independence and control, minimize taxes, while affording adequate liquidity.

Stock awards will be made to key employees under an Incentive Stock Option arrangement geared toward long term payouts, as the company gains value.

General counsel, Don Dubendorf, of Williamstown, Massachusetts, will develop company bylaws, statement of ownership and purpose, and arrange for stock establishment. Accountant, Charles Saunders, of Greenfield Massachusetts, will review the incorporation for tax advantages and adequate control. Closing with Garden Way Incorporated is set for June 30th.

This says "things are under control," and in the hands of high priced mechanics. In fact, I negotiated all accounting fees to be picked up by the selling corporation, and attorney's fees on a "pay when possible" basis. Figure on $10-25,000 total.

Potential

Following capitalization, the business will commence operation on July 1, 1983.

Because of the demand for information, in readily accessible formats, it is anticipated that the growth of the business will be rapid and healthy.

The longer term objectives include the growth in asset value of the corporation, the development of new forms of information transfer, and the assumption of a leadership position in the field. With a low debt ratio and limited dependence on heavy capital investment for either plant or equipment, SCI should be particularly well suited for fast growth. And because of the continuing favorable ratio of paper and printing costs to price, its margins should become increasingly attractive in the days ahead.

(Philosophical) Background *This tells how you're just a bit different without getting in the way of the business.*

In proposing the formation of this new business enterprise, we've focused on several key business objectives described above. The philosophical objectives are also simple...to help talented and like-minded business people achieve their basic goals in life.

We expect the organization of this group to be unique, and to be based on a sound philosophy of healthy enterprise:

1. A strong emphasis on individual freedom and fulfillment.

2. Positive cash flow for the participants.

3. Professional respect among key partners.

4. A sense of fair play for customers and teamwork for employees.

5. Identifiable and diverse responsibilities for motivated and talented people.

Maybe the best selling line in the whole document, thanks to my consultant brother-in-law Edgar.

In short, the partners in this organization would expect to work like hell and have fun doing it. They would share an entrepreneurial spirit, have a strong desire to do something extremely well, ability to set goals and achieve them, willingness to take reasonable risks and ability to profit from feedback.

Since a fundamental objective of this idea is to enhance one's personal, or not-for-business-only life, most participants would share a well-defined personal philosophy, that would be obvious in daily practice, including perhaps:

1. A sense of faith, and commitment to ideals broader than one's self.

2. Strong family and home ties, and dedication to friends.

3. A sense of pace and humor balancing leisure time with business interests.

Additional business and financial details concerning SCI follow in Appendices A-E.

The Computer Directions Group, Inc.

40 East 34th Street, New York, N.Y. 10016 / Phone (212) 725-1555 / TELEX 645 242

May 17, 1983

Mr. John Storey
Storey Communications
98 Ide Road
Williamstown, Ma. 01267

Dear John:

You have asked us for a general evaluation of the worth of the
Garden Way mailing list.

Our experience shows it is permissible to take a figure equal to
the amount spent on acquiring the list and valuing that amount
over the "life" of the list. The list rental life is 2 full years.
After 2 years, the names are virtually worthless from the list
rental standpoint.

I should also point out that, in our opinion, this list should
rent in its entirety, a minimum of 10 times per year. The 700,000
names therefore, should result in 7 million names rented at a price
of $50/M. This translates to $350,000 gross, or after brokerage
and management commissions, and after fulfillment costs, approximately $230,000 net profit per annum.

Sincerely,

James H. Knox, Jr.
Executive Vice President

JHK:lk

A very helpful letter from a sales representative on an Asset that doesn't even show up on the Balance Sheet. This is "gravy" from the banker's perspective.

WOODRUFF STEVENS & ASSOCIATES, INC. / NAMES UNLIMITED, INC. / CDG DATA CENTER, INC. / DATA BASE MANAGEMENT, INC.

63

ASSET LISTING	PURCHASE PRICE
Work in Process	$24,000.
Prepaid Paper	15,000.
Accrued Royalties	29,000.
Inventory of Finished Goods	300,000.
Furniture and Fixtures Lease/Buyback	
Mailing Lists 700M Names	
Imprint/Trademarks/Copyrights	
Authors Contracts & Reprint Rights	
GW Book Packaging Contract	
GW Name License	
Goodwill	100,000.
	$468,000.

Here's where the pencils come out.
I say it's worth $468,00. The banker
says he'll give 60% on Work-in-Progress,
Prepaid Paper and Inventory, and nothing
on Accrued Royalties and Goodwill.
So he may support you to the tune of
$203,000. You'll want to accept the
$203, while arguing for more. We
wound up adding a $600,000 receivable
which he "stretched" to 80% on, for
initial, first round financing from
our local banker of $691,000!

Appendix B  *Editorial Program*

Soft, but shows you're planning 2 years ahead and expect to be in business for a long time to come.

<u>THE FALL 1983 GARDEN WAY PUBLISHING BOOK LIST</u>

    <u>Solar Projects for Under $500</u>   Mary Twitchell, Author

    <u>Feeding the Birds</u>   Jan Mahnken, Author

    <u>The International Vegetarian Cookbook</u>   Kristin Skaarup,
                                                 Author

    <u>Home Wine Making, Brewing and Other Drinks</u>   Charles Foster,
                                                      Author

    <u>Award-Winning Passive Solar House Designs</u>   Jeffrey Cook,
                                                 Author

    <u>Garden Way's Compact House Book</u>   Don Metz, Author

<u>SPRING 1984</u>

    Garden Way's <u>Joy of Gardening Cookbook</u>
    Garden Way's Joy of Gardening Workbook
    The Berry Cookbook
    The Poultry Cookbook
    The Horse Book
    Houseplants
    Photovoltaics
    Plant Propagation
    Post and Beam Construction

<u>FALL 1984</u>

    <u>Home Maintenance</u>
    A-Z Hints for the Harvest Kitchen
    Apple Cookbook
    Garden Way's 1985 Calendar
    Garden Way's Desk Diary 1985
    Garden Way's Gardening Annual 1985
    Butchering

<u>SPRING 1985</u>   (Tentative)

    Garden Way's Personal Independence Library (Mail Order)
    Cookbook Continuity Series (Mail Order)
    M. O. Continuity of JOY: Partworks with Cassette
    Garden Way's Complete Guide to Sunrooms and Solar Greenhouses

<u>FALL 1985</u>   (Tentative)

    Book from Cloverdale-Indoor Gardening
    Janet Ballentyne Cookbook/Tools & Appliances
    Desk Diary-1986
    Annual 1986
    1986 Calendar
    Garden Way's Complete Guide to Country Living

Important early statement of solid background and experience, within the industry, of your key managers.

Appendix C - Key Management

M. JOHN STOREY   Chairman, President   Storey Communications, Inc.

Storey, 39, married, has 17 years of Publishing experience with Garden Way (President and Publisher, Garden Way Publishing), Hearst Publications (Director, Mail Order Marketing), Time Incorporated (Business Manager Time-Life Books/Time Incorporated Book Clubs). Formerly Vice President and Stockholder, Garden Way Incorporated. Founded Venture Marketing and Practical Gardeners Newsletter 1976. Board of Directors, Direct Marketing Idea Exchange, New York City. Featured International Speaker Direct Marketing Association, New England Direct Marketing Association, 100 Million Club, New York University. Director, Williamstown Advocate. Masters Degree, Johns Hopkins. Bachelors Degree, Williams College.

JAMES BRADY   Associate Publisher   Garden Way Publishing
Division

Brady, 48, married, has 17 years of Publishing experience with Garden Way (Director of Sales and Marketing), Time Life Books (Mail Order; International, Special and Retail Sales Manager), U.S. News Books (Sales Director). Delegate American Association of Publishers. Extensive domestic and international bookselling experience. Masters Degree, Loyola. Bachelor of Arts, Loyola.

ROBERT H. SHIELDS   Publisher   Marketplace Division

Shields, 40, married, has 16 years of diversified business experience, the last six in publishing with Garden Way Publishing (Director/Publisher of the Garden Way Marketplace), Greenleaves Magazine (General Manager, Co-Publisher and Partner). Corporate experience with Mead Johnson, and Humble Oil. Masters of Business Degree, Indiana University, Bachelor of Arts Degree, Indiana.

ALAN HOOD   Marketing Director   Garden Way Publishing
Division

Hood, 42, has 20 years experience in the book business with Stephen Greene Press (Marketing and Sales Manager), E.P. Dutton (Sales Manager/Distributor), David McKay (V.P. - Sales), Henry Regnery and G.P. Putnam (Sales/Representative). Hood formed Alan C. Hood, Book Services, a consulting arm, in 1981. Bachelor of Arts, Williams College.

RICHARD SALMON   Business Manager   Storey Communications, Inc.

Salmon, 42, married, has 19 years of book publishing, business and marketing experience with the MIT Press (Business/Credit Manager) and Time Life Books (Assistant Business Manager). For the past three years he has served as Telephone Marketing Manager for the Garden Way Manufacturing Company. Salmon launched his own publishing business, Brattle Publications, in 1979. Bachelor of Arts, Manhattan College.

IRVING GARFIELD   Production Director   Garden Way Publishing

Garfield, 60, married, has 35 years of book production and manufacturing experience with Time Life Books (Production Director, Planning) Time Incorporated Book Clubs (Production Director) George Braziller Inc. (Production Manager). Garfield established his own book production consultation company in 1980.

Garden Way Publishing Publicity in the Works

-CHEESEMAKING authors rescheduled for NBC's TODAY SHOW, early May
-PICKLES, possible mention by Gene Shepard on National Public Radio's
    "All Things Considered"
-May 3rd, TODAY SHOW, Gene Shalit's Critic's Corner on Gardening,
    may include JOY OF GARDENING or ROSES LOVE GARLIC
-DESSERTS FROM THE GARDEN, planning local publicity and possible
    ACROSS THE FENCE appearance.

-Review copy mailings completed:
    PICKLES & RELISHES, 175 copies sent, with special note to
        top women's and cooking and self-sufficiency magazines.
    ROSES LOVE GARLIC, 205 copies sent.
    HEATING THE HOME WATER SUPPLY, 139.

-Review copy mailings in the works:
    DESSERTS FROM THE GARDEN, press release, and special "harvest
    hints" note to editors.
    RAISING YOUR OWN MEAT FOR PENNIES A DAY, target to country
    living and self-sufficiency publications.

A touch of show business which will get you no more capital, but a sense of national recognition.

NBC TODAY SHOW
May 5, 1983
Gene Shalit

GOOD NEWS!

Garden Way's JOY OF GAR-
DENING book was featured
on NBC's TODAY Show on
Thursday morning, May 5.
Gene Shalit devoted his
"Critic's Corner" to great
new gardening books, and
saved the best, the JOY
OF GARDENING, for last!
Gene Shalit mentioned
JOY at the end of his
review of books, saying
it was one of the best
gardening books of the
season!

PUBLISHERS WEEKLY
Jan. 1983

GARDEN WAY'S JOY OF GARDENING,
Dick Raymond. Garden Way, $14.95 to
May 1, then $17.95 ISBN 0-88266-319-
4, hardcover $25 ISBN 0-88266-320-8
The author of previous successful gardening guides here incorporates advice
on using many innovative methods to
lessen chores and reap richer harvests.
Raymond's conversational approach is
an asset and so are the numerous illustrations: color paintings and photos,
charts, etc. The pictures show the grati-
fying results of adapting the wide-row
process—broadcasting seeds across a
long strip, from 10" to 25" across—
rather than in single rows. Raymond
also introduces tools designed to make
gardening easier, such as an in-row
weeder that doesn't disturb wanted
plants. Perhaps readers will appreciate
most the book's complete coverage of
measures to combat marauding moles
and other animals, birds, insects and
diseases—identified in pictures and described in the text. But there are many
other features that can teach gardeners
how to minimize pest and maximize joy
they can get from fruits and ber-
ries or even as small as a window box
or in plots of all sizes. Raymond's syn-
dicated TV show, with the same title as
the book, will promote its sales. *30,000
copies, contributed first printing*
—*March*

NEW YORK, N.Y.
NEWS
D. 1,483,333—S. 1,888,324
NEW YORK CITY METROPOLITAN AREA

APR 22 1983

Housing books are intriguing

By GENE AUSTIN
Knight-Ridder Newspapers

NE OF THE MOST exciting trends in housing is the recycling of old structures—sometimes very unlikely old structures—into houses. Accompanying it is another movement in which homes are built from inexpensive or unusual materials.

I think it's interesting and delightful when someone makes an attractive home from an old silo or abandoned church or uses discarded lumber or tamped-down earth to build a livable dwelling. It is also extremely practical, of course, because millions of people find it difficult or impossible to buy a conventional new or existing house because of high interest rates for mortgages and high prices.

A couple of new books chronicle some examples of these recycling movements, and I recommend either or both to anyone who despairs of ever owning a home, to those who need reminders that American ingenuity is alive and well, and to those who are just bored with townhouses, condominium apartments and suburban Colonials.

THE BOOKS ARE "Renegade Houses" by Eric Hoffman and "Getting a Roof Over Your Head".

Hoffman's book, subtitled "A Free-Thinker's Guide to Owner-Built Homes," describes some genuine curiosities, including a house built in an old water tower, another built mostly from used railroad ties and a discussion of the rammed-earth technique of building houses.

The rammed-earth system, which involves tamping earth into forms until it becomes hard as concrete, isn't really new. It was used in building China's Great Wall as well as in some Great Depression-era housing, and it is making a comeback in some areas.

"RAMMED-EARTH WALLS are dry, fireproof, rot-proof, soundproof, termite-proof, excellent passive-solar collectors—and best of all, dirt cheap," said David Easton, a engineer trained at Stanford University whose techniques are described in Hoffman's book. Easton is building rammed-earth homes in California, and thinks they can revolutionize housing construction.

"Some people conclude dirt construction is for backward cultures and poor people," Easton said. "That's wrong. When you combine earth and modern construction technology, the result is a superior product."

Hoffman's readable and well-illustrated book can be ordered by mail for $8.70 from Running Press, 125 S. 22nd St., Philadelphia, Pa. 19103.

"Getting a Roof Over Your Head," compiled by Garden Way editors, includes 16 examples of self-built housing with such intriguing chapter titles as "Learn From Thoreau," which describes how New Englander Roland Wells Robbins built a small, inexpensive house much like Thoreau's at Walden Pond, and "Scrounge," which tells how a Colorado couple built a livable house for $2,500 with salvaged materials.

OTHER CHAPTERS describe how to act as your own contractor in building a house, learn building techniques by attending an owner-builder school and recycle old buildings such as schoolhouses or churches.

"Those of us who wrote this book had no difficulty finding success stories," says a preface to "Getting a Roof Over Your Head."

"Getting a Roof Over Your Head" is available by mail for $11.45 from Garden Way Publishing, 2538 Ferry Rd., Charlotte, Vt. 05445.

THE THEME THAT runs through both books, and I think it is a valid one, is that most people can have their own house if they want it bad enough and are willing to settle for something less than the American-dream home with three bedrooms, a two-car garage and 2½ baths.

Putting up a high-quality storage shed

By Gene Austin

BUILDING A STORAGE shed is a popular spring project, and many do-it-yourselfers want the sturdiness and permanence of wood construction.

The simplest and foolproof way to build your own shed using wood framing and siding is to buy a high-quality kit. The kits, which contain plans and most or all of the building materials, are widely sold at home centers and lumber yards.

Here are some things to keep in mind when shopping for a kit shed:

● Look for dealers with completed sample sheds that can be inspected. Some kits skimp on framing or have flimsy sheathing or roofing.

● Kits that include special carpentry connectors of galvanized steel are easiest to assemble and are strongest when completed.

● Some kits use waferboard in exposed positions, such as for siding. If exposed to weather, waferboard should be primed and painted.

● Carefully check the list of contents for the kit. In some cases, extra materials such as roofing shingles and paint will be needed.

● Find out what kind of foundation is required. A concrete slab or concrete blocks on concrete footings is best.

● Check the building code in your municipality by calling the building inspector's office. In

is as easy as 1-2-3-kit

many areas, a permit is required to build or erect any type of shed.

Another way to build a shed partially of wood and avoid the tricky job of erecting wood framing is to use a steel-frame kit. The frame kits have hot-dipped galvanized parts.

HERE ARE two other possibilities for those who want to start from scratch to construct outbuildings:

● Craft Patterns offers complete construction plans for several sheds and small barns. The Home

Ideas Book listing the projects is $1.50 from Craft Patterns, 2200 Dean St., St. Charles, Ill. 60174. For fast delivery, add $1.50.

● An excellent book, "Building Small Barns, Sheds & Shelters," by Monte Burch [$10.95 paperback, Garden Way], gives the basics of constructing small buildings and includes plans and designs. The book can be bought by mail by sending $12.45 to Garden Way Publishing, 2537 Ferry Rd., Charlotte, Vt. 05445.

Knight-Ridder Newspapers

Appendix E (Financial Plans)

This section should be as long as the previous 25 pages, going into extraordinary detail, and trying to anticipate every single financial question, challenge & concern.

° Profit and Loss Estimates

° Asset and Liability Sheets

° Cash Flow Analysis

° Divisional Performance Analysis

ASSETS	1983	1984	1985	1986
CASH&INVESTMENTS	2000	2000	2000	2000
ACCOUNTS REC.	207562	250468	288028	312123
INVENTORY	262108	313606	365418	410028
OTHER CURRENT ASST	2000	2000	2000	2000
TOTAL CURRENT ASSI	473670	568073	657446	726150
FIXED ASSETS-NET	47600	83200	68800	54400
NON-CURRENT FIXED	0	0	0	0
TOTAL ASSETS	521270	651273	726246	780550
LIABILITIES				
ACCOUNTS PAYABLE	31174	37570	43204	46818
NOTES PAYABLE	169843	139941	-283082	-674824
CUSTOMER ADVANCES	8635	9398	10417	11155
ACCRUED EXPENSES	15000	15000	15000	15000
ACCRUED BONUS	0	0	0	0
ACCRUED INCOME TAX	-26671	49682	270513	356103
TOTAL CURRENT LIAB	197941	251591	56052	-245748
OTHER LIABILITIES	0	0	0	0
TOTAL LIABILITIES	197941	251591	56052	-255048
EQUITY				
NET INCOME YTD	-26671	76353	270513	356103
RETAINED EARNINGS	350000	323329	399682	677095
TOTAL EQUITY	323329	399662	670195	1033198
TOT.LIAB.& EQUITY	521270	651273	726246	778150

Show your summary awareness of how a Balance Sheet works and provide considerably more detail by later time periods. e.g. what's the A & L going to look like in May of 1985?

PROFIT AND LOSS STATEMENTS
FOR THE PERIOD 1983-1986

	1983	1984	1985	1986
GROSS SALES	2776999	6977702	7666112	8190363
DISC,RTNS,ALLOW.	1222423	3063802	3231417	3401898
NET SALES	1554576	3913900	4434695	4788465
COST OF GOODS	887992	2029155	2054583	2102601
GROSS MARGIN	666584	1884745	2380112	2685864
MARKETING EXPENSE	205000	536000	581500	673270
CONTRIBUTION	461584	1348745	1798612	2012594
DIVISIONAL EXPENSE				
EDITORIAL	72000	180000	180000	180000
FINANCE/ADMIN.	189000	480000	480000	480000
CORPORATE FEE	108000	240000	240000	240000
CUSTOMER SERVICE	132804	265300	333655	365390
TOTAL DIV. EXPENSE	501804	1165300	1233655	1265390
OTHER INCOME (EXP)				
LIST RENTAL	25000	50000	100000	200000
PRODUCT DEVELOP.	-25000	-55000	-130000	-235000
INTEREST EXPENSE	-13122	-25739	6067	0
TOT.OTHER INC(EXP)	-13122	-30739	-23932	-34999
TOTAL NET INCOME	-53342	152706	541025	712206
TAXES @ 50%	-26671	76353	270513	356103
NET AFTER TAX INC.	-26671	76353	270513	356103

Start with 3-4 year summary and work your way down to every product, program, channel g distribution, resource and cost item.

Figure 3-1. SCI business plan, with annotations.

convinced, and this led to his commitment to proceed with a loan in excess of $600,000. I am convinced that without Maurer's active support, this would not have happened. Don't forget the courtesy of talking to your sponsors in advance, and thanking them afterwards.

I suspect the banker called Maurer because the title "President, Hearst Magazines, New York City" was as high level a contact as a banker in Bennington, Vermont had ever approached by phone or in person. It worked.

The creation of the business plan is not an overnight job. If conditions allow, it's better to think about and shape it over a year's period than to try to do it in a week.

If you find yourself thinking, at an early business age, that you would like to own your own business down the road, create a rough business outline and begin to store notes that you think would be helpful or relevant to your plan, just as if you were doing a college research paper. In my own case, I used a 4 × 6 notecard file and filed notes under the various sections of the business plan for at least a year before I actually wrote it.

It is also helpful if you can set aside a solid block of time, removed from the office, and take a crack at doing a rough draft, well in advance of when you want to make your move.

I did this in the summer 1982, months before we launched our business. We went to the South Jersey shore, one of my favorite places, and I spent four hours every morning working on the business plan, having it typed by a local typist, and came back from vacation, tanned and with a full-blown plan. The plan was a business which, in the form I outlined, never got off the ground, but which made the initial launch of Storey Communications that much easier.

Another good rule is to try for complete honesty in your business plan. Integrity comes through and a plan which says, "Our sales assumption may not work out as quickly as we've outlined" adds great credibility to your presentation.

Perhaps there will be some completely unattractive aspects of your plan. Should you throw those out and act as though they don't exist? I wouldn't.

By showing your banker or pontential investing partner the "warts" on the plan, people will believe in other parts of the plan and the easier it will be to get money.

Nor do you have to act as though you have the answer to every single question that comes up. You don't. No one does. Let your partners, bankers, and investors know that there are some things which are not perfect about the plan. And, if you don't have the answer to something, you will get back to them the next day with it.

PREPARING

Don't try to do the plan in a hurry. I have one friend who everybody pitied because he commuted two hours each day from Ridgefield, Connecticut to midtown Manhattan. He used every means of transportation imaginable to get from Ridgefield to the West Side of Manhattan; his car, a train, the bus, and then finally, a cab. While everyone was feeling sorry for him, he was spending an hour and a half each way, or three hours a day, for two years, putting together one of the finest business plans that has ever been completed. What others saw as a negative, Don saw as an opportunity. He started compiling data and asked himself every day, "What if I had my own company?" It is a real mistake to try to drop everything and do a business plan hastily, overnight. You will invariably miss important major questions that have to be considered methodically before launching into this, the most important investment decision of your life.

Once completed, test everything that you have in your plan. How can you sharpen each part of it? How can you poke holes in the weak areas and get harder information to make the plan more palatable? How realistic is the sales portion of the plan? Without sales, nothing else happens. Look at the market you are entering. Why do you think you are going to succeed? Why have others failed? Research that market and industry extensively. If you are in publishing, what are the market niches that Time, Inc. CBS, Grolier, and Gannett are not filling? Where is the industry going?

At Garden Way Inc. in the 1970s, we rode a company from $30 million to $130 million in 8 years, primarily because the market for gardening products was hot. What makes you think your market is going to be "hot" in the balance of the 1980s and 1990s?

RESEARCHING

You can get some extremely helpful information from investment bankers. Call any of the major houses and ask for their analysis of the publishing industry, or whatever industry you are a part of. These are prepared by some of the best research departments in the country, are clearly written, can be analyzed quickly, and will allow you to protect greater awareness and knowledge of your industry with your banker, your investor, or your partner.

Your plan can also be strengthened through informal market research. Any major corporation would invest considerably in market research before launching a new venture. You can't afford to do the kind of quantitative and qualitative research that a Xerox, or a General Mills would use in launching new products. But you can get considerable bang for the buck, and add dramatically to your business plan, by doing informal market research of your own.

Pull 5 or 10 of your friends together. Explain to them what you are trying to do. Ask them to poke holes in your ideas. Show them some proposed advertising for your proposed products. If you want an unbiased, impartial coordinator, hire a market research person for the evening at a cost of probably $150 to lead a discussion that can give you substantive insights, copy points, and leads as to what will work and what will not work. Your banker will be very impressed that you went to the extent of testing your idea in front of a group of people.

Don't miss the opportunity in your business plan to point out the clients that you have. And you should have them going in. List them all. John Davies, III, now general manager of the Denver office of the very successful Krupp Direct Marketing Agency, tried to launch his own business in 1979, but started with no client in the bag or any significant financing. His partner and he were living hand to mouth, and finally, after six months, had an opportunity to bid on, and eventually win, a major account from a cosmetic manufacturer in Israel. They borrowed to the limit to develop the business, but had not planned adequately for the staffing that was necessary, staffing that they could now neither afford personally nor borrow for. Out went the business, the doors were closed, and both of them went back to work for others.

Davies says today that when he looks back on it, he would have spent the first three months arranging financial backing to make it possible to do what he knew they could. The moral of the story in that kind of business is to make sure that you have an adequate business plan, adequate financing, and at least one major client before you order business cards and office space.

REVIEWING

Now comes the testing of your business plan. Start by meeting with your accountant for an hour or so to give him a complete feel for what you are doing, and outlining the assumptions of the business to him. You will be paying for this time, at perhaps $50 an hour. If he's good, he'll push you. He'll ask you some pointed questions like, "How do you actually plan to create the sales to result in the cash flows that you are showing in your document?" "What is your time table?" "What are your fundamental assumptions?" "What if you're wrong?"

A good accountant will walk with you step-by-step through each line of the revenue assumptions, the cost assumption, the overhead assumptions, and the profit assumptions. He will be the first primary hurdle for you to get over, and will forge a stronger document with you, if you give him adequate time. He will also, with the help of a personal computer be able to extend all of your assumptions out over a one-year, three-year, or five-year period. This mechanical job of extending the numbers will give you a document that is roughly twice the size of what you have prepared so far. (In my own case, approximately 25 pages of text, and 35 pages of financials.) You'll make dozens of changes which, with the help of a personal computer, can be painlessly incorporated.

Every banker, investor, or partner will be looking for this excruciating detail, and for you to try to do it manually with a hand-held calculator will take you the next decade. So hire the accountant to do the job for you, but only after you've done the conceptual, assumption development, and sales and marketing plans.

Ron Hume, one of Canada's most successful direct marketers, who now operates a $75 million-a-year Toronto-based publishing business, was asked recently why his new business plan had succeeded. He responded simply, "I had an answer for everything." It is this kind of detail—data, data, data—particularly on your assets and your projections that are critical in convincing the banker that you know what you are doing.

Two of my early mentors told me the exact opposite thing. Paul Hush, a business manager for whom I worked at Time, Inc., once told me to concentrate only on the profit-and-loss statement. He said, "Don't worry about your assets and liabilities; if the profit-and-loss statement is working, the A and L will fall into place."

Years later, Bill Blair, who had launched the very successful *Country Journal* magazine, told me on the phone, "Forget about your profit-and-loss statement. Nothing matters except how much cash you brought in today, and how you are going to be able to pay your bills." After about a decade of cash receipts watching, Blair and his partner, Dick Ketchum, cashed in their chips in a sale for several million to *Historic Times*.

This is the age-old difference between the big corporation and the entrepreneur. In the end, Blair is more right than Hush. It is the daily cash, the ability to pay the bills, that allows you to gain credibility and develop your business through the fragile early stages into something more stable and substantial. I will tell you this, I know every morning by 9:00 what our receipts are for the day. I only worry about the profit-and-loss statements once a month.

Prepare various scenarios as a part of your business planning, perhaps a mid-range, maxi, and mini set of expectations. This will allow you to answer easily bankers' questions as to what you're going to do if your sales projections don't materialize. It is a critical piece of work.

After the accountant has finished, put the whole thing back together again. But this doesn't complete the task. Find the smartest business people you know, and ask them to take time to criticize your plan. Tell them that you can't pay them anything for it, but that you'd greatly appreciate their expertise. You will get it every time. In my case, I asked Jim Edgar, my brother-in-law and a managing partner of Edgar, Dunn, and Company consultants in San Francisco; Rick Sommer, a New Canaan, Connecticut entrepreneur; and Prescott Kelly, a long-time friend with product brand management and direct marketing experience, to do it. They tore it apart six ways to Sunday, tested my assumptions, and forced me to go back through another two weeks worth of digging and work. It was all worth it. If you don't ask somebody else to tear it apart, the bankers or investors will. Don't give them the opportunity.

After you have done the re-research, sit down, and quietly write your very best final draft. This is your Pulitzer. Critique it yourself one final time and you're ready to go.

The final printing and packaging is not an insignificant piece of work. The printing should be of high quality to match the work that you have put in. The packaging, including folder, binding, and presentation, is equally important. Spend the money to make your business plan look as good as it really is.

Unfortunately, once people have completed their original business plan and secured their financing, many put it on the shelf and let it go into oblivion. Remember that you have put hundreds of hours of work into it, and it should be your business plan for the first three years of operation. Use it, modify it, make it work as an exciting and dynamic business tool for you as you try to get your business off the ground, into the air, and flying high. You will find that all of the work that you put into your business plan will pay you back many, many times over. It will tell you whether you are on schedule, meeting the expectations that you put into it, or whether there are critical flaws in it which the sooner corrected, the better. It is a precious document. Remember, it talks about your dream, and how you are going to achieve it, which we will talk more about in Chapter 4.

The nicest thing that anybody ever told me was that mine was the best business plan they had ever received. I asked the banker who said this what percentage of people applied for loans with and without a business plan. "Oh," he said, "the vast majority come in with no plan at all. Over 90 percent." I asked him what percentage of people get loans. He smiled and said approximately 10 percent. I knew, from that conversation, that there was no coincidence in those statistics. Aim to have the very best business plan that you could ever create, and to be part of that special 10 percent that gets the funding they need to get going. You can do it.

4

The Master Mechanics: Your Accountant and Lawyer

You are convinced of the merit of your idea. You have worked hard at putting a strong selling plan together and on paper. Now what do you do?

If you're smart, you'll get down to the task of finding yourself a good accountant and a good lawyer pronto. Why? Because, quite simply, they'll lead you to capital and give your deal a better chance of succeeding. John Suhler, partner in the Veronis and Suhler investment firm in New York, put it this way, "I've seen more good deals loused up because of the absence of complete numbers and a decent negotiating lawyer. There is probably no single reason why more deals fall apart than the absence of good professional accounting and legal help."

WHY YOUR ODDS GO UP WHEN YOU HIRE PROFESSIONALS

I think of them as highly paid and professional mechanics: highly paid because they'll get your business vehicle going; mechanics because they know how to make business deals work. They'll start with your business plan.

In talking with a banker recently I asked him, "Just out of curiosity, how many people come in here with a full blown business plan?"

"About 1 out of 10," said the banker.

"How many are professionally prepared?" I then asked; "About a third of those."

"What percentage of your applications wind up getting bank support for their projects?" I asked.

"About one out of 25," said the banker.

Coincidental? On the contrary.

There's a very strong probability relationship between your having put together a professional plan with the help of an accountant and lawyer and your ability to get that magic ingredient to get this whole thing going—money. In talking with my own accountant, Tom Gajda of Gajda, Marlow Associates, I was amazed at what he shared with me. "About 150 people come to me with proposals for new firms every year," said Tom. "Most of them shouldn't. They haven't thought things through, or asked themselves what's going to happen if an assumption doesn't work out." Lesson: Before you begin to spend between $50 and $100 an hour for a good accounting mechanic, you should have a very strong sense of business direction as reflected in your own plan. Brief your accountant on this.

This might be as easy as your saying, "Here's our plan for a business which we think can do $1 million in sales in one and one-half year and $5 million in three. But we need your help in analyzing and projecting it, and if the review is favorable, in helping us to get it going." Obviously, this is an area where you should plan on spending some money. But think also of accountants and lawyers as brain surgeons—you don't go to a brain surgeon and say, "I think I have a headache." You get real precise before you begin to spend real money.

Ask yourselves, "What do I really need an accountant for?" Why? When? And who should it be?

You'll want counselors who will continuously review the financial plans that you have put together for your new enterprise in terms of profits, losses, costs, prices, margins, and risks. Particularly early on.

This is an area that you really don't want to skimp on. If you do, you're likely to pay for your cheapness three times over in the future.

Victor Kiam, noted entrepreneur, put it this way in a phone interview, "I think the fellow you need today is an astute tax accountant. With the tax laws the way they are, how you structure your deal financially is so important. You can structure it one way and pay a lot of tax, or another way and not pay much tax, and both ways are legal."

Your lawyer and accountant actually will be working for you as your legal and finance departments when you first get going. Their help will be needed in preparing or reviewing such instruments as your letter of intent to buy or sell, asset and inventory statements, auditor's reports, financial forecasts, financial statements, sales agreements, promissory notes, mortgage deeds, security agreements, releases from liability agreements, lease transfers, noncompete contracts, and many other business documents. Failure to understand all of these properly could cost you severely, and bleed your modest capital unnecessarily. If your deal is more complicated, you may need their help with stock structuring, trade name protection and complicated issues of tax basis. But at the very outset, you will want your accountant to test your idea, test your plan, lead you to capital, and ultimately get you going.

You're not alone. Every businessperson requires an accountant at some point unless you happen to know a great deal about financing, taxes and bookkeeping and accounting. Obviously, the less you know about these specialties, the more you need this kind of specialized help, and the greater potential for failure if you don't afford yourself an accountant.

Tom Frederick, an accountant and lawyer who practiced with the "Big 8" firm of Peat Marwick for many years before buying into a going industrial supply business, said recently, "You'd be amazed at how many businesses go down the tubes early because people don't think that bookkeeping and accounting are that important. They lose information, fail to meet critical dates and leave no trail whatsoever for the helpless accountant after it's too late!"

TRADITIONAL ACCOUNTING FUNCTIONS

So how does an accountant help? You go to an accountant for basic services of a financial and arithmetic nature, such as:

Help in preparing your business plan

Aid in securing financing

Bookkeeping, helping to set up the books and actually keeping the books for you in the early days

Analyzing the profit-and-loss statement, the asset and liability statement, the cash flows

Help in financial planning

Finding hidden assets in your business, such as a mail order list, a paper inventory, or in one case I heard about recently, $70,000 worth of grain that no one else had noticed

Preparing quarterly tax returns for federal, state and local authorities.

Filing the initial documents for taxpayer identification numbers, sales tax numbers, and helping you get registered with D&B to establish credit

Help in avoiding taxation, within the limits of the law

He will also advise you as to the most beneficial business structure for you to pursue. For instance, the establishment of an S corporation or Section 1244 stock (stock Issues in a small company which allow any loss to be taken personally in the form of an ordinary loss thus allowing you to maximise personal deductions) could be particularly advantageous to a new business where there is an intent to lose money in the first year or two of operations.

An accountant can also provide simple, detailed descriptions of the difference, in terms of organization, between limited partnerships and research and development partnerships, C corporations and S corporations.

Particularly in the tax restructuring underway currently in the United States, it is critical to hire an accountant to aid you in selection and delineation of types of organizations.

For instance, several provisions of the new tax law should make it considerably more attractive to structure your business as an S corporation instead of the regular C corporation status. Without getting into the detailed benefits and liabilities attached to an S corporation, we want you to know that, in an S corporation, losses pass directly from the corporation through to you as the shareholder. This is then used to offset income and reduce or eliminate taxes on your personal income tax filing.

There are limitations and requirements involved in the formation of an S corporation, including the number of share holders that you can have, a number of states that will not allow it, and selection (very carefully) of operating years and filing dates. But it is something to be sure to check out very carefully with your accountant and lawyer. And without their advice on this subject you could be missing a significant opportunity that could be costly, both initially and in the long run.

Your accountant will also aid you in establishing immediate controls, particularly in the asset area. Who will have access to inventories, receivables, cash on hand and other principle assets? These controls are critical to put into place early, and to observe. You think you can keep an eye on things yourself? A recent investigation turned up an employee who was systematically removing money from the business by writing checks to himself on a top check, and covering by making the carbon out to various suppliers. He would then catch the cashed and canceled checks himself in the monthly bank reconciliation without others in the office being aware. Another bookkeeper used her boss's rubber stamp signature to provide herself with $50 in weekend spending money almost every week.

Your accountants will help you avoid these problems. They'll also provide a stream of financial information, as mundane as employee withholding taxes, and as important as changes in tax law that can affect the way you handle investments, investment tax credits, cars, and leasing versus buying decisions.

They will also provide you with general advice about how to maximize your own personal financial situation. This will depend on whether you are trying to please a banker, a group of investors, or yourself. But there are dozens of different ways to handle the expensing and capitalizing of costs as they come in. There are benefits to each. They can result in tremendous differences in the way a business is portrayed.

A client approached his San Francisco accountant with a large profit surplus on December 24. The accountant said confidently, "I have never seen a $100,000 problem that we couldn't do something about." Certainly accounting law is clear, and you don't want to be foolishly aggressive, but an experienced accountant can create and eliminate reserves, write off inventories, produce charitable contributions, and much, much, more.

Your accountants will help you in longer-range planning as well, helping you to define what your goals are and what they might become, for instance, considering something as far ranging as going public, what that entails and how to go about it.

They will aid you in contingency planning. What if you get into trouble? How do you get out, fast? What if you have surplus profits on the other hand? They know ways that will allow you to either minimize taxes or maximize profits, depending on what you are trying to achieve at a particular point.

When you get to the question of refinancing, they can help you seek out different banking relationships, combine banking relationships, or find additional investment capital. Remember, an accountant is in the financial marketplace every day, dealing with many different investors, and is aware of people whose problem may be the absence of write-offs in a particular year. This could bring them to you as willing investors, swapping cash for write-offs.

Your accountants can help you in minimizing your own taxation and maximizing your personal liquidity. They will show you how to borrow money from your corporation and how to establish a minimal interest and repayment structure. They will show you what assets can be treated as personal and which as corporate, and how to do this in a way that will insure a successful outcome if an audit should come your way.

WHEN TO HIRE AN ACCOUNTANT

These are just a few of the many reasons "why" an accountant should become a prime member of your team. Many people then ask "when" is the best time to hire an accountant?

The accountants will tell you the earlier the better. "There are so many deals that we could have improved if we had heard about them earlier rather than later and having to bail someone out," said Gajda. Frederick confirmed that. "The people who spend about $1,000 with us in two meetings, reviewing the assumptions, uncomplicating the deal or plan, and allowing us to package a complete financial document are the ones who wind up getting support."

The idea of developing a full-blown plan, then ramming it through, is far less attractive to an accountant or a lawyer than if you invest in a short, perhaps one-to-two hour consultation with each of them before you actually begin to polish your already highly defined business plan. In that session you can also get a strong sense of whether your accountant feels that you have a chance of getting traditional bank financing or whether you'll have to go to less conventional sources. He'll also check your major assumptions and discuss any critical flaws within your plan.

It is harder to bring in an accountant later, even if you intend to do much of the planning work yourself, because you will have already churned out a considerable investment in time and energy that you and the accountant may be less likely to want to adjust or reconcile. This is the very common "but I've already got it all printed up" syndrome.

So bring both accountant and lawyer in at as early a point in the process as you can. Once you're successful with financing, they will also help you get off to a faster start with the administrative mechanics of the start-up, including all of the permits, licenses and fees, and can aid your initial hiring decisions. Hiring advice, particularly as it relates to personnel procedures, operating routines, and systems that you are going to want to put into place can be critical. In my own case, my accountant happened to have a publishing background. We were trying to take a giant step forward by getting beyond our manual operating system and installing a system for order processing, accounts receivable, inventory control, and general ledgers. One of the most attractive options was with the Storage Technology Corp. which was offering a turn-key system at a cost of $50,000. We were told that it was a major opportunity since the system had been developed at an investment of millions of dollars, and that it was marked down from $75,000. I was enthused, but our accountant strongly urged us to pause before leaping.

Looking at the contract on a Thursday afternoon, which only required my signature, I decided to let it wait until the next Monday morning. On Friday morning I picked up the *Wall Street Journal* and read a lead story describing Storage Technology's Chapter 11 bankruptcy filing. I was stunned. I would have a very unwise decision, and only through the pause that my instinctive accountant gave me did I not sign a deal with Storage Technology.

Eventually, we were able to develop our own system internally at considerably reduced expense, a system that we have continued to add on to and modify as we have matured and our business has changed.

Today, virtually all accountants are familiar with data processing operating systems. I would not consider hiring an accountant who was unfamiliar with systems. Their advice in the computerization of your business is invaluable, from the moment you put in your first standalone personal computer to your first integrated micro system to your first major mainframe. They will show you how to set up systems and controls and make suggestions on how to maximize the capacity of your system. They will also help you find the right systems people who can immediately make a difference in the return on investment you can achieve from your hardware and software decisions. In our case we moved from manual, to IBM PC/XT, to a 17-user Fortune Micro System in the first four years of operation. The investments were labor at stage 1, $10,000 at stage 2, and $25,000 at stage 3.

I made no moves without the involvement of my accountant and a key systems person in the development of our data operations.

Another reason it is important to have an accountant on board early is that the successful negotiation you have with your banker will translate itself into a not uncomplicated bank document. These can take many forms and carry a lot of "mumbo jumbo." Accountants are obviously familiar with all of those different forms and will encourage you to sign this or add that. An accountant will simplify this process and keep you from feeling that you're reading a *magna carta* which requires 15 years of law school to really understand. Your return on this alone will be many times the fee you pay.

CHOOSING AN ACCOUNTANT

Accountants, like all professionals, come in all sizes and shapes. They will range from the retired, 71-year-old corporate chief financial officer who is now delighted to get $75 a day, three times a week, so as not to exceed his Social Security limitations, to a young MBA who is moonlighting, and picking up experience at the same time as a junior accountant, to a senior bookkeeper, to a "Big 8" firm.

The best place to start is with your brother-in-law who probably knows an accountant. This allows you to have an informal conversation about accountants without "the meter running." An hour invested with a friend at a time like this is important because you will learn the differences between levels of accounting sophistication and expertise. Dick Hug, president of Environmental Elements, an insider or leveraged buyout of the Baltimore division of the Koppers Corp., put it this way; "I decided that I was going to be with the very best law firm and the very best accounting firm that I could find. I engaged Arthur Andersen, the accounting firm whose managing partner was a lawyer I had known for a number of years here in Baltimore. He has now come to work as my partner, executive vice president and chief financial officer of the company. I also engaged Basher and Howard, the number one law firm in Baltimore. Both of them were crucial to making this deal go."

There is a big gap between your brother-in-law and Arthur Andersen, so the questions that you must ask yourself are: Who should my accountant be? How much depth do I really need? Will a single, small-town practitioner be enough or is your business going to be complicated, so much that you need the support of a medium size or even a "Big 8" firm?

In deciding this, the question of previous experience is critical. In my own case, my accountant had spent a number of years working on the Houghton-Mifflin book publishing account for Peat Marwick in Boston. Obviously, the experience that he derived from that account has helped him to help me in the narrower areas of publishing law, even though he's now a small town proprietor. So the guiding questions should be, "What have you done recently that is similar to my kind of business? What kind of specific contacts do you have in this field? Are we a good match for each other?"

Directness with your accountants is a time saver. Are they willing to be initially honest with you, telling you that they can't provide you with the specific services that a big eight firm can? Will they tell you that while they will charge you a lower rate than the big eight firm, when you get into specialized areas, such as complicated stock structuring or preparation to go public they won't be able to help and will push you along to someone who can? It's that kind of message that you're seeking.

We looked at three very different approaches to accounting, ranging from small town, small office practitioners to a long-term conservative IRS agent who had formed an accounting office with 20 people, to a medium-size (100-person) accounting firm in Albany, New York. For our start up, the former IRS agent was the most qualified and most specifically practiced in the area of S incorporations, and he made a big difference to us in getting going. The person who is perfect for you during start up may not be perfect for you as you grow. Three years into our venture we determined we needed someone with stronger publishing background, and we were fortunate in being able to fill our needs locally. This has helped us to grow, and to understand our business enormously.

Growth, in the form of additional sales volume, does not mean that you won't have to continue to spend proportionally in the bookkeeping and accounting areas. Hoge, the aforementioned president of Huber-Hoge Associates in Long Island, tells of a near disaster when his business grew rapidly and the accountant insisted on continuing to do it all herself. "Before we knew it, we were backed up two months in our accounting, didn't know what our real financial picture was, and had a near disaster on our hands."

Another example was a high flying direct marketing corporation in Chicago run by Joe Sugarman, who, before he knew it, had a seven-to-eight week backlog in his order processing and record keeping causing complaints to be filed with the Better Business Bureau and then the Federal Trade Commission (FTC). They moved in demanding every imaginable detail, and in the process closed his business. That was an awful tough way to find out about the importance of bookkeeping and accounting. A good accountant will keep you briefed on state and federal regulations, such as the FTC 30-day shipping rule, and help you with serious problems.

CONTROLS FOR YOUR BUSINESS

A good accountant will also help you to plug in the small controls that you need to keep from "getting beat."

In fact, a recent story in *Inc.* magazine tells of a chief financial officer who convinced the owner of his business, after about six months of favorable employment, to allow him to open a small discretionary account that he could use on Fridays and Mondays when the boss wasn't around. Fortunately for the owner, a bank employee made a phone call on a Friday afternoon to his home asking whether he really intended to have his entire line of credit, $800,000, transfered from the commercial account into this new discretionary account. He did not, and that was the end of the chief financial officer.

There are many ways that you can be beaten by shrewd employees. Don't let this happen to you. Ask your accountant to help put controls in place, and to provide regular audits.

This also gets back to your fundamental decisions on new employees. Obviously intense scrutiny devoted to resumes and the completion of background checks and probing interviews can raise your chances of hiring talented and honest people. Don't let yourself get beat.

A friend of mine recently left the big eight practice of Touche Ross and became the chief financial officer of a fast growing company in our area. I asked him why he made the shift. He replied, "Too many unenjoyable clients." I asked him what the characteristics of a good client were and he said, "Someone who understands his business, watches his shop, spots the trends that are developing, and is willing to take advice."

This may seem obvious, but many people go into business areas that they know nothing about, finding it difficult to understand what's happening in their industry or any of the trends that are underway. They fail, frequently after rejecting their accountant's advice.

Probably the highest success rates come to those who move into an area they already know extremely well, and find a niche for themselves and for the business within that area— "niche" marketing as it were.

Accountants also look for people who have the information they need, but who are willing to listen to professionol opinions. Recently there was a proposal for a new supermarket to be formed out of the purchase of an old supermarket in Berkshire County, Massachusetts. The proposed new operators knew everything about the supermarket business but were unwilling to allow their accountant to go through and test the assumptions of the business plan and, as a result, financing didn't materialize. On the other hand, another recent business launch, the Delftree Corp., which specializes in growing and wholesaling gourmet shiitake mushrooms, was tremendously aided by the involvement of an accountant who was able to package both the financing and business planning, and aid in the securing of the money needed to effect a buyout of the business. The business now ships 2,000 pounds of mushrooms weekly.

ACCOUNTANTS ROLE IN FINDING MONEY

Help with financing is obviously one of the major areas in which an accountant can be of assistance. Starting with the question, "Is the loan amount reasonable and realistic?" an accountant can quickly assess, based on his experience with local and regional lenders whether you are even at the right level of the game. For instance, someone looking for $25,000 to $50,000 may be able to get a bank loan with only an accountant's letter.

On the other hand, anything over $50,000 is probably going to require a strong, sound, formalized business plan, because the bank needs very specific sales plans and identifiable assets. Additionally, anyone seeking $50,000 or more who would like a Small Business Administration guarantee will definitely require an extensive and full-blown business plan.

Now here comes a relatively bitter pill. In virtually every start-up situation, personal guarantees are going to be required by a banker. You must understand what this implies: Your corporation, no matter how cleverly structured, cannot shield you, eventually, from having your house, your car, or your daughter's silver flute repossessed. Banks don't like to do this, but it can happen. In our own case, we anticipated and accepted this banking reality during the first year, but after a full year of results were in, we negotiated a second-year line of credit which was more sizeable and which eliminated the personal guarantee. I remember vividly my lawyer telling me to tell the banker that, "This isn't a Mom and Pop doughnut store any more." It worked.

Accountants can help enormously in steering you through city, state, and federal opportunities for funding. This is an intricate path, and it is unlikely that the individual with average knowledge of state sources can be lucky enough to come up with much support. Recently, my accountant called and indicated that the governor of Massachusetts had just introduced legislation to reduce small business taxation by 50 percent. By informing me of this potential development, we were able to consider a simple restructuring of our business in such a way as to take maximum advantage of that likely change.

While it is important to get advice in areas like the form your corporation should take, and the documents that you have to fill out and the details regarding S and C corporation status and Section 1244 stock, the most important piece of accounting advice comes in the form of financing alternatives, and how to secure firm commitments. The accountant can truly help you shine during the organizational phase. Jim Edgar, former managing partner of Touche Ross, West Coast operation, who now runs his own highly successful practice in San Francisco, put it this way, "We put six months of work into our business plan, went to three bankers and they were impressed that we had every answer to every financial and accounting question that came up. We got our money."

Accountants will also ensure that you pay attention to your bookkeeping from day one. This is an area that cannot be neglected or done "when you get time to do it in the evening." It is critical to be prudent, cautious, and concerned every day about the money that is coming in and going out.

Your accountant will help you to appreciate the role of the computer in your organization and to assess how you move from a manual order processing and shipping system into new applications one at a time. First, a word processor, then order processing, then accounts receivable, then inventory, general ledger, and finally sales and marketing and production information. This step-by-step approach, with the total involvement of the accountant in each phase of it, has allowed us to have an orderly support for our growth.

At the same time that you do not want to act solely out of tax motivation, it is important to be aware of the tax consequences of everything that you do. It is rather silly, on one hand, to rush out on December 30 and buy $10,000 worth of supplies just because you are trying to avoid paying taxes on a small profit that developed for the year. You are probably better off paying the tax, and not tying your money up in supplies that won't be used for three years. I know one firm that is still using toilet paper they bought five years ago.

The flip side of that coin is that you don't want to do things procedurally to improve the appearance of your profit-and-loss statement in the fourth quarter of the year that could potentially hurt the underpinnings of the business.

During the late 1960s at Time-Life Books, the publisher would distribute a memo every fourth quarter indicating that expenses should be deferred until January 1. The purpose was to enhance earnings, apparently. The practical effect of that was to move planned advertising expenditures, one of the few things that can be mapped late in the year, out of one of the most effective promotional selling seasons of all . . . pre-Christmas. This had an apparent short-term "improving" effect, but negative longer-term consequences.

It is also important not to ignore the rest of your business in order to master every single aspect of accounting. That is why you have accountants. You don't have to understand every nuance in amortization and depreciation schedules, but you do have to have someone who can make sense of it for you, so that you can make reasonable judgments as to the best way to go.

ACCOUNTANTS' ADVICE FOR YOUR EMERGING GROWTH COMPANY

After you successfully emerge from your start up, you'll begin to wonder if either partnership money or debt financing will be adequate to sustain the rate of growth that you want to achieve. You may begin to wonder whether going public is something that you want to consider seriously. This absolutely requires a heavy involvement on the part of your accountant and lawyer. Understand that while any underwriter will tell you that the "going public" time schedule is six months, the actual process, to be done cleanly and well, might take as long as two years.

This is because your accounting systems must be absolutely squeaky clean, including clean balance sheets and numbers that may even have to be managed for a period to provide the apparent profitability that any business contemplating a public filing with the Securities and Exchange Commission (SEC) must have. Obviously, you can't do this overnight, and two years may be a reasonable target. An SEC filing will also require three years of audited financial statements from a recognized big eight accounting firm, which will probably be different from your local accounting firm.

Public offerings are time consuming and complicated. Do not underestimate the money and effort required to carry them off. Don

Dion, chief financial officer of the Patten Corporation and formerly with Arthur Young in Boston, advises that his firm's public offering took six months and cost over $350,000 in legal, accounting, and printing bills. This is clearly the "big leagues" and should not be taken lightly.

I had to laugh the other day when I read in the financial pages of the newspaper this "Rule of Thumb from the Silicon Valley: After two profitable quarters, go public." Obviously, you are in your business for the long haul, and you are not looking for get-rich-quick schemes through public offerings.

On the other hand, an extremely well-planned public offering can yield major benefits to both the corporation and to individual investors. The Patten Corp. of Stamford, Vermont, a unique marketer of rural land, went public at just the right point in the 1986 stock market with an offering price of $10 per share, and it recently traded as high as $30. Many people got wealthy, at least on paper, and the firm gained the debt-free capitalization it was seeking in order to expand.

A commonly misunderstood procedure is the year-end evaluation that your accountant does for you. Simplify this by understanding that there are really only three levels of review. From least involved to most involved, they are as follows;

1. *An opinion.* An opinion means that no audit has taken place and the accounting firm is unwilling to take any position on the health of the company or the completeness of the financial statements. As it stands, they'll offer "an opinion."

2. *A review.* This means that a compilation has been completed of the records of the business in financial statement sequence and order, but that no independent verification has taken place. This is twice as expensive as an opinion.

3. *An audit.* This is where your accountant will apply rigorous standards and take a position of independent verification of the assets and liabilities of the business. This can be expensive and carry some liability for your accountant and auditor, and therefore is three to four (and even more) times as expensive as a simple compilation.

When you get going, you will require nothing more than an opinion, unless your banker insists on it. As you take on additional investors or partners, or additional levels of equity or debt financing, you may well be required to move from opinion to review to audit. Know what you need and spend accordingly.

Hopefully you can see the tremendous value that an accountant/partner can have on your business. Now let's take a closer look at the lawyer.

YOUR LAWYER AS YOUR FIRST PARTNER

Your relationship with your legal council is apt to be your closest, and most personal. It is your task to consistently supply your lawyer with enough details about your business, your plans and your directions, in short, the grand design of your business so that he can make calculated judgments about the way to structure the best organization and to deal with the many different players involved.

This results in your doing a fair amount of education of your lawyer, at your own expense. Don't be surprised when after sending your lawyer an interesting magazine article that relates to your business, you get a bill for $25 for his reading it. (This may also cause you to be somewhat selective about the articles that you send his way!)

My attorney, Don Dubendorf, of Williamstown, Massachusetts, tells me about the time a brand new client came in his doors and said he was launching an artificial intelligence business in town. Don's first response was, "Jeff, I'll be happy to help you, but you should know that it is going to cost you a fair amount of money to educate me."

Jeff gladly did that and the relationship has been an extremely productive one over the last three years, with a consistently high payback on time invested up front.

Why have a lawyer at all? Simply because the right one will save you his fees 10 times over in structuring your business, structuring your deal, negotiating and drafting contracts on your behalf, and closing.

I saw in my own contract with a major corporation how as few as two words can save a person hundreds of thousands of dollars. I noticed that Don had inserted the words "from stock" as it related to how inventory would be transferred. This put me in a position of being able to request inventory as I chose, rather than being stuck with the carrying charge of that inventory myself. In short, you want your lawyer to be more than an employee, and less than a professional servant. What you are really looking for is a partner.

You might ask, "Isn't it terribly expensive to have a lawyer?" It cost me $10,000 in legal fees to get my business going, and I am convinced that I got a $100,000 worth of advice. I am also convinced, after four years of experience, that without his help and guidance there were several times (about once a year) when the entire corporation would have gone under. With evidence like this, I think you can convince yourself rather quickly that it is worth the money.

More importantly, ask yourself what kind of a lawyer do I need? Do I need a technician, a negotiator, or a creative deal maker?

The best place to start, again, is with family and friends who have had some experience with lawyers. Pick the friend most approachable and see if you can spend an hour discussing the range of services that different types of individual practitioners and law firms offer.

Try to determine how much advice you are going to need. Remember, at about $100 an hour you are dealing with a brain surgeon, not a bone setter. It is critical to have this professional in the game early. Explain, as early as you can, what kind of business you are talking about and the kind of business advice you think you are going to need. Don't get hung up on corporate form, permits, licenses, and fees right away. (You don't even need a lawyer to get a sales tax number.) Rather, try to convey a specific idea about the kind of business you are getting into and where you see it going over the next five years. This professional will help you, for certain, by drafting contracts and stock purchase agreements and helping with your other various forms and documents, but it is the early involvement and understanding of your vision that you need.

After that one-hour consultation, show the business plan that you have developed. Look for the same kind of reaction that you expect from your accountant. He or she will probably spot ways to immediately improve your situation by virtue of his or her understanding the way in which the business will work over periods of time. Again, if you expect losses early on, the S corporation will be a great benefit to you. On the other hand, if you expect profits, perhaps the C corporation is the form recommended by your attorney. Talk about this, as well as your profit and personal expectations.

One of my friends told me two years ago he had found a legal "clinic" that could do the job. He felt it was effective and inexpensive for simple, technical and fast legal forms, documents and services.

However, these people are unequipped for helping you to define, negotiate and establish a business, or to aid in developing relationships with clients. For this you should expect to invest $500, minimum, for your lawyer, with other state ($150) and miscellaneous fees in addition.

CHOOSING A LAWYER

In trying to measure a lawyer, there are probably three major areas of consideration. First, is he or she competent in your business area or willing to learn about it? I am not arguing for a narrow specialist here—for example, publishing contract law—because you really don't need one at this time. You need somebody who is experienced, savvy, a fast problem solver, and therefore intelligent, but who is willing also to take the time to learn your particular business interests.

In my case, I spent a fair amount of money educating my lawyer early on in the publishing business and all of its quirks. "Do you mean to tell me that you ship books out today and they get sent back to you from Walden two years from now?" asked Don. "This isn't a business, its a consignment attic!"

However, once he understood the nature of returns, he helped me to structure a virtually unique four-tier marketing program, equivalent to a beautiful recycling system.

What you are trying to do is enable your lawyer to be creative in adding value quickly to your business. As you go on, you may need specialization. Our company has run into needs in the trademark and licensing areas that went beyond Don's ability to give us advice. He picked up the telephone, contacted a colleague at Foley, Hoag in Boston, where we pay a big city $125 an hour instead of a rural $80 an hour. But they are specialists whose services we enlist when necessary.

Second, is your lawyer willing to talk money with you? If you feel awkward talking about this subject, you should broach it at once. Do not ask your lawyer to be a speculator, but assure him or her you will pay the fees whether you come out plus or minus in your situation, and that he or she will not be at risk because of your venture. Also before you engage an attorney, determine how much you are going to be charged. Ask how long it will take to do the work you require. And make sure everyone is aware of your desire to limit legal expenses.

Fred Steingold, a lawyer from Ann Arbor, Michigan, details 18 ways to cut legal costs in his *Practical Legal Guide for Small Business*. These range from talking about fees up front, to trying to settle cases out of court rather than litigating, to insisting on itemized statements each month, to guaranteeing a minimum number of hours of work, and numerous other ideas. Talk, in detail, with your lawyer about ways of containing legal costs.[1]

Ron Hume whose Hume Publishing Company is now approaching $100 million in sales tells about his lawyer who said to him in the early days, "Ron, I believe in the venture that you are getting into. Take all of my legal bills and put them in your upper right hand drawer. If you are successful, pull them out and pay me some day. If your business goes down the drain, forget about them." While Ron wasn't sure that that was exactly the way that he wanted to do business, he remembered that conversation vividly and later, after the business had been launched and was underway successfully, he not only paid the bills but he asked the lawyer to become a partner. That lawyer partner is not at all uncommon in business start-ups. Many people have a lawyer in key positions of responsibility.

The third major question to ask yourself about your lawyer is whether you have confidence in the person. Quickly, you will learn that their judgment is either consistently solid or spotty. Their knowledge of the facts of law may be impressive at the outset, but without good judgment gained from years of negotiating and doing deals, all the facts of law mean nothing. How about their problem-solving ability? Are they creative in refashioning or remaking your plans? Do you feel comfortable with them? Look at their offices. "Status offices," that result in $125 to $150 an hour because of thick carpets and thirty-fourth floor locations overlooking harbors are things that you should avoid like the plague. It may be at some point you will need a "name," but at the outset it is the last thing you want

---

[1]Fred Steingold, *Practical Legal Guide For Small Business* (Englewood Cliffs, NJ: Prentice-Hall, 1982).

to spend money on. They can be located in $5-per-square-foot space as long as good, legal work can be done and effective long-term communications can be developed.

Your first meeting with your lawyer should be geared toward getting across as quickly as possible the gist of your business concept. This should be an all-cards-on-the-table kind of meeting where you pass on what you know and admit to what you don't. Under no circumstances should you try to out-lawyer your lawyer. Legal knowledge is what you are paying for. Take your idea, your vision, your goals, and your plan; and show him or her how you are creating a new niche. Ask for the lawyer's best advice on capitalization.

Ask what technical, organizational, or legal issues he or she can see right off that your new business will face. Whether it be a corporate structure or a zoning problem, detect chinks in your armor early.

Tell him or her that you expect help in negotiating, formulating contracts, and in defining precise relationships—such things as purchase/sale agreements, supplier relationships, landlord relationships, purchase orders, and invoices.

Ask for help in setting up a simplified method of hiring and in communicating with your employees. Potential problems with discrimination, equity, and fair play can all be minimized with simple discussion upfront.

Tell your lawyer what you think are the most important assets of your business, the "tools of your trade," and ask for assistance in protecting those assets. They may be ideas, they may be machinery, they may be, as in the case of Larry Bird, a 30-foot jump shot. But all of these things can be legally protected. You should enlist the aid of your lawyer to line up the insurance you require to cover them.

Don't make too much early on of the importance of the corporate structure, otherwise you might find yourself "all dressed up with nowhere to go." On the other hand, do take the steps necessary to have everyone take you seriously. And these include initial capitalization, federal ID number, the leasing of office space, and stock agreements.

THE FINE POINTS OF NEGOTIATION

From my point of view, one of the most important areas of support from my lawyer has been in negotiations. This may be something immediate—your first lease—or it may be long term, such as the acquisition of another business.

Victor Kiam, in his book *Going For It!* discusses the importance of negotiations: "You must try to view the proceedings through the other person's eyes as well as your own."[2]

Since negotiating strategy is one of my average-to-fair abilities, I placed a great deal of emphasis on negotiating ability when I sought an attorney. This is what we learned together in the process of negotiating the buyout of Garden Way Publishing.[3]

In our buyout of Garden Way Publishing, we were all cooperatively, even happily, involved with the firm's top officers in thinking up creative ways to make our deal work. At this level we were treated as part of the solution.

Then we moved on to review details with finance, tax accounting, and warehousing, and suddenly we became part of the problem.

During this difficult period, some of the top officers became inaccessible. In one case, when we finally were "slid in" to a busy schedule, the meeting was limited to five minutes when we needed an hour.

However, successful negotiating should solve problems for both parties in a friendly, win-win way. That's your best position and one that will be weakened if you focus on subsidiary factors.

"In a successful negotiation everybody wins," according to Gerard I. Nierenberg. "The objective should be to achieve agreement, not total victory. Both parties must feel that they have gained something."[4]

Keep the negotiations fair, friendly, and nonconfrontational. Be reasonable despite their responses. *Listen* to your counterparts.

Negotiate on the merits of the deal that will work to the best advantage of both sides. An insider buyout will only happen if both perceive they are coming out ahead.

Don't negotiate from too rigid a position.

Try to close the deal early.

We asked several persons to cite the most important thing to them in their own business negotiations.

"Hang tough for the key issues," said Vaughan Beals of Harley-Davidson. "Don't take the easy, expeditious way out."

Doug Baker, Vermont innkeeper, said the most important thing in negotiations was, "One word, patience."

[2]Victor Kiam, *Going For It!* (New York: Morrow, 1986), p. 159.
[3]Donald Dubendorf and M. John Storey, *The Insider Buyout* (Powal, Vermont: Storey Communications, 1985).
[4]Gerard Nierenberg, *Fundamentals of Negotiating* (New York: Hawthorne Books, 1977).

Patience is an unnerving sign of strength. Patience can serve to wear down and divide the other side and make an early resolution more important than the adoption of certain values or terms. It also provides time to probe and educate.

"You're in negotiations not only to win your own point but to come to some type of resolution to the situation, and usually there is a middle ground where you meet, and you have to learn to accept that middle ground," Baker said.

"You learn that in negotiations you always ask for more than what you really want . . . so that when you get to where you want to be, if the other side will give in a little, you'll actually come out a winner.

"A lot of people don't know that art—asking for more than you want—simply because most people are basically honest. They go into negotiations from a position they will have to give up. You can well afford to give up what you never expected to win," Baker said.

To complement and bolster your overall friendly, win-win negotiating strategy, you and your counselors must agree on the specific tactics you will use during the talks.

Our suggestions include the old favorites: Respond to their concerns. Meet their needs. Lead to their strengths. Invent options. Build trust. Act, don't react.

What these negotiating tips add up to is a process of getting all the facts and concerns out on the table where they can be discussed.

Additionally: Keep your emotions and your ego in your briefcase. This is no time for loose cannons on the deck.

Also: be your own casting director. You're the reigning expert on the business on the table. Tell them how you are going to solve their problems.

Most important: Use the ABC negotiating and sales technique: that's Always Be Closing.

If the negotiations take some surprising turns in an attempt, you suspect, to intimidate or pressure your side, don't reveal your anger or impatience. Remain true to your image of yourself as manager of sales, deals, and buyouts.

When the going gets tough, change the pace. Let your counselor take over and play tough for your side.

Regularly, during insider negotiations, you need to steer the conversation back to square one.

You might say, "Let's remember why we're sitting here—to solve these problems. It's true we seem far apart on this issue, who's going to pay for this. Let's go back to the fact that the corporation wants this to happen. Let's invent a solution to this problem.

"If you win this minor point, you might be threatening the very life of the new entity which would cause a public-relations problem and end the flow of cash back to the corporation."

Be prepared for unexpected changes in the price or terms of the deal that could lead to a deadlock in your negotiations.

A deadlock can result when one side attempts to raise or lower the stakes. Or it can result from new information or perceptions that appear to change the balance.

Perceptions aside, deadlocks are real and can be costly in time and money.

One thing's for sure: it takes two sides to make a deadlock.

For the most part deadlocks will be the result of legitimate business issues. But insider buyouts are frequently fertile ground for deadlocks caused by emotional, petty, and not-so-petty personal and personality problems.

You should also watch for deadlocks that are imposed as a negotiating tactic to confuse you and wear down your patience.

Do not be intimidated by the threat of a collapse in your talks. Approach deadlocks with patience by continuing to talk about solutions to genuine problems.

Be calm and confident, not cocky or combative. Try to appear relaxed. Study everybody's body language. Maintain friendly eye contact with those who have authority to close the deal. Break the ice: Tell a family joke or arrange for your attorney to tease you about something trivial.

Ask questions about the issue that has caused the deadlock. Listen carefully to the answers.

Don't focus on their statements of position. Probe to discover the reasoning behind their positions.

Two sides can play this game. Respectfully change the subject. Answer only a part of the question. Answer a different question. Ask for the question to be reworded or rephrase it to suit yourself. Or excuse yourself while you make an important telephone call back to the office.

However, don't get too cute. If you're negotiating the purchase of a company, continue to sell the strong points of your deal as if you were negotiating with a lender. Make your pitch to the sellers and steadfastly refrain from jousting and becoming competitive with their attorneys. The sellers are the only ones who have the authority to close the deal. This is not the time to become impatient or indignant.

Patiently try to discover the real reason for the deadlock by narrowing your focus. Is this an unexpected logjam or a planned stall imposed as a tactic to intimidate you and weaken your position? Offer to take the time to research and redefine the issues. Sometimes the threat of another delay is just the ticket for dissolving a deadlock.

Leave all the doors open. Don't burn any bridges. Find a way around the deadlock that will satisfy both sides.

Be prepared to yield to reason and principle if the deadlock is warranted. But avoid being pressured into adding any sweeteners to the deal unless there is quid pro quo.

Remain firm in the face of unwarranted pressure.

And never stray very far from your basic reasons for suggesting a purchase/sale. Recall the original sentiments expressed by both parties.

Remind them that the goal of the talks is agreement in solving a mutual problem, not victory for one side or the other.

The stickiest, trickiest negotiations in our Garden Way Publishing buyout came just before the closing when headquarters announced its insistence that accounts receivable be included in the deal, a move that increased the price of the deal by over 250 percent.

Originally headquarters had wanted to collect these accounts, which was fine with us. Later, they realized this could be a mistake. In the crazy book publishing business, trade retailers are allowed to return unsold books for credit. What appears to a publisher as a receivable account may turn out to be old inventory and a cash liability. Headquarters had become concerned that without a publishing division, the company would have no way to process a stream of unsold books flowing back from retailers. The proportion of returned books to books sold may range from 10 to 30 percent.

The last-minute change in our deal meant enduring some negotiating over the value of the outstanding accounts, especially since we started talking with a 30 percent difference in the valuation of these accounts.

Our buying the accounts receivable meant we could open the mail on Day One and find checks enclosed. But the proportion also meant we were scurrying for additional last-minute financing and beginning our new business by focusing on past mistakes—ours and everyone else's—while we tried to collect old accounts.

The banker relationship was absolutely critical at this point. By now we had lined up financing, but it didn't include the receivables. We walked our banker-partner through the restructured deal, and after ten minutes, he said, "If the rest of the deal makes sense, this part makes real good sense." Knowing when to leave, we left.

Others have had similar problems. Dick Hug said of his July, 1983 buyout of Environmental Elements from Koppers, "Until April, our relationship was good. But when we got down to the nitty-gritty negotiations, obviously I wanted to get as good a deal as I could, and they in turn . . . got a little bit testy. I began to wonder whether this thing was going to work. Then, on the other side of the fence, there was a lot of wondering on the part of Koppers people whether they ought to sell this business."

It was at this point that a memo that Hug had written came back to haunt him during the final negotiations:

"Several months before this began [in September 1982], I had written a five- or six-page memorandum to the president and chairman of the company telling them why they should not sell the Environmental business—for all the reasons that I bought the Environmental business. The future was there. The position we had in the marketplace. Our technology.

"I gave them facts, figures, forecasts, and performances. I think the longer this thing played out, the longer they had to think about it. They began to wonder if this was the right decision.

"If we had not completed our deal in July [1983] as we did, it may never have closed."

Remember, closing the deal is in effect closing the sale. This is no time to relax and give up your responsibility as sales manager for the deal. This is the time for you to move into your new role as the president, chief public spokesperson, and sales manager for your new company.

Meanwhile your attorney will be responsible for preparing all the necessary agreements and documents.

However, in your haste to get on with running your new company, be sensitive to your attorney's concerns about tying up all loose ends of the deal. Hold the handshakes and champagne until your attorney signals he is satisfied all the specifics have been met.

Then, when all is said, signed, and transferred, congratulate the sellers. Make your sellers believe they won. Because if you and your counselors did it right, there will be *no* losers among the parties involved.

"We learned something," Gura said. "They are not all barracudas out there. When you're really giving it your all, when you've maintained your integrity with people, the people you do business with are very supportive. They are not out to rape you. There's always an exception—and we had a couple. But generally they lined up behind you and they cheered for you. It was terrific."

In our case, the closing was an anticlimax. The homework had been done thoroughly on both sides. Two checks were drawn. I signed five papers and went home and kissed my wife.

I think all this supports how very important it is to find the right lawyer that you can work with. Another entrepreneur, Larry Munini, Genysys Software Systems, said, "Early on, in my series of phone calls seeking advisors, I called a neighbor who was an attorney. I gave him my spiel about how I was going to start this company. Would he like to put in money? He said, 'No, but I have all sorts of clients, all sorts of private investors who do this all the time. I'll introduce you.'

"I said I need an attorney to represent me, will you do that? He said, 'Gee, that would be a conflict of interest if I were representing an investor. Let me give you the name of a buddy who lives across town.'

"Basically, he put me in touch with a gentleman who ultimately wound up as my attorney. A very fortunate pass along, because that attorney turned out to be my most valuable advisor over the next six months."

Munini said his attorney and his venture capitalist served on the Genysys board of directors. The attorney is also corporate counsel, a job that takes about one day a week.

Another view on the importance of a lawyer is expressed by Jay Jordan, venture capitalist, who best described the key strength of lawyers and other professional counselors bring to the deal. "*Knowing*, that is the key to success in negotiations," Jordan said. "The guy who hasn't been through it before is not going to know when to give, when not to give, what to say and what not to say. An experienced person will know. The experience may result in a nontransaction, and that might be good."

This is a case when apparent losing might in the long run be winning.

All of this by way of saying that the selection of a lawyer is one of the most important decisions you are going to make.

Tips on Selecting a Lawyer

1. Try to determine your legal needs
2. Do your homework about lawyer selection
3. Ask yourself how much value your attorney can add to your business
4. Will your lawyer encourage you to take calculated risks?
5. Don't make him or her defensive or try to out-lawyer your lawyer
6. Look for confidence, competence, and previous success
7. Minimize the number of people in contact with your lawyer
8. Ask the names of the law firm's accountants and bankers
9. Don't skimp on legal service or advice; you get what you pay for
10. Remember that other questions may be far more important than corporate structure

I asked both my accountant and my lawyer to join my board of directors. Both said no. I was surprised, but I learned.

I learned they both felt strongly that they could give the most detached, unbiased advice by being participants in the board meeting, but not directors.

They have done that, and in addition led us to numerous contacts that have resulted in new business.

So pick these high-priced mechanics carefully and well. They will pay you back many times over.

5

Finding Money: Partners, Bankers, Governments, and Venture Capitalists

After your lawyer and the accountant have reviewed your plan, it's pretty obvious what your next step is: finding someone to give you the money you need. Maybe you have a $200,000 early corporate retirement package on one hand or a rich Uncle Gus on the other. Most people don't. But everyone has assets, and some source of capital that they can turn to.

Why can't you just go to the bank? Banks, for the most part, aren't that interested in brand new, and let's face it, high-risk ventures. And while you may be able to secure some financing from a bank, that's just about the tip of the financing iceberg. We'll cover over 20 ways to fund your new venture, a number of which may surprise you.

Some people feel that they don't want to borrow money at all. Ed Stern, president of Hilary House Publishers, felt very strongly about this, "I worked evenings and weekends on a new publication while I was employed as vice president of Grosset & Dunlap Publishers. We now produce two successful annual reference directories, and rather than seeking bank or outside financing, I was able to finance my directories on my own. This gives me 100 percent ownership of my corporation and permits me the lifestyle that I want."

On the other hand, if you're already used to borrowing, or you get an idea for something major as Herbert Boyer, a gene splicer, and Robert Swanson did in 1976, you may need $100 million before you can really get your venture into full gear. Their idea, Genentech, was the Wall Street sensation of 1980 and went public in order to produce the $100 million worth of funding required. Genentech predicts $1 billion in sales by the early 1990s. Whether you're an Ed Stern or a Genentech, the money is going to have to come from somewhere.[1]

That's what this chapter is all about: finding money. After you've read it, we hope you feel your options are many. Remember, there are many many people who would like to see you succeed. Whether it be a supplier counting on future business, an accounting firm happy to provide startup space for your "emerging growth company," a bank looking to make predictable and safe interest on its loan to you, or a venture capitalist striving to "beat the market" by identifying initial public offering possibilities long before they go public, there are many people who would like to see you be a winner. Your task is to show them how you're going to do it.

Financing your venture may take a while, so don't be discouraged if you have to look beyond a single source (in our case we talked to five different bankers before getting our loan). There's also no reason why you have to think about getting all your financing from the same source. In fact, there are advantages to creating a multilevel financing package. We'll show you how to do that, in simple step-by-step fashion, where every bit of capital gained attracts new capital, and allows you to build momentum.

Keep in mind, also, as you weigh various financing options, that in virtually every case you will have to give up something for the financing you need. You may have to promise equity, control, future profits, royalties, or rights to technology, but in return you'll be given the break you've been looking for—the opportunity to finally get your business off the ground.

[1]Thomas D. Kiley, "Successful Transitions," at *The Challenge of Growth: The Fourth Annual Conference on Entrepreneurship*, May 18, 1985, Stanford Center for Entrepreneurship, Stanford, California.

An important early decision is whether you'd rather give up equity in your firm or carry a higher debt load. For many, the notion of either is unappetizing. After all, your major reason for doing this is to gain increased personal independence, so why give up equity and control in something that's yours? On the other hand, you may never have been comfortable borrowing large sums of money. In my case, the maximum that I had ever borrowed before was $50,000, and that was for a house. Suddenly I found myself asking for more than 10 times that amount, without concern. Actually, I was numb.

You're simply playing in a new ball game, and the stakes are higher. My advice is to hang on to as much ownership of your company for as long as you possibly can, because this is the fundamental reason you're venturing in the first place. If you wanted you could certainly work for another corporation, but there is no likelihood that the conditions in the new corporation will be much different from the conditions that you're leaving. Rather, this is *your* "new frontier," it's *your* new break, so why not hang on to as much as you can for as long as you can. That means maximizing the debt quotient of your financing and minimizing equity financing.

You may well change your mind as you proceed. Ron Hume started on his own, quickly added a partner, and now believes deeply in taking a smaller equity position in what can become, through equity distribution and stock incentive to key managers, a larger, faster-growing corporation. "100 percent ownership of a million dollar business is not as much fun as 20 percent of a $100 million business," said Ron recently.

Let's also recall our concept of leverage. Just as the cavemen used the small stick to move huge rocks, you're now trying to move business mountains through leveraging whatever modest financial assets you have. That's what leveraged buyouts are all about—some of them billion dollar deals—where the amount of actual cash put up to make the deal might be relatively tiny. The seller, and the lender, are banking on future earnings for the deal to work.

Victor Kiam illustrated this recently in his book. Says Kiam, "For a total cash package of $750,000 representing money given to vendors, I had become the sole owner of a $25 million company."[2]

In my own less dramatic case, I was able to become the owner of a

[2]Victor Kiam, *Going For It!* (New York: Morrow, 1986), p. 192.

$3.5 million company with no money down, by leveraging small assets, contacts and promises into ownership. Thousands of others have done this.

PINPOINTING THE FINANCING YOU NEED

One of the first and most important things to do is to determine as precisely as you can the exact amount of your financial need. Sound silly to you? Sometimes your exact requirements are not so obvious, and one of the worst mistakes you can make is asking for too little or too much money from the wrong source. The key is to match your needs with the right lender or investor.

After putting hundreds of hours into my business plan I remember turning it over to Rick Sommer, a Connecticut-based consultant and friend. Sommer read it for about 10 minutes and told me that I would need approximately twice the amount of capital that I had asked for.

"But Rick," I said, "I'm asking for $300,000. That's six times the amount of money that I've ever borrowed before."

"Three hundred is fine and I think you can get it," said Rick, "but to stay in business for the second six months you'll be real happy if you have another 300." Ask for it!

Rick's "rule of 2 times" proved to be right. As I looked at many business prospects over the past four years, I realized that one of the most common problems of new entrepreneurs is reluctance to ask for the money they need. Think about the amount of time and effort you've put into your plan. Now is the time to have confidence in it, and to remember that shooting high can frequently bring a result that's completely acceptable, even if lower than you request.

This was corroborated in our own financing when the largest of the five banks, Bank of New England, provided a very favorable initial response in a phone call from lending officer Gary Adams. Adams called from Boston, asked some very insightful questions, and then said politely, "John, we like your prospectus a lot. Why don't you give us a call in a year or so when you're looking for some real money?" The real money ($600,000!) that I was looking for apparently didn't seem like all that much to the Bank of New England. At the same time there was an expression of strong interest in the plan and in the future of the business.

In putting your business plan together, you should know exactly the amount of external financing that you'll need immediately, as well as in years two, three, and beyond. This should come right out of your cash flow projections. Your final meeting with your accountant should allow you to know exactly what you need and when. Some businesses will need millions to get started and will be comfortable borrowing that. Others don't want any external financing to set up shop. Let me tell you about one of the latter.

A firm by the name of MacKenzie-Childs Ltd. was founded in Aurora, New York as an outgrowth of a ceramic pottery hobby business. The owners made ceramic dinnerware for themselves and for friends as gifts, but soon ran out of funds. They approached a New York store, which purchased $7,000 worth of merchandise—the beginning of their business. With no money down, no investors, and no bank loans, the couple began production, entered a designers' show in New York and accepted orders for pottery. In the first year, they sold $25,000 worth of dinnerware, funding their operations through their own cash flow and small overdrafts on their local Aurora bank. The main goal of the business was to generate as much cash as possible so the firm did not need either to borrow money or sell equity. By 1984, sales had reached $92,000; in 1985, $370,000. Because of a strong balance sheet and sufficient cash flow, financing is now provided by a Syracuse bank, the New York State Job Development Authority, and the local Cayuga County Industrial Development Authority. In addition, a $100,000 line has been arranged for short-term needs. So here's a case of a couple taking an avocation and turning it into a business. Their primary motive initially was to raise enough money to send their daughter to ballet school. Now they're approaching seven figure sales and employ 45 people!

On the other hand, a company like Teknowledge, Inc., formed in 1981 by 20 computer science professors and researchers from Stanford University, launched an artificial intelligence business at a time when no market even existed. They raised $100,000 from local investors and have raised many millions more since. Revenue in 1985 reached almost $5 million with 50 percent annual growth predicted in the years ahead. In this case, substantial moneys were raised from investors who knew the risks as well as the potential rewards.[1]

[1]Lee M. Hecht, "Organizational Transitions," at *The Challenge of Growth: The Fourth Annual Conference on Entrepreneurship*, May 18, 1985, Stanford Center for Entrepreneurship, Stanford, California.

It really gets down to your attitude about borrowing. How much debt are you comfortable carrying? How much risk do you want to take? Do you know precisely what you are looking for? Do you need seed money? Working capital? Long-term permanent capital? A real estate loan? A revolving line of credit to solve cash flow problems? Or a combination of several of the above?

Two of the most common causes of business failure are undercapitalization and cash flow problems. They may or may not be the same thing. Undercapitalization is really a function of poorer than expected business results and can arise from inadequate sales, heavy operating expenses, receivables difficulties, inventory carrying difficulties, excessive fixed assets, or more. In fact, it is really a poor excuse to say, "We didn't have enough capital at the beginning." And this gets back to the original business plan. Make sure you are looking for enough capital to get your business going, and also to run and maintain it after it is underway. Ron Hume likes to talk about <u>his</u> rule of 2 times: "Everything you plan will take twice as long, require twice as much money, and be half as profitable as you expected it to be." While this may seem gloomy, it is realistic. Ron speaks from 25 years of hands-on entrepreneurial experience.

PERSONAL ASSETS, HIDDEN AND OBVIOUS

Let's try to identify where your seed money will come from. The place to start is obviously with your own personal savings and assets.

It may not have to be a huge sum. Walter Marshall, a long time magazine and newsletter advertising agent, started a small company called C.M.S. with a total capital investment of $300 in 1982. Four years later he had achieved $1.5 million in annual sales and employed seven people full time. His attitude was, "Why borrow money if you don't have to?"

Perhaps you've been putting a little money aside each week as you work toward your dream. A close friend decided to have his employer deduct 15 percent of his monthly pay check. He started in 1980 at a salary of $30,000 and left six years later at $70,000—and with nearly $50,000 in savings. He'll start his own firm and do well.

In Chapter 2 we discussed the assessment of your own personal assets—liquid, less liquid, and frozen. Take another look at those assets. You may have more leverage than you think. Most small start-up businesses are financed at least in part by their owner's personal assets. After all, if you really believe deeply in your idea, you should be willing to put most of what you have into the venture. You may do it in order to maintain 100 percent equity, or to convince a banker that you are completely serious about it. But the trick is to take a number of cash-triggering steps, like putting a mortgage on your house, cashing out a life insurance policy, and turning all of your family savings over to the business. Any money you had invested alternately will probably have to be drawn out and put into your own new business venture, or at least put into a collateral position.

Assets like passbook savings accounts, money market funds, stocks, bonds, and life insurance policies can be ready sources of cash. Let's start with borrowing against your life insurance policy, a fast way to get liquid. Terms vary with your specific policy, but it is possible to borrow against ordinary, whole life, or universal life insurance.

I had a $25,000 whole-life policy begun for me at age 18. By the time I was 35, it had a borrowing value of $20,000. Here's how it works: A certain percentage of the policy premium goes toward your actual life insurance protection, but the rest accumulates as cash value, after an initial period, generally about two years. So, your policy has (1) a cash value and (2) a loan value which accumulates over time, usually equal to about 85 percent of the cash value.

You will find the terms of the loan are in a table in the policy itself. Getting the loan is fairly simple: Write a letter to the company or your agent, they'll send you a form to fill out, and within a week to 10 days you will receive a check. This can be particularly inviting because the interest rate of the loan is set at the time you buy the policy. Today it is about 7 percent, 20 years ago it was probably about 3-to-4 percent. In the event of your death, the loan amount is simply deducted from the face value of the policy before benefits are paid. Life insurance is just one asset that can be leveraged. Another potentially larger asset might be your house.

Let's take a house that you bought in 1977 for $100,000 with a $50,000 mortgage and $50,000 in equity transferred from the sale of your previous house. Basically, you are now trying to refinance, either completely or with a second mortgage, to take advantage of: (1)

the reduced mortgage, (2) your ability to carry higher monthly payments, and (3) the increased value of the equity.

It's 10 or more years later and your $100,000 house is worth $200,000, your old mortgage is now down to $40,000, and you have $160,000 in home equity.

How do you get cash? Relatively easily. You make application to the bank. The bank will send one or more appraisers to your home who will assess its value at $200,000 (or thereabouts) on today's market, and the bank will decide to give you 70-to-90 percent of that value without risk. Of course, the bank will want to determine independently that you have the ability to make the higher payments of the new loan but here your prior favorable credit experience will kick in and help you. At the 90 percent figure you should be able to borrow up to $180,000 on the home. Perhaps you can pull out as much as $150,000 for your venture. Timing is important here too. Make application for the refinancing while you still have your old job. Bankers prefer employed people.

A second mortgage operates similarly, and is often called a home equity loan. Simply stated, this is a new line of credit which is revolving, and gives you a new personal line of credit for 70-to-90 percent of the equity (market value minus first mortgage). It is set up as a personal line of credit and you simply draw on it and repay it as you would any other current line. Check out your options here carefully. For instance, one bank may offer no payment requirements on principal for 5 years, and is then willing to roll it over to a second mortgage. Another requires no appraisal, simply the borrower's assessment of value.

When refinancing or adding a second mortgage, you should carefully evaluate the costs, hidden and otherwise, that are associated with the changes so that you are not blind-sided. Legal fees, premature payment penalty, points and other closing costs could amount to several thousand dollars.

Additional sources of cash range from stocks, bonds, jewelry, and furnishings on one hand, to the liquidation of property that you may have accumulated in an earlier time when your interests and priorities differed. How about that small vacation home or that piece of land you bought 20 years ago? Find every single asset you can, because cash is king. In my own case, I've been in the book business for 20 years, and probably bought and accumulated 5,000 books over that period of time. As we opened our own small publishing business we experimented with a retail bookstore and converted many of those books into cash. Sales of these and over 200 other titles amounted to perhaps as much as $30,000 during the course of the first year. So you may surprise yourself in terms of small hidden assets that can be converted to money.

If all of this sounds painful, understand that sometimes it is. But if these decisions allow you through self-finance to avoid paying interest on a loan or giving up equity in the venture, then it may be worth it. I should note here the important involvement and support of your spouse and family in your venture. All must understand, and believe in, what you are trying to achieve. Frequently, the spouse and family find themselves in a position of doing without and feeling a bit sorry for themselves as you toil away in your mine. Unless they are completely committed to the venture to the degree that you are, you will find that despite a good business plan and good financing, you may not make it. Many have tossed in the chips for family tranquility.

THE ASSETS OF OTHERS

After you have exhausted your personal savings and assets, you should look to family and friends who might be willing to help you finance. Let's say that you have been able to squeeze $50,000 to $100,000 from your various insurance policies, home equity, and sale of possessions. A good approach at this point is to have breakfast with your dad or other close relative.

"Dad, I am putting $100,000 of my own money into a new business which I believe in deeply. Can I share my dream, and business prospectus with you?"

Dad will probably say yes, and when he reads your prospectus he will be impressed. He will most likely ask the simple question, "How can I help?" You now have two options. Tell him the amount of money that you are looking for and express your willingness to repay with interest over a definite time period, or take him in as a partner and first stockholder.

The loan has the benefit of allowing you to retain complete ownership of the venture so that you won't have your father or father-in-law looking over your shoulder to see how his 10 percent of the firm is doing. Beyond the fact that you may be able to get the lowest interest rate from family or friends, they may be willing to give you a loan when the banker isn't. But start with the premise that while you have every intention of paying them back, this may be later than you would have to pay back a standard loan. What you might do is ask them what their lowest-yield asset currently is as well as their longest-payback asset. Tell them that you would be delighted to replace those two assets with a better one — *you*.

Another approach is to go to successful friends or other well placed business contacts and ask them if they would be willing to serve as a director of your company. I wrote to Pete Willmott, a long-time friend, who is chairman of the Carson, Pirie, Scott retail conglomerate in Chicago. Willmott called me one night at 10:30, told me he was in town, and wondered if I could have a beer with him. I was at the Williams Inn within 10 minutes, had a nice chat and learned that for business reasons he would not join my board but would be happy to be helpful as an investor if I wanted. It made me feel good.

WHEN TO TRY PARTNERS

After borrowing, the second avenue is to sell equity in your business. One of the most difficult aspects of this at the outset is to know what value, if any, your company has, and what to charge others for it. This is key, because if you cannot determine precisely what the value of the company is, you cannot determine what a share of stock is worth. Ybur investors, of course, are hoping that the worth of their shares will increase over a period of time, despite the fact that they are essentially worthless at the time of incorporation. This form of financing allows you to generate capital relatively quickly with no immediate payback requirement, but the major disadvantage is that it is not yours any more and you may lose control.

Five years ago a newspaper was launched in our town and the entrepreneur behind it made 30 personal visits asking potential investors for $1,000 each. The approach worked in raising the capital that was required, but in this case the majority of the business belonged to others. In each of the last three years, the business has shown increasingly better operating margins and has become more self-sufficient, but its founder has left, and the original investors are yet to see one penny returned on their dollars invested.

Another local venture, Thermius Inc., required $100,000 in capital to support the production of electronic wind chill gauges. The entrepreneur sought units of $5,000 each from 20 investors. Because of a fundamentally faulty premise, this business failed in under a year, and 20 people found themselves $5,000 poorer. A wonderful book on the subject of investigating venture capital opportunities from an investor's perspective is Venture's guide to *Investing in Private Companies.*[4]

Another way of selling equity in your business is simply to take on a single substantial partner. Technically, anyone who owns a bit of stock in your company is a partner, although most small investors are inactive. (They've got more important things to do.) For some small business owners working with a partner, a co-venture is the best thing they could possibly have done for their firm, while for others it's a disaster. Successful partnerships generally operate when the entrepreneur honestly determines his or her area of weakness and works hard to find a complimentary partner whose strengths are polar.

Rapp and Collins, one of the most successful direct marketing agencies in the United States, was created when Stan Rapp, a solid account man teamed up with Tom Collins, one of the true creative geniuses in the country. Each partner brought substantially different personal characteristics to the partnership. It has lasted for decades.

Each partnership is unique in some way. Some are happily split 50–50 between two operating partners while in others an investor will provide much of the financing while you run the show. The silent partnership can work to everyone's advantage.

One of the points made regularly by entrepreneurs is the fundamental reluctance to bring on anyone else. Kiam points this out in his book when he says, "Entrepreneurs don't look to share their equity with anyone."[5]

Another discovery is that happy partnerships and friendships may not always mesh. Generally speaking, good friends don't make good

---

[4]Arthur Lipper and George Ryan, *Investing in Private Companies* (New York: Dow Jones, 1984).
[5]Victor Kiam, *Going For It!* (New York: Morrow, 1986), p. 134.

partners. One example of this came from Donald Shading, a former Kodak employee, who began a graphic arts supply store with a friend as a partner. "We found out that good friends don't usually make good business partners." The results were that they folded the company and moved on in different directions. When asked about his decision to start up with a friend, Shading said, "I worked for two years for nothing. I made a bad decision."[6]

At Storey Communications, we take on partners on a selective project basis, never allowing the basic equity in the firm to be shared with anyone other than ourselves and key employees. Nonetheless, at this time we have two successful joint ventures going which were based on outside partners bringing specialized skills or properties to us. It is very important from the outset to understand who controls the assets and what the terms of a break-up might be. One of the advantages of a project partnership is that it is a good source of capital and may add experience, contacts, and expertise to your venture, while reducing your personal risk, and without yielding a stake in your overall firm.

The disadvantages are that you do lose some control; and when differences of opinion emerge as to the direction the specialized venture should take, you can frequently run into a clash without an agreed on procedure for resolving such a problem. Breakups occur frequently.

There are many sources of "noncash" support that may come from informal partners. Frequently accountants and lawyers become informal partners. Although they haven't put up funds, they can have a vested interest in the success of your business and may provide valuable advice by serving on your board of directors. In our own company we have a regular quarterly financial review and an outside board of directors who have never been offered cash. After a dinner party at which we gave each of the directors a basket of Vermont ham, maple syrup, and cheese, Don Dubendorf, our attorney, stood up and said, "I can't believe I'm doing all of this for a piece of cheese." He was and continues to.

[6]Amanda Bennett, "Laid off managers of big firms increasingly move to small ones . . ." *Wall Street Journal*, July 23, 1986, p. 23.

BANKER LOANS: TYPES AND AVAILABILITY

Let's say you have lined up perhaps as much as $100,000—$50,000 of your own equity squeezed from personal assets, $25,000 from your Dad and $25,000 from your father-in-law. Now you may want to think about the banks.

As stated earlier, banks are frequently reluctant to provide any seed money, or initial financing, for brand new ventures. Basically, banks want to lend money to people that don't really need it. But if you can show them some sort of track record and why you're a great bet, and even suggest to them that you may be using them as secondary or back-up financing, they may be much more interested in giving you the loan. Be realistic. Remember that only about 10 percent of businesses that apply to banks get any money, but your chances are already dramatically higher since you're prepared to present a full-blown business plan.

I carefully packaged up my new business prospectus and delivered it to five bankers. One of them, Knute Westerland, of the First Vermont Bank in Bennington, Vermont, was the first to respond and ask to come to talk and take a look at the assets I was purchasing from Garden Way. He drove about two hours, spent three hours with me, went back with prospectus in hand, and began his process of seriously evaluating the plan. He liked my plan. In addition, good prospects for clients, contracts, and a good reputation within my industry were important. When he saw that I was staking my own future on the venture and recognized my willingness to put up my own assets, he became seriously interested.

He responded within a week that he wanted to go forward with the loan, asked a few more questions, and gave me great confidence. I was fortunate. And the hard work paid off. On the other hand, don't be discouraged if you get turned down by the first banker. You're in good company. If you do get a rejection, request a complete and candid explanation as to why you were rejected. It could be valuable in your next discussion with another banker. Bank of New England told me they were looking to invest a million and up apiece on emerging growth companies. I didn't qualify.

It is more the exception than the rule that the bank will finance a new venture completely. Once underway, it is a different story. The banks will call you and be eager to provide second- or third-round financing or a new credit line. Don't burn any bridges—you can always use that promise of future interest and support at a later point. One of the banks that was lukewarm to us initially has been pursuing us aggressively now that we are through the third year of operation. Keep in mind also that there are hundreds of banks out there that *could* be interested in supporting you. Let them know that you are serious and that you want to work quickly. We received complete financing commitments within three weeks. Despite the apparent reluctance of bankers to finance start ups, try to encourage your banker to see the uniqueness of your proposal and *always* demonstrate how they are going to be repaid. A local bank is currently running an advertising campaign that says, "City Bank . . . your business is our business." Call them on it. Tell them that you want them to be your partner. Then invite them in as a lending partner.

Another pointer: Have your own, small-scale "banker relations program" under way at all times. Keep your name in the news, send samples of your work, and perhaps once a year send an update to interested bankers on what you are doing. It will pay future dividends.

Before you approach a specific banker, you had better do some in-depth research. There are many different banks with varied services. There is no sense in wasting your own time or theirs if they are basically not in the commercial lending business. Simply stated, you want to go to a commercial banker if you have assets that you can borrow against in your business. Let's say that you need $100,000 and have an accounts receivable worth $50,000 and inventory worth $50,000. The "worth" part is where you and the bank may differ. They will look at the receivables and say that in a crisis they could get 70 percent for those receivables, and if you had to liquidate the inventory they might be able to get 50 percent. So, they will take your request for $100,000 and say, "I'll be happy to lend you $60,000." For the other $40,000 you need, they will ask you for a personal asset-and-liability statement in order to identify assets the bank can secure. These might include your house or your car. In all likelihood, you will get the $100,000, but you will also give up a small piece of skin and a little bit of blood.

Before you go into the banker's office, be prepared. Know the specific services that the banker can provide, who he or she reports to, what his or her lending limit might be. This can be done relatively easily. Start by going into the bank and picking up the publicity and public relation pieces that are laying in the lobby. Get a sense from asking around town who does business with whom, and talk to clients of the bank before you approach them yourself. Discover any quirks, idiosyncracies, or special policies of the bank. Determine if any loans have gone bad recently and how long the loan officer you would be dealing with has been, and is likely to remain, around.

When you do go in, say "I appreciate very much the time you're giving me. We have worked hard in putting together a plan for a new growth business that is going to be located down the road. We see it growing from $100,000 this year to $1 million in five years, becoming profitable quickly, and creating approximately 40 to 50 jobs. We are going to need some inventory and receivable financing, and also longer-term credit to allow our growth to occur. I would like to share the plan with you which I have here, and I'd like to show you how we are going to do what we say we're going to do in the prospectus. We think we have a high profit potential and would like to enlist your support in helping us to get going."

In all likelihood, a banker will be complimented that you have sought him or her out, impressed by the amount of work that you have put into your business plan, and anxious to dig into the pages of financials that you will have included. But you should have a good sense of the stage that he or she is on as well. How's the banker's record? Are there significant changes going on within the organization of the bank? Is it likely that someone might replace "your" banker sometime soon? Are any bank acquisitions or mergers planned? All of these things could affect your relationship dramatically.

Also try to become familiar with the types of loans the bank has available. There is a bewildering array of types, terms, uses, paybacks, and interest rates. In the appendix of this book, we have tried to simplify the various types of loans that are available. Your accountant can help you here, but in short, lending works on either a cash cycle basis, pegged to your current assets (normally short term with a revolving loan, including short-term equipment loans, accounts receivable loans, short-term commercial loans, and inventory loans), or on a longer term "cash flow" basis up to five years, commonly used for real estate or equipment investments.

Before you go to meet with your banker, your accountant can be of great help. I would not invite the accountant along, but I would pick his or her brain for background on the four or five different people that you are going to be speaking with so that you can know something about them. Who do they loan to? What do they like? Who specifically are you meeting? What is the individual's position in the bank? How long has he or she been there? All of this background can be infinitely valuable to you before you sit down to make your pitch.

I would also advocate preparing your pitch just as you would a presentation or a speech. This means standing up in front of your family, or in front of a mirror, or dictating into a tape recorder and listening to it 30 times before you go in. There should be total preparedness on your part, and an ability to answer every question that is raised.

As a new small firm you are viewed by a bank as being a very high risk lending opportunity. Therefore, you must overprove yourself. Here are some of the major areas that a bank looks at in making major loan decisions. I call it my "big eight."

Character
Credit worthiness
Collateral
Capacity
Capital on hand
Clients
Contracts
Contacts

Any and all of these can help make your case. I have been told time and time again, "I lend on character." This means it will be easier for you if you have been in an area for 10 years and have a positive reputation, and no intention of going anywhere else. On the other hand, having a large client on hand as you start up is a tremendous boon. Lee Epstein, president of Mailmen Inc., struck out on his own after years in the lettershop business, with only his reputation. He quickly struck a deal for one big client, rolled that into bank financing, built his plan and is highly successful in a very competitive business.

Don't be too concerned about giving the bank the impression that you have all of the answers. It is perfectly okay to say, "That's a good question. I'm glad you asked it. I don't have the answer to it, but I will tomorrow." This compliments the banker, which very few people ever do. Think about it.

Equally important to the banker is the kind of a management team you've gathered. He or she knows you don't have all the skills required to run the entire business, and is therefore impressed if you have plugged those areas where you need help with a good solid production or financial person.

Don't be too quick to think of yourself as "small potatoes." You might be a sizable fish in a local banker's pond. In our own case we were launching a business in the rural southern Vermont area, with a volume of approximately $3 million per year. This made us a relatively unusual, and attractive, business target for the local bankers, who were more accustomed to applications for $25,000 to $50,000. We would have had a much harder time in a large city which recalls the old lesson of being first in the village rather than second in Rome.

You can easily determine, and be prepared for, the relative success or failure rate of your enterprise based on historical standards. It's a fact, for instance, that restaurants and contractors have a higher failure rate than drug stores and accounting firms. These kinds of statistics are available through D&B by calling a local office and requesting their current published data on business success and failure. This is broken down in every conceivable way, and is a very helpful document in preparing your own loan request.

The bankers themselves consult this kind of material through the American Bankers Association or through an organization such as Robert Morris Associates in Philadelphia. All of these kinds of statistics are helpful in responding to a banker, "Yes, I've thought about that and here's how we intend to avoid that problem."

GOVERNMENT MONEY

From time to time, a region, county, or even municipality aiming to create jobs, will launch a bank loan pool. Recently, the Berkshire County area of Massachusetts, a traditionally high-unemployment area, created a $1 million-plus loan pool with a $200,000 maximum borrowing limit and found that there were very few takers for the money. The attractiveness of this pool was that it carried a subsidized interest rate and was available for higher risk enterprises. As of this writing, a good portion of the pool is intact.

The purpose of such a pool is basically to create jobs. Bankers love to see this money go into bricks, mortar, and equipment for manufacturing and operational activities, because in their minds this is what creates jobs. On the other hand, something like the North Adams General Store, a second location of a successful "country store" retail operation, was able to tap into this venture capital pool without being a manufacturing organization. So the rules obviously can be bent.

In addition, less traditional sources include small business administration guarantees, direct government assistance, state, county, agencies—the "alphabet soup" of the banking world. These are worth understanding and taking a look at, but be prepared for high administrative fees and paperwork. Just applying for a $200,000 to $250,000 industrial revenue bond, for instance, can require an investment of $20,000 to $25,000 in legal, accounting, and trust fees.

One thing you will definitely find is that neither government bureaucrats nor bankers are much interested in talking about the intangibles. Again, they are looking for hard assets to collateralize. This is frequently unfortunate, because some of the best assets of the company may not be reflected on a standard balance sheet. In the case of the direct marketing world, for instance, mailing lists have never been accepted as collateral. Yet, in our own case, we received $250,000 in mail order sales from *previous advertising* expenditures and $50,000 in list rental income from assets that weren't able to be reflected on the balance sheet.

This is not to say that an intangible asset can't become a positive feature of your presentation. Point it out. Show that despite the fact that it isn't on your balance sheet, it will result in a stream of income, which is historical and demonstrable. You'll get attention and pick up points here.

BEYOND THE COMMERCIAL BANKS

The bankers I have been describing thus far are associated with commercial banks. Their approach is to look at your hard assets together with your established cash flows and loan in a conventional fashion.

It might be advantageous also to look at the "thrifts." These are savings and loans, mutuals and co-ops typically, that loan on an asset base and on your own personal resources—typically realty assets. They are willing to loan somewhere in the neighborhood of 75 to 80 percent on realty.

There are also commercial finance companies such as Beneficial Finance or Commercial Credit. These organizations loan just like commercial bankers, on the basis of your assets, but at a somewhat higher interest rate—perhaps 3–4 points higher traditionally, although the margins are currently closing up.

Why the higher rates? From their point of view, your loan request is simply a higher risk and a more expensive loan involving monthly audits and test checks of the assets. This activity is reflected in the higher interest rates.

If you are borrowing strongly on the basis of your background, your experience, and your proven track record, be prepared to refer the bank to people who can vouch specifically for your abilities.

No banker will be overly interested in you unless you have something significant at stake personally. This could be in the form of equity, your own cash investment, or your commitment, creating the very best concept and business plan imaginable. The bank will almost certainly check your personal credit history from consumer credit files, something you should verify for accuracy yourself from time to time.

Ask again, "Am I asking the right banker for the right amount of money?" A lending officer may have a limit of $200,000 or it might be $1 million. Asking a banker with a limit of $100,000 for $1 million is not a good use of anyone's time. These lending limits are difficult to discern in advance, but you can do so by talking with others who have done business with the bank. Determine *who* is the right person at the bank to talk with, and what the review process will be. Lending limits are also based on whether the loan is going to be secured; that is, by real estate or liquid assets, or unsecured, which is by collateral of another sort.

Before you leave the bank you should let the banker know that you want an answer within a two-to-four-week period. Don't be bashful about insisting you have to know by a certain date, and ask whether that will be sufficient for the bank.

Once your loan has been okayed, you'll be categorized as either a cash cycle borrower or a cash flow loan borrower. In the first case, that of cash cycle, you will be expected to repay the loan in one year or less. In the latter case, you will be expected to pay out of long-term profits. It is important to the banker to categorize your loan properly, to save administrative work. Obviously from your point of view the longer the term, and the lower the security arrangements, the better.

Your banker is looking for a good long-term relationship with few surprises. To accomplish this you've got to be absolutely honest and share the good news as well as the bad as you proceed.

THE BANKER'S RED FLAGS

Following are typical red flags that the banker will look for:

- [ ] Delayed financial information
- [ ] Inquiries from other creditors, requests for split financing
- [ ] The accountant's inability to provide interim information or explanation of changes that have occurred
- [ ] Changes in accounting procedures or practices
- [ ] An absence of activity or changes in the way your building and operations appear . . . machinery that is not in use
- [ ] A change in your D&B trade credit rating
- [ ] Asking for a meeting with your lawyer and accounting firm

The best situation, from the banker's point of view, is to lend you money on a term or revolving basis against your receivables and your inventory. The rates against inventory might be 40 to 60 percent, and the rates against your receivables might be 60 to 80 percent. This is a securing of those assets, and serves as your collateral.

Going much beyond those percentages is difficult for the banker, and he or she is unlikely to do it without heavier personal guarantees on your part. Beware of nonbank sources that go beyond the bank's percentages. Any number of people in New York City would be happy to lend at perhaps 95 percent of receivables and 85 percent of inventories, but they will exact a price for that. Also, you can count on those people becoming very active in your business, showing up on at least a monthly basis to check both receivables and inventories.

The most extreme and least favorable route are "factors" who will pay you cash for your receivables and then collect it themselves. You no longer own it, and your old accounts may not like that very much.

WHEN THINGS SOFTEN

Your banker will likely want a monthly check of your inventory and receivables, lunch perhaps four times a year, and a monthly phone call to get a sense of how the business is going. He or she will check on how your line is operating, up and down, from within the bank.

When business gets more difficult, a banker might want to visit with you more frequently to get a personal look at how things are going. Frequently, if there is concern, your banker will show up unannounced simply to wander through your plant. When things begin to soften, with sales not materializing, inventory not moving, you may find tighter scrutiny yet will be put on you so as to avoid the "workout."

What's a "workout"? Just like it sounds, it's the point at which the bankers have given up hope of repayment on the conventional terms as agreed and begin to roll up their sleeves and flex their muscles to "work out" the problem. Typically, the banker (or bankers, as there may be a primary and a secondary lender) will call all of the parties together in a big room at the bank, and insist on seeing accurate, timely, and complete financial data. They will then proceed to test the financial data—calling accounts, checking stock, and so on—to see if it accurately reflects the condition of the company.

Next, they will bring in their "workout specialist," in effect, to run the company. This will include opening the mail in the morning, personally pulling out the checks, and applying them against the bank loan.

If your business is in less serious shape, the banker will decide that perhaps a one-month time frame might be allowable for the owners to work their way out of the problem without declaring bankruptcy. Something as serious as a workout can be avoided by good, ongoing communication with the banker. This means, again, sharing the good news as well as the bad.

If the news is bad, don't be concerned that he or she is going to ring the chimes and call the loan. The pressure on the banker is every bit as great as is the pressure on you. He or she is the last one who wants to concede that a loan has gone bad, and you should work with him or her as your ally rather than an adversary. Believe it or not, bad news, coupled with a thorough plan of attack and remedy for action, can show your banker what you're made of. A "can do" attitude and even a sense of humor can help here. At one of our toughest points in the first year, my controller brought a small gym bag to the meeting. After the "crisis" was over, he opened it up and pulled out a small oxygen tank. "Anybody need a whiff?" he asked. The room exploded in laughter and all tension was gone. Frequently, when times are tight in your business, you will be tempted to bring your outside accountant or lawyer to a meeting with the banker. This is generally unwise. Showing up with your accountant or lawyer will almost certainly be construed as a sure sign that things have changed and that you are concerned about the condition of the business. On the other hand, bringing your chief financial officer, or your in-house accountant or bookkeeping people, is construed simply as a way of passing along maximum information to the banker.

If failure occurs, in the form of bankruptcy, your banker will do everything to collect maximum asset value quickly without tarnishing the bank's image. Obviously, marching up your driveway, planting a for-sale sign in your front lawn, and asking for the keys to your car are the last things local bankers want to do. But they will if they must.

Rather, they would prefer to control the situation in other ways. One other way a banker can control the relationship is through the term of the loan. The shorter the safer, from the banker's perspective. It could be as short as three months, it could be as long as two years, but in the early stages bankers will opt for a shorter term—perhaps six months—and extend this as the business conditions become apparent. Longer term is in your interest. You may point out to them that the administration of a 12-month loan is easier for them than a 6-month loan. They'll likely agree.

Many people will go beyond the single bank loan and cross-collateralize. What do we mean by this? Cross-collateralizing is really a method to increase the amount of money that people will lend to you without your increasing your asset base. For instance, your first loan of $50,000 might be backed up by a personal guarantee of $50,000 based on some portion of the value of your home. You might maintain that $50,000 line and add another $100,000 line with the same, or a different banker, using the same collateral, your house, to back up that second $100,000 loan. This might go on, with the house being used as the primary collateral indefinitely. You're risk of loss of collateral obviously increases with the number of lines that you open up; but at the same time, there is no way that you can lose the house six times. A good example of cross-collateralization is seen with the ski apparel manufacturers, C.B. Sports in Bennington, Vermont, and Glens Falls, New York, which borrows up to $15 million annually against sales of $30 million. As C.B. Vaughn himself puts it, "Everything I've got is cross-collateralized this way, that way, and back again."[7]

In short, your banks don't want surprises any more than you do. But they can be great allies if you share news with them as you go along. The worst thing to do is to think of them somehow as your adversary. Get it squarely into your head that the bank is your partner.

THE SBA

There are additional borrowing possibilities for small businesses that do not accrue to larger businesses. For instance, the SBA will help with business loans to many new companies. The SBA helps new or growing businesses to meet their financial needs, counsels them with problems, offers special assistance to minority-owned, women-owned and veteran-owned businesses, helps small businesses secure government contracts, and acts as a special advocate with other federal agencies, with state agencies, and within the private sector. The SBA offers two basic types of business loans: (1) Loans that are made by private lenders, usually banks, and guaranteed by the SBA. By law, the SBA can guarantee a portion of a loan made by a bank or other private lender, however the SBA guarantee cannot exceed $500,000. Or (2) Loans made directly by the agency. In general direct SBA loans carry interest rates slightly lower than those in the private financial markets. They are generally available to applicants unable to secure private financing or an SBA guaranteed or participation loan. The SBA publishes a wide variety of documents, and you

[7]Jeffrey Seglin, "Growing by their bootstraps," *Venture*, July 1985, pp. 48–52.

can get the full information from any SBA office. I've enclosed a recent listing of SBA Regional Offices, along with their phone numbers in Appendix C. The easiest way to find the location nearest you is to refer to your telephone directory under "SBA."

The SBA as a guarantor can provide you with assistance in getting bank financing. In general, however, SBA-backed loans can be more complicated than straight bank financing. Why? The application process is more extensive because you have to work both through the SBA and your bank, and it can be time consuming. It often takes up to a year for the SBA to decide if it will back your loan or not. So, if you can get it without that kind of help, fine. If you can't, look on it as perhaps a longer-term support opportunity.

VENTURE CAPITAL

Let's pause for a moment. I'm assuming that some combination of the above has yielded successful results. So at this point, you may have $200,000 in your pocket. Fifty thousand dollars of your own, $50,000 from your father and father-in-law, and a matching $100,000 from the banker. If this does not meet your financing needs, don't despair. Some of the more interesting and attractive financing options are still to come. You are, in effect, building a capital pyramid, and this requires some architectural creativity. It may include venture capital, research and development partnerships, corporate partnerships, or private equity placements.

How does venture capital work? What does it mean? Simply, you can get capital, but you will be relinquishing control of a good chunk of your venture. Money for equity.

Many people believe that venture capital is the first place you should go when looking for financing for a start-up venture. While venture capital can be a logical source, it can be every bit as difficult to secure as conventional financing and has some serious disadvantages to it. In reality, only about 1 percent of all start-ups are financed through venture capital operations.[8]

Don Dion, a CPA and lawyer, put it this way, "Most of the action in the Boston-Cambridge-Route 128 area is venture capital driven. Two bright young guys will spin off from Digital or Analog and

[8]Stephen Robinett, "Blood from a rock," *Venture*, January 1985, pp. 38–45.

come in with only the seed of a good business idea. Since the accounting business is so competitive, virtually every one of the big eight firms has created an 'emerging business group' that will provide tax accounting and EDP support to these would-be entrepreneurs, and, when ready, match them up with venture capitalists. Companies like KEL, Matrix, Software, and others were all formed this way. Basically, the accounting firms will do start-up work for nothing, hoping that a strong relationship will develop and the success rate will be high. The firm will provide the entrepreneur with a business plan, set up the books, get basic relationships going, do some hiring, some administration, even recommend phone systems. The venture capitalists like this because they are dealing not with just a bright guy with a good idea, but with a solid business plan and a sober accounting firm, Dion continued.

"We'll then introduce these people to venture capitalists in Boston and New York . . . generally not bankers because bankers are not particularly interested unless the guy has $3 million in his pocket. Money from venture capitalists comes in the form of preferred stock with convertible features, or convertible debt. In most cases, the entrepreneur will give up 50 to 75 percent of his equity in order to get his idea off the ground. The venture capitalists, for their part, will take a 50 to 75 percent position, owning convertible shares with the right to convert them into common the day before the business goes public. This has a double effect, because it protects the capitalist during the start-up phase by allowing them, in the event of bankruptcy, to regain their assets before the owners do; and second, before they go public, they can convert their shares to common stock."

Venture capitalists are actually less involved on a day-to-day basis than you might think. So, the concept of giving up all managerial control is not generally valid. They offer access to corporate contacts and to a network under the guise of "helping your business to succeed." But they are not really interested in managing the business. They are already thinking about their next deal and moving on to it. They will probably show up at a monthly directors' meeting, and look at results tied to a business plan or to a sales plan.

Eighty percent of businesses launched with venture capital support fail within the first two years. Most people in the venture capital business understand this. Their trick is making far more money on the winners than they lose on the losers.

It is also a highly competitive business. There are about 600 venture capital firms nationwide, (see *Pratt's Guide to Venture Capital*, Venture Economics Inc., Wellesley Hills, Massachusetts). Most of them will typically finance only three to four new ventures a year, but they might read 20 business plans each week. Realize that competition is high, and be prepared for rejection.

What are venture capitalists looking for? James Anderson, of Merrill, Piccard, Anderson and Eyre, put it this way, at the Stanford University School of Business. "The key ingredients are (1) an experienced management with relevant industry experience and actual job function experience; (2) a distinctive product line that fills a real need, that is, unique, defensible so that it can't be copied, cost effective, and provides a dramatically superior solution to the customer's problem; and (3) large and expanding markets."[9]

Dion put it differently. "Venture capitalists are looking for people who are willing to work 7 days a week, 12 to 15 hours a day, that have superior problem-solving ability and can tough it out in difficult situations."

With $200,000 committed, and a fresh idea uniquely presented, you may get venture capital support of another $200,000 for your venture, so that brings you to $400,000. This won't be easy, and you'll need help from your accountant and lawyer on the "term sheet" and purchase and sale agreement, working and legal understandings. These require negotiations on many points including percentage ownership, price to be paid, and who will be on the board of directors. This is a long and complicated process that cannot be covered appropriately here. Ask your lawyer and accountant for help.

OTHER SOURCES OF CAPITAL

What other possibilities may exist? Let's go through a few;

1. *Commercial finance companies, such as Household Finance.* They may be more willing to finance your venture, but will charge a higher interest rate.

[9]James Anderson, "High-Tech Venture Capital," at *The Challenge of Growth: The Fourth Annual Conference on Entrepreneurship*, May 18, 1985, Stanford Center for Entrepreneurship, Stanford, California.

2. *Suppliers.* One morning, one of our accounts called and asked for 90-day billing. If I said yes, I would have become an investor in his business. The basic rule of business is net 30. That means that you will pay someone within 30 days. If you get somebody to provide you with 60 days billing you have free financing for 30 additional days. The best way to achieve this is to establish a good credit rating with your suppliers and to maintain a solid D&B rating. In our case, at the outset, the paper suppliers from whom we were buying about $150,000 worth of paper a year gave us the following terms: cash, all of it, up front. When we asked for 50 percent cash and 50 percent on a 30-day basis, we eventually, (year two) got that. In the third year, after testing other suppliers of paper, and having paid our bills successfully for two years, we were able to get Westvaco, our first supplier, to grant 30-day billing; and by that time had worked out preferable relationships with additional suppliers. The same process worked on $200,000 worth of printing; so if you take a look at your major cost areas, and try to get your suppliers to play ball with you, you can get "free financing."

3. *Credit cards.* Don't overlook your credit cards. This will, by its very nature, be in limited amounts, but don't eliminate this as a source of existing credit. It's also slightly more expensive, but it has pulled more than a few businesses through at a tough time. Bernice Bush, president of a brokerage firm in Huntington Beach, California, took a $500 Christmas bonus, and started a list management business. To fund the travel needed to line up clients and lists to manage, she used a MasterCard and paid the monthly minimum. She took no salary for the first 10 months, and at the end of the first year was able to pay off the MasterCard. The company today employs 15 people full time, and is the largest list management firm specializing in the evangelical Christian market.

4. *Regional development authorities.* Any corporation that promises to provide employment, particularly in a depressed area, will learn of additional financing possibilities. I checked around locally and just within Berkshire County, Massachusetts, there are five major areas of support: (1) Community Development Corporation that gives goal loans of up to $300,000; (2) The Northern Berkshire Loan Pool, seven local banks that work together and offer $200,000 to $250,000 loans available at three-fourths of prime rate; (3) Urban

Development Authority, which grants federal money for land, not buildings or equipment; (4) Industrial Revenue Bonds, a federal program which is administered by the state and puts long-term money into buildings and equipment; and (5) Training Assistance Grants, which result in 50 percent payroll reimbursement for people hired by a qualifying business.

I found these five without looking very hard. There are probably more in your area. Check your telephone directory or ask around about industrial development, regional development, country development, city development and see what kind of programs are available.

5. *Lease-buy financing.* One of my friends, Tom Frenz left a major New York list management company and needed a computer to get going. With an initial investment of $60,000, and careful planning, "List Advisor" acquired a low-cost, high-powered mini-computer system with a small initial investment, and the objective of stretching capital as far as possible. Through lease-buy financing they acquired office equipment, furniture and computers with payment stretched over two-to-five-years. At the end of the lease term, with one additional monthly payment, they will own the equipment. Within a year they were able to establish an extremely active business with a positive cash flow. So look into lease-buy financing.

6. *Corporate bridging or seed money.* Many firms encourage their employees to develop entrepreneurial activities and are willing to provide initial financing. You may be required to make your technology compatible with theirs, or there may be other strings attached, but don't overlook the corporate parent to help you get going. This is exactly what happened in our case. When we bought certain assets from Garden Way, we included in the purchase and sale agreement a three-year book packaging contract worth $300,000. This was as good as cash-in-hand to the banker.

Or you may consult, under contract. In one case, Stauffer Chemicals allowed former employee Loren Hov to consult for them for a period of time and got him started in his own consulting business. (*Wall Street Journal,* July 25, 1986) Many of my friends have done this very thing.[10]

---

[10]Amanda Bennett, "Laid off managers of big firms increasingly move to small ones . . . and then often consult for their ex-employers," *Wall Street Journal,* July 23, 1986, p. 23.

Richard Jordan, president of Jordan Creative, an advertising agency, struck a deal with his former employer, Rapp and Collins, contracting to them a certain percentage of his services during his first year of business. They provided him with a guaranteed income while he built his outside clientele, and also helped the agency by cushioning the shock of his leaving. By the end of the first year his outside consultancy was booming. It now provides an income that runs well into six figures.

7. *Corporate separation plans.* You may not be close to getting fired, but you may have an opportunity to take early retirement. Or, simply to sit down with your employer and say, "What would the company be willing to do for me if I did leave?" Kodak, which has been looking to thin its management ranks over the last several years, was more than willing to do this for William K. Sponn, who received a $50,000 sweetened early retirement plan. Such separation pay can sustain you for a period of time, and from there, hopefully, you can make enough money on your own. Sponn recently turned down an offer to rejoin Kodak.[11]

8. *Customers.* Customers may be willing to finance a new business from which they will benefit. For many years at Garden Way Inc. we ran a customer reservation plan on the Troy Bilt Rototiller, where a person would send in 20 to 30 percent of the sale price, allowing us to operate with a float of $2 to $3 million at any given point in time. Another example, Brook Trout Technologies, used a creative financing approach where six investors from Computer Telephone Corp. (CTC) (a distributor as well as customer), and CTC itself, put up financing in exchange for 28 percent equity in the new firm. The rest of the financing came from a private investment company which guaranteed a bank loan in exchange for 6 percent equity interest in the company.[12] Don't overlook your customers as a source of seed money.

9. *Corporate partnerships.* Similar to corporate seed money, but in this case you approach corporations with which you have no previous ties. Tell them that you will operate as their research and development arm, or their publishing arm, or their insurance arm. Many

[11]Amanda Bennett, "Laid off managers of big firms increasingly move to small ones . . . and then often consult with their ex-employers," *Wall Street Journal*, July 23, 1986, p. 23.
[12]Stephen Robinett, "Blood from a rock," *Venture*, January 1985, pp. 38–45.

corporations will be attracted to your reputation and the lower over-heads that you bring to them.

10. *Research and development (R&D) partnerships.* "This is a company with an idea for product which forms an R&D partnership which then sells limited partnerships to investors, and pays the company to do the actual development. If it wishes, the company can acquire sole manufacturing and sales rights to the product. The advantages of this are that financing appears on the company books as revenue, not debt, so the borrowing power is not diminished. Company owners are spared dilution of equity. The disadvantages are that royalties to partners can mortgage the product's future, and undercut the incentive for marketing."[13]

11. *Barter.* Amazingly, there are companies that will take old assets that you have, pay you a certain amount of cash or barter credits, and give you services that you might need over the course of a 12-month period. Nike moved $16 million worth of outmoded sneakers in Formosa under this plan. Check out barter possibilities and shift slow moving inventories into prepaid assets.

12. *Go public.* Although for most people this is somewhere down the road, going public is a process that allows you, once you have proven your ability to generate positive cash flow, to expand your business dramatically through public offerings without having to pay it back. Richard Thalheimer of San Francisco launched his *Sharper Image* catalog, and built a $100 million mail-order business with 15 retail stores out of self-generated profits. In order to advance it more rapidly, he decided to take it public in 1986. The standard route for doing this would be to devote two years to a planning period to clean up your accounting systems and to make sure you have unassailable balance sheets. The actual process of filing with the SEC is a complicated one that entire encyclopediae have been written about. But basically, you're registering your securities, and providing three years of audited financial statements by a recognized big eight firm in order to have the opportunity to take your corporation public, resulting in stock money coming in to you for a fee. You will pay an underwriter, such as Drexel or Morgan Stanley in New York, somewhere in the neighborhood of 6 to 7 percent for their effort in raising the money.

[13]"Financing Techniques for Start-ups," *Nation's Business*, May 1985, p. 24.

The actual process of legal and accounting work and printing will take about six months and cost you up to $300,000, so it is not a casual decision.

In the process of going public you will get a tremendous amount of free advice from investment banking firms that will advise, counsel and urge you to press forward. Often, however, they are motivated by a desire to become your underwriter and generate the fee for themselves. Going public presumes that you have made tremendous financial progress in your business, have a projectable formula, and are ready to achieve a whole new plane of development. That's what we all want to attain. Good luck scaling the summit. In Chapter 6 we'll show you how, with financing intact, to begin to structure your business operations to maximize its value.

6

Important Start-up Decisions: Making Them Correctly and Leveraging Them to the Maximum

There are hundreds of different reasons why brand new small businesses fail. For one thing you're starting with no inertia, you've just worked very hard and been successful at finding appropriate financing; but remember you're entering a brand new market, you have to develop strong supplier relationships, you have to hire and then train employees. It's no wonder that so many brand new ventures have trouble getting out of the starting blocks quickly.

In this chapter I'll tell you how to sprint, and begin to consolidate your earliest gains. We'll show you how every penny you spend can be turned into asset value, equity, which enhances your worth daily.

On the first day that I entered our brand new business to start publishing operations, a flush of pride quickly gave way to reality—the scurry of squirrels and mice through the building, which had an ignominious history, having been used as a motorcycle shop and then a pottery/ceramics kiln operation.

My one employee, my wife Martha, was busy trying to get our one phone to work and there wasn't a carpet in sight. It was a far cry from the grander corporate days I had just left. But I realized quickly that there were extremely important decisions to be made, and as soon as I was able to clear the dust off of an old desk that had been left behind by the potters, I was able to begin to focus on the job at hand—getting the business up and going quickly.

The sooner you get at this and stop worrying about your old corporate surroundings, or whether you have all of the experience and management skills required, or whether your business is undercapitalized, the faster you'll be able to build some new value.

In this chapter we'll cover three major start-up decisions, how to make them successfully and how you can begin immediately the leveraging process that will allow you to continue to find more money for your venture while keeping your costs completely under control.

Those critical first decisions include your name and image and how you will communicate that to others, your location and facility, and your first staff and recruits.

WHAT'S IN A NAME?

When you sit down to begin business on the first day you should pull from your shelf perhaps the only book that's on it, your business plan. In there you will have stated what your objectives are, your raison d'être. Your name should certainly be a reflection of what you are, what you're going to do, why you are in business and what your philosophical approach is going to be. This part of your document should be shared with any of your new employees or suppliers. In mine, we talked about having quality publishing products, superior customer service, a decent employee working environment, and most importantly, positive cash flow. These four principles became from day one, guiding principles for getting going.

In my first draft of a prospectus I referred to the various publishing and other activities that we were pursuing and tried to find a name that was impressive and formal. The best I could come up with was

"The New England Communications Group." This, to me, sounded like something that had been around awhile and had a ring of authority and formality which I thought would help us get going quickly. When I shared that with one of my business friends, he said "it sounds just like a new regional operation of the telephone company. What the hell does that have to do with you?"

When I talked with Ron Hume about how he decided on a name for his company he said "Well, I wanted to do it right, I hired the best advertising/image company that I could and spent thousands for them to come back and tell me that the name of my company ought to be a direct reflection of myself. We wound up calling ourselves 'The Hume Group.' "

I thought about that and also thought that I might save $5,000 for myself by following my instincts and going with something that simply reflected who I was and what I was doing. It was true that "Storey" had the potential for a play on publishing words ("Storey Books") and it was also true that I wanted to be in the *communications* business so as not to lock myself into a single, narrow form of publishing. It could grow as we grew and changed. "Storey Communications" resulted and has served us well from the beginning.

I should tell you that on the first day of business, I went down to the post office to see if there was any mail for us and indeed there were three letters. Two were congratulatory notes about the opening of our business and the third looked to be either an invoice or a check. Praying for the latter, I opened it up and my eyes bulged out of my head. Inside the envelope was a check for $250,000 payable to "Storer Communications," a considerably larger Miami-based communications corporation that had about 30 years and a billion dollars more in revenue than my brand new Storey Communications had. All the same, it was a wonderful way to start the business and gave us all a good laugh.

Think carefully about what you want your name to do for you. Once you've selected it, think about how it can begin to build equity immediately. We sent out an announcement immediately (Figure 6-1) to communicate to as many people in the publishing and direct marketing world that a new entity had been born.

One of the fastest ways you can build credibility is to license the name of a product line or company that is up and going. In our case, one of the strong selling points to our banker was that we were

Announcing

The formation of Storey Communications, Inc.

an independent publishing company

which has agreed in principle to acquire

the assets of Garden Way Publishing Company.

May 3, 1983

Ferry Road
Charlotte, Vermont 05440
802-425-2171

Figure 6-1. Announcement of a new enterprise.

accelerating our launch with a licensing agreement that gave us the use of the Garden Way name for a five-year period. It also gave us a running start with both suppliers and accounts, and allowed for a fast transition. In effect, we were doing business on day one with 5,000 accounts nationwide through the use of that Garden Way Publishing licensing accord. We had authors submitting to us, suppliers seeking to do business with us, and bankers calling us on the strength of that name. And we paid for it on a simple royalty basis. Take a careful look at licensing, and ask your lawyer how to structure a deal most simply. Corporations view it as a nice, "new" profit center and will be happy to talk with you.

COMMUNICATING

If you happen to be buying something from your previous employer or from another corporation, suggest to them immediately that it's in your mutual interest to get out a communication to all of their employees, previous suppliers and customers as well as to the press to announce the fact that a change has occurred. Ask them to pay for it. Once they agree to this, or even to splitting the cost, you have the opportunity to use that mutual interest to your advantage. In our case, we communicated with approximately 1,000 companies alerting them to the change. We also sent the announcement to the local and trade press, which picked up on the event as well.

You should begin immediately to have a no-cost, "press relations" campaign which takes every shred of publicity that you can squeeze out, about anything, and leverages it into more publicity. For instance, your local newspaper is certainly going to be willing to run an article about your new venture (or a convention you're attending or speech you're making), as is the alumni magazine from your college or university. In trying to get broader coverage than that, clip the articles that have appeared on you and your new venture from the local press together with their masthead in an official-looking announcement and send that off to larger publications, which will then give the event more credence than if you simply sent out your own press release. This leveraging factor is one that you can do over and over again.

Spending no more than a few dollars, we were able to come up with publicity that landed in *USA Today* (see Figure 6-2) only about a year after we launched our enterprise. How did we do it? A local free-lance writer wrote a good run down on our company and what we were trying to do for the local newspaper. (Don't be afraid to ask for a prepress draft so that you can "correct any technical problems.") We then reprinted that article with masthead and sent it off to a number of national media including *Publisher's Weekly* and *USA Today* which, unbeknownst to us, was doing an article on the decentralization of corporate America and the move of many people from Madison Avenue to Main Street. They caught a glimpse of our article and said, "Perfect . . . just the kind of example we're looking for." We wound up on the front page of the *USA Today* Business Section. Circulation? Millions. Results? We're still hearing about it. In fact, when I was in New York last week, I bumped into an old friend from college who introduced me to a friend of his from the Doubleday Publishing Corp. Before I could say anything, Jeff's friend said, "Are you John Storey from Storey Communications in Vermont?" I said "Yes, how did you know that?" He said, "I think I read about it in *USA Today*."

Country publishers help others make move

By B.J. Roche
Special for USA TODAY

POWNAL, Vt. — Once you've decided to buy a business in the country, what's the next step? John and Martha Storey, owners of Storey Communications Inc., are hoping you'll want to pick up a book — theirs.

The company's new Country Business Library is aimed at city folks who want to make the move to the country.

The first book, *How to Find and Buy Your Business in the Country* by Frank Kirkpatrick, will be released through Harper and Row Publishers Inc. in April, followed by *Licenses, Permits and Registrations*, a guide to business regulations in New England.

Other books, including one on running country stores and inns, are in the planning stages. They will instruct the reader in

THE STOREYS: They're capitalizing on country know-how.

By Elizabeth E. Johnson

the basics of advertising, bookkeeping and evaluating business opportunities.

"We have found there are many people sold on the idea of moving to the country but facing the real and very practi-

cal question of how they will make a living if they make the move," says John Storey.

The Storeys have firsthand experience in the urban-to-rural transition. John Storey worked in New York publish-

ing for 17 years before they decided to start their business.

In May 1983, they founded Storey Communications, which publishes gardening, cooking and self-sufficiency books, as well as the twice-annual *Gardener's Marketplace*, a direct-mail vehicle that pulls in such advertisers as L.L. Bean, Vermont Castings and *Organic Gardening* magazine. Sales from their publishing and marketing efforts are expected to total $3.5 million this year.

It's not always easy doing business far away from an urban area, but Storey says the Vermont location is worth any problems it causes.

"The Vermont address gives us some credibility," he says. "The whole theme of gardening would almost be inconsistent if we were in a skyscraper in midtown Manhattan. People who buy from us want to think we're not a big corporation."

Figure 6-2. Front-page coverage (*Source: USA Today*, B. J. Roche January 3, 1985. Copyright © 1985, Reprinted with permission).

The whole point of this is to increase your *apparent* stability, the seriousness with which your customers, your suppliers, your investors, your bankers, and even your employees take your fragile new venture. In this regard every single bit of credibility helps. In developing this press campaign, work hard to show people what the uniqueness of your venture is. At the time we launched our company, "country" was hot. Barbara Mandrel was singing "I was country, when country wasn't cool." We decided to hang our new company image on getting away from the city and getting out to the country. This was a hook that most media picked up on and ran. I personally mailed a letter a day to possible media, and developed a list that now has over 1,000 contacts.

In the case of *Publisher's Weekly* (PW), the major trade journal of the publishing field, Editor John Baker happened to enjoy visiting Williamstown, Massachusetts and its Clark Art Museum. We invited John to stop by our fledgling country publishing business and he said he would be delighted to do so. He kept his promise and showed up on the most beautiful day of June 1984. We had a wonderful lunch and a spirited conversation about the decentralization of publishing. I was not surprised to hear from John a few weeks later that a favorable article on us would be appearing in *PW* shortly. [See Figure 6-3.]

Garden Way Puts Down New Roots

The former publisher of gardening books, under new management, is taking aim at country consciousness

by John F. Baker

It doesn't make much difference what kind of a day it is when you visit most publishers. A visit to Garden Way Publishing, aka Storey Communications, however, is another matter. Since it is located by the side of the road in the foothills of Vermont's Green Mountains, a little above the Massachusetts line, and looks out over acres of meadow and forested hillsides, a visitor certainly hopes for sunshine. And when *PW* drove up on a shiny day in early June, it seemed like the best place in the world to have one's headquarters.

The man who chose this particular location, in Pownal, is John Storey, who with his wife Martha started Storey Communications a little over a year ago, licensing the name Garden Way Publishing from Garden Way, Inc., predominantly a manufacturer of rototillers. It was a rather circuitous route that brought Storey and his wife to the head of this operation, which, appropriately enough, publishes gardening books and is now branching out into related cookbooks, books about building methods, and doing business in the country.

With a background at Hearst and Time-Life Books, where he was involved with marketing on the *Time-Life Encyclopedia of Gardening*, Storey eventually launched a gardening newsletter—"which is when I got to know the Garden Way people. They made the Troybilt rototillers, and began the publishing operation as a sort of sideline, putting together gardening books as premiums for their customers." The Storeys sold their newsletter to Garden Way, then spent the next seven years with the firm, "investigating possible products and services. Eventually they decided they wanted to concentrate on their garden products, and we had a chance to buy the book publishing and packaging operation, licensing the Gar-

den Way name for our books."

As for the new location in Pownal, Storey is a Williams grad and lives in Williamstown, only a few miles to the south. When he joined, the Garden Way publishing operation was in Charlotte, Vt. "I wanted to move it closer to Williamstown but keep the Vermont feeling." Eventually he found a former ceramic workshop, just in front of a school, and moved in. "We've just decided to buy the building." (For those

L. to r.: James Brady, John Storey and Roger Griffiths at their conference picnic table

interested in such things—as most Manhattan-based publishers are—he estimates the cost of space in the Pownal headquarters office, and in a separate warehouse building just down the road, as about $3 a square foot.)

There are two acres, including a newly started garden for employees, and a rustic picnic table that doubles as a conference table for the more informal planning sessions involving the Storeys, editor-in-chief Roger Griffiths, associate publisher James Brady, sales manager Alan Hood and business manager Richard Salmon—though there is a more formal one indoors for use in rainy or cold weather.

And there is a lot of planning to do because, as Storey puts it, "in terms of our publishing operations we had to go back almost to square one and rebuild." A fast decision had to be made on distribution because the parent company had originally done it, marketing

largely to nurseries and garden stores and without much emphasis on the book trade. Storey chose Harper & Row to distribute Garden Way, "and they've helped us through a very difficult transition." To put the company more firmly on the publishing map in New York, securing attention and reviews, they hired consultant and publicist Carolyn Anthony. And they have been busy combing the lists—currently there are 180 book titles and smaller-scale "bulletins" in print—to prune out the flops, decide what needs revising, and launch new titles and lines.

And then, of course, there was the problem of the Pownal mail service. The company is heavily into promotional mailings and mail order, and when John Storey went down to the local post office to discuss it he found the postmaster delighted at the prospect of new business—until he found out that mailings of a million pieces at a time were contemplated, followed by about 60,000 replies. "His eyes rolled up into his head." In the end, an expansion was made and all was happily resolved.

Backing up all this activity is a hard core of successful backlist titles, headed by Dick Raymond's *Joy of Gardening*, which, tying in with a successful TV series, has sold over 375,000 copies. (This has recently been followed up with Janet Ballantyne's *Joy of Gardening Cookbook*, the new Garden Way's most ambitious project to date, an all-color simultaneous hardcover and trade paperback.) There have been strong sales of books discussing new approaches to building: *The Underground House* and *Pole Building Construction* have both sold 200,000 copies, and some judicious retitling (*The Zucchini Cookbook* instead of *Cooking with Squash* and *Carrots Love Tomatoes* rather than *Companion Planting*) have revivified sales of old standbys. Under the old regime, directed toward vegetable gardening, flower gardening books were not encouraged, says Alan Hood; now they can be done. The cookbook line is now growing faster than the gardening books, though books on energy saving, once 20% of the list, have dropped to about 5%.

The new approach that most excites Storey and his colleagues at present is the Country Business Library, to be launched in the fall with two titles, *How to Find and Buy Your Business in the Country* and *Licenses, Permits and Registrations: New England Edition.* "There's no doubt this is an area of enormous and growing interest," Storey says. "The latest figures show the growth of exurban America dramatically outstripping that of the urban centers. People want to get back to the country, and these books will tell them in practical terms how to do it."

Another string to the bow is *The Gardener's Marketplace,* a sort of catalogue with advertising space sold in it to dozens of garden product firms, which goes out to a million names twice a year (the bane of the Pownal post office).

Bob Shields, director of special sales, explains that currently about 50% of Garden Way books go into regular trade outlets, 30% into special sales (including 2000 hardware, feed and seed stores and nurseries) and up to 20% mail order. He has placed books in 200 out of the 700 Agway stores nationwide, and is aiming at new major accounts like Norpro, a large chain operating out of Oregon. There are plans to actively expand telemarketing, and Garden Way display fixtures, to carry 15–20 titles, are being improved.

Hood, who is here on a part-time consulting basis (and is also marketing director at Countryman Press), led a major assault on the trade marketplace recently by taking a team of eight to the ABA in Washington. He sees his markets as being principally in the Northeast, the Upper Midwest and the Northwest rather than the South or Southwest; "it's a matter of the kind of climate our books are written for."

Despite its rustic location and subject matter, Garden Way is electronically sophisticated. All manuscripts are keyboarded onto disks and sent out to local printers; at the warehouse (and future telemarketing center) down the road, orders are processed and letters prepared on five PCs.

For editor-in-chief Roger Griffiths, a

Garden Way staff preparing a vegetable garden outside company headquarters

veteran of the old Garden Way since 1974, the country location is no problem. He recalls that at Charlotte all the staff members had vegetable gardens and used to prepare their own salad lunches—and is confident that in Pownal "it will come." He is very much a practicer of what his books preach, and could hardly be imagined in a New York office building. Griffiths himself works on about 12 books a year, and has three part-time editors to help out. "I'm not close with agents, so that doesn't matter—but I read magazines in the field carefully for writers and ideas, read other books. But since we're defining our own areas as we go along, it's more a matter of finding writers to do books we want rather than hoping someone will come up with something." He gets about 10–15 manuscripts a week over the transom—"mostly old ladies with recipes, some poetry, some fiction." Copy editors and proofreaders, mostly part-time, are no problem, with northern Massachusetts and the Berkshires, and the Albany area, both within 40 miles.

There are in fact 15 full-time employees currently and about a dozen part-timers, though their number will grow as the company does. Their joint efforts bring in net revenues estimated to reach about $3.5 million this year, and with hopes for considerably beyond that in 1985. Storey is "trying hard to expand the list" and aiming at creating a new line each year, Hood is working to improve trade distribution, Salmon is streamlining the invoicing and making ambitious telemarketing plans.

"We've still got a lot to learn," says Storey thoughtfully. "We're focusing inward, on how we can do things better than they were always done in the past. And in any case," he decides cheerfully, "you can still say we're the biggest publisher in Pownal—and probably for 20 miles around." □

28

Figure 6-3. Text and illustrations reprinted from *Publisher's Weekly* article (*Source:* August 3, 1984), published by the Bowker Magazine group of Cahners Publishing, a division of Reed Publishing USA. Copyright © by Reed Publishing USA.

The combination of location, weather, and uniqueness of our business put John in the right mood and he wrote a most helpful article on our behalf.

Luck? Hardly. If you throw out a hundred lines, you're going to catch some fish.

None of this has cost us very much (mailing a letter a day costs about $75 a year). In a very short period of time, public recognition of Storey Communications *has* increased. We consider it a poor day when we can't take something that has occurred in the press world and repackage it for prospective customers and clients. We're now, four years later, subscribing to a national press clipping service which, for approximately $150 a month, will send in all of the articles involving our company or our products that appear in newspapers around the country. In our case, we get approximately 150 to 200 clippings a month that we then redistribute to sales representatives, to authors, and to customers. This total publicity campaign costs approximately $20,000 per year, for a company with $3.5 million in annual sales. I believe the return that we are getting on that investment to be somewhere in the neighborhood of 10 to 20 times.

All of your communications should be done with consistent style and tone. This gets down to some pretty mundane matters such as letterheads, envelopes, business cards, invoice forms, and rate cards. Decide from the very beginning that you want to have a consistent and uniform look about what you're doing. If you decide in week one to do something in a classic typeface and format and then on week six decide to do something in a frilly or expansive typeface, you will begin to confuse your audiences from the outset. Remember that you are trying to present a "together," integrated look. Make sure that you put your name, address, and phone number on every piece of correspondence and promotion that you send. You shouldn't be cheap (choose your printer carefully) when it comes to these first investments in your letterhead, your envelopes, and your business cards. You should present a high quality image and design so that you can get across to people the classiness of your operation and your absolute intention to be a success.

On the other hand, you don't have to spend a huge amount of money on it. We developed a high-impact Rolodex card (see Figure 8-1) with the Storey name on it and mailed it out to 500 of our potential customers. The entire printing for this cost under $100 and we still hear from many people that they "see our name popping out of their Rolodex before anyone else's." This "David and Goliath" approach has proven to us again and again that you don't need slick and expensive four-color to get your image across to people.

Be systematic. You do want to create a method of keeping your name in front of your clients and your prospects regularly. You can do this with the reprints of magazine articles that you have written, other news on your corporation, or even occasionally with a thoughtful premium, something that they will keep on hand to remind them from time to time of your name. Set up a planned mailing schedule at the beginning of each year. Figure 6-4 shows how it might look.

Don't be bashful. Let people know about the various events you've been involved in, good words that clients and customers have for you, and developments in your company. During our first year of operation we won a coveted "Tastemaker Award" presented by the R. T. French Company for our *Apple Cookbook* published in our first year of business. This was presented in New York at the Park Lane Hotel to my wife Martha, who was seated between Random House and Harper & Row! We were able to parlay the publicity surrounding our "best single subject cookbook in America" into a much higher recognition of our publishing program. The point is to get your publicity up and going promptly and ensure that the integrated name and image of your company is getting out in front of people's noses every single day. It's as effective and considerably less expensive than advertising.

CHOOSING A LOCATION AND BUILDING

Location is your next major consideration. By this I mean both your general location—geographic—and your specific facility location. This is another important first decision, one that planned properly will allow you to get going and grow comfortably for the first few years of your operation without getting into costly changes, additions, moves, as you outgrow your building or wrong location. Entering into the location decision will be image, costs, access to markets, transportation, labor, and even proximity to your home.

For starters, you could do worse than asking yourself where, exactly, you would like to be. There is tremendous value in being where

January 1	"What's New at Storey"	500 pieces
January 31	"Revolutionary Medium Drops to 1,000,000 Gardeners"	2,000 pieces
February 28	"New Books: Announcements"	1,000 pieces
March 31	"Visit Us and Meet Our Authors at ABA" mailing	1,000 pieces
April 30	"The Birth of a New Publishing Concept"	1,000 pieces
May 31	"Surprising Developments in Direct Marketing"	1,000 pieces
June 30	"Christmas in July Special Ordering Plan"	1,000 pieces
July 31	"666,000 New Businesses Started in 1986"	1,000 pieces
August 31	"Innovative Direct Marketing Techniques— Visit us at DMA" mailing	1,000 pieces
September 30	"New Book Announcements"	1,000 pieces
October 31	"Celebration of 40 Years in Print"— best sellers mailing	1,000 pieces
November 30	"New Book Announcements"	1,000 pieces
December 31	"What We Believe 1988 Will Bring"	1,000 pieces

Total number of pieces 13,500.   Cost $6,500.   Returns Incalculable!

Figure 6-4. 1987 Pub mailing campaign.

you want to be. When we announced that we would move all operations from Burlington, Vermont to Bennington, Vermont we were able to do two things at once: bring *me* back to Williamstown, Massachusetts *and* reduce $750,000 worth of corporate overhead. We simply ceased many functions that had grown like weeds in Burlington. People who lost jobs were also able to explain their loss more easily to others, simply by saying "my company moved."

Ask yourself also, is your choice a place where others would like to be. How about employees? Customers? Suppliers? We get a steady flow of people from Boston and New York publishing worlds, typically on Fridays and Mondays because of the attractiveness of Vermont as a four-season recreational and vacation community. An advertising sales fellow drove up from New Jersey en route to Stratton Mountain, left his wife and family in his station wagon with the motor running, and ran in to do some business with me in order to write off a portion of the weekend! We'll take it, however it comes!

What about transportation—both in terms of getting you and your goods out and getting others and your supplies in? We are right on the Vermont, Massachusetts, and New York borders which gives us easy access to Boston (two and one-half hours), New York (three hours), Montreal (four hours), Burlington (two and one-half hours), and Albany (one hour) by car. Access to other cities around the country is easy through the Albany and Hartford Airports, and a good Amtrak train system from Albany directly into midtown Manhattan. Ask yourself about your business environment. As we made our decision, we were very much aware of the fact that both Vermont and Massachusetts were working hard to develop entrepreneurial small business growth in Bennington County and Berkshire County. This ultimately proved extremely beneficial to us, both in terms of lower cost of doing business and assistance. Seek out development agencies immediately.

Finally, ask yourself how attractive is your location promotionally. We could have been in New York, Massachusetts, or Vermont by moving the business about a mile in either direction. But we knew that when we're on the road and we say to people "we're from Vermont," the impact promotionally is considerably greater than "I'm from New York" or "I'm from Massachusetts." We have used that "beautiful, small state" image to good advantage over the last several years.

There should also be some relationship between the kind of business you're doing and the location you've picked. Because our business is primarily concerned with selling books and advertising space which relates to country living, our Vermont location has proven to be one of our most valuable assets. There would be a certain contradiction if we found ourselves "talking country" from the top floor of a skyscraper on Columbus Circle in New York.

If you're a national mail-order house you may locate pretty much anywhere you want, and certain decisions may drive you in one direction or another. Our neighbor to the north, the Orvis Company, recently decided to close its Manchester, Vermont operations and move everything to Roanoke, Virginia, because of a larger labor pool and the dramatic savings it could experience in the form of reduced United Parcel Service (UPS) shipping (UPS hub is in Roanoke).

On the other hand, it you're a computer consultant there may be real advantages to being near your customers. One of my friends who lives in Garden City, Long Island is on call evenings and weekends, much like a doctor, to service IBM's major account five minutes from his home. Proximity to his customer is critical.

You should check out very carefully whether it is more expensive to do business in one locality or state than another. You'll also want to incorporate where you think you will be doing most of your business. If not, you'll run into the requirement to register in other states as a foreign corporation and pay taxes in both states. But, in your selection of location, keep in mind your whole basic reason to be getting out on your own.

Once you've selected the area in which you would like to work and live, you'll be surprised by the resources available to help you find a specific site that fits your needs. Most cities and towns have development corporations that are familiar with all of the current possibilities that exist in terms of facilities, labor, and other available inducements. They'll also be versed in the zoning laws of the area and can help you avoid legal battles.

Obviously, each different kind of business will have a different requirement in terms of location. Retailers require—location, location, location—places with predictable street traffic and good parking, while an industrial company will be more concerned with low-cost overheads, transportation and parking for their labor force, and the ability to increase the size of the facility.

Work with confidence, because you have something to sell. People will want you to locate in their area, on the premise that you will create many new jobs for their community. You should keep this very much in mind and, while promising nothing, listen to everybody's offers. Allow yourself to be wooed. Do not overlook any state, county, city, or municipal government for assistance. Every state has a development office, and don't forget the federal government has SBA offices in every state. All of these people will be looking to help you with your site selection and inducements to locate there.

I announced that we would be moving to the Bennington, Vermont area. A newspaper article appeared. This did not keep people from Pittsfield, Massachusetts from calling and saying that "we have good reasons for you to consider seriously putting your business in Pittsfield, in Williamstown, or in North Adams." On the northern front, the Bennington County Industrial Commission came forward and began immediately to coordinate an effort that resulted in phone calls from friendly bankers, an offer of free space in a Bennington County "incubator" for new business, and tremendous cooperation and early friendship.

All of this makes you feel good. You should also be thorough and cautious at this moment and plan to take at least two to three weeks to make your decision on location, so as to maximize your longer-term opportunities.

In an article in the *Wall Street Journal*, authors Axel Kotlowitz and Dale D. Buss reported on the tremendous competition that existed in and among localities in trying to lure companies into their respective areas. Tax breaks, business loans, and outright grants have been plums for relocating and start-up companies for some time.[1]

Be realistic. If you are a brand new start up with no track record and nothing but the promise of future employment, the states of New York, California, and Michigan are not about to drop everything and seek you out. On the other hand, the town of Bennington approached me aggressively, offering space at no rental cost initially, and eventually a rental of $2.50 per square foot in order to get me going. Their particular incubator was started by the Bennington County Industrial Corp. in the late 1970s and offered 150,000 square feet of space, which at the time of my interest housed 36 firms. Of encouragement to the new entrepreneur was being told that companies that had "hatched" from the BCIC Incubator building had enjoyed a 90 percent success rate. The price of $2.00 to $2.75 a square foot included heat, insurance, sewer, and water, cutting down on the entrepreneur's need to worry about those kinds of details.[2]

Another prize example was a company called Bio-Teck, a medical technology company, which started in a Burlington, Vermont incubator two years ago and now employs 200 people.[3]

Sometimes the interest of the community goes well beyond tax bills and grants. Des Moines, Iowa has created something recently called "The Gold Circle Loan Guarantee Fund" that in effect goes beyond the SBA loan guarantee program. To qualify, a business must meet two criteria: "The loan must finance a project that will create or preserve jobs in the Golden Circle," an area within a 50 mile radius of Des Moines; and "a majority of the borrowers new business must

[1]Axel Kotlowitz and Dale D. Buss, "Localities' giveaways to lure corporations cause growing outcry," *Wall Street Journal*, September 24, 1986, p. 1, 27.
[2]Marguerite Lyons, "North Bennington incubator ready for sale to private sector," *Vermont Business*, September 1986, p. 9.
[3]Phillip K. Dodd, "Incubator schemes take on new importance," *Vermont Business*, September 1986, p. 9.

be done outside that area, bringing money into the region. The guarantees are available for loans between $50,000 and $250,000."[4]

Chicago is a prime example of a community/municipality going after corporations aggressively. In 1980 a *Wall Street Journal* article said, "the city provided Playschool, Inc. a Hasbro-Bradley, Inc. unit with $1 million industrial revenue bond with a promise from the company that it would create about 400 new jobs."[5] These things don't always work out perfectly, and Chicago and Playschool are battling with each other now because of Playschool's closing. The article went on to say that "states now are emphasizing education and worker retraining in small business assistance."[6] A local retraining program provides our company with up to 50 percent of compensation of certain new employees.

Many consultants feel the location selection is the most crucial decision that a new business owner makes. Certainly if you're in the retail business this is true. Don't let your emotion be your guide here. In order to have the traffic to support whatever kind of retail store you're opening, make absolutely certain it's going to be there. Watch the traffic patterns every day for a month, then go back a month later and see if the traffic patterns are similar. Watch it in June *and* November. Get traffic counts from other local businesses. Make absolutely certain that there's nothing seasonal or changing about that location.

We thought that the opening of a retail country book store in a section just north of us on Vermont Route 7 would allow us to take advantage of a high traffic pattern on that highway. In fact, the retail store was a failure because people simply didn't want to slow down long enough on the 50 miles-per-hour "strip" to stop for books.

Consultants also warn about a decision to move to an entirely new region of the country at the same time that you're starting your new business. They advise strongly against it, pointing out that these are two of the most intense and emotional involvements that you'll ever have. Doing both of them at once has been traumatic for some. Ideally, you can move your business to your own community. This

[4]Stephen P. Galante, "Des Moines has its own way to back small-business loans," *Wall Street Journal*, September 29, 1986, p. 45.
[5]Axel Kotlowitz and Dale D. Buss, "Localities' giveaways to lure corporations cause growing outcry," *Wall Street Journal*, September 24, 1986, pp. 1, 27.
[6]*Ibid.*

should be a critical question to ask any person from whom you're considering buying a business.

I remember a long-time native of Bennington, Duncan Campbell, saying to me "let the community embrace you." In the case of a small business you'll find that you'll have many immediate fans, from the banker to the board of selectmen or town council to the gas station operator, who will be cheering for you.

Ask yourself whether there is an advantage to being located close to a particular metropolitan area. It is no coincidence that square foot costs in New York City and Boston are dramatically high—in some cases between $50 and $100 per square foot. Many people find that they can squeeze out far more business from $50-per-square-foot space in metropolitan areas than from $1-per-square-foot space in rural areas.

Kiam puts it this way: "Business is where you are."[7] This occurred to me recently when I was in New York and going from one meeting with *Better Homes and Gardens* to a lunch date at the John Wiley & Sons offices. While on Third Avenue I bumped into a fellow that I had not seen for some time who asked me "What are you doing now?"

I opened by briefcase on a trash can and began showing (and gently pitching) him our services. While I was doing that, another old friend who I had not seen for a year came by and I suddenly had an audience. I began to look and feel like the sleight-of-hand artists who do their card tricks quickly before the police can find them; or rather, as one of these fellows said, "A publishing hooker working Third Avenue." But it is the case, as Kiam suggests, that your business is where you are, particularly at the very outset.

Obviously, if you are in the high-tech business you are looking for a Cambridge, Massachusetts Route 128, or Silicon Valley location. These are the places to be for many start up high technology businesses, both in terms of the brain power and intellectual community, as well as venture capital to support them.

While your choice of location should please you, don't think it necessarily is going to solve all of your problems. The environment in which you work is a very important one, but there will be days when nobody will come your way and you'll have to hit the road. Being a

[7]Victor Kiam, *Going For It!*, (New York: Morrow, 1986), p. 107.

happy country business owner doesn't mean you're not going to have to get out and scrounge up some business when the mail doesn't come and the phone doesn't ring.

Once you have decided on location, finding an efficient facility is your next job. I would strongly advocate renting before you consider buying anything. Amazingly enough, many people decide that; "Now that I am in business, I need a building of my own" and go out and spend what precious capital they have on a facility. This is the last thing that you want to spend money on. Alfred Knopf said recently, "It's the publishing start ups with too much money, not too little, that fail."

A different approach is to negotiate a rental with an option-to-buy clause for later purchase. You can make this offer, either way, with properties advertised for rent or for sale. This is something that you probably won't want to exercise before at least two years of business experience is under your belt. Things can change quickly.

Figure how much space you are going to need. Look at your five-year plan which carries assumptions about personnel, and look at the maximum number of people that you expect to have in the five-year period. Multiply that number by 100 square feet per person and see what that adds up to. In our own case, we estimated that we would have 30 people within the first five years, and that gave us a need within that period for 3,000 square feet for office purposes. We found a building with 3,000 square feet for sale for $55,000. We negotiated a rent-option-buy with all rental ($3 per square foot) applicable against purchase price, which we exercised two years later. We also needed a separate warehouse facility, and were able to do that in a large, very low-cost ($1 per square foot facility) 25 minutes away.

Be sure, in this early decision making, that you have some room to expand, because it is incredibly disruptive and costly to have to close down and move to a different facility. It is also complicated, as we discovered, to have a remote facility even if it is only a few hundred yards away. We had to install two telephone systems, two computer systems, and found that communications among departments and employees became extremely difficult. I consider this now a $30,000 to $50,000 mistake that we didn't have to make, and I would avoid like the plague ever doing it again.

Bigger corporations make this mistake all the time. Garden Way Inc., primarily because of the desires of three different owners, had locations in Westport, Connecticut, Troy, New York, and Burlington, Vermont. All systems and many corporate departments were duplicated, and it led to an extremely high cost and low return on investment. Now consolidated in Troy, New York, the corporation has saved millions in lower-cost, better integrated operations.

The questions that you want to ask the owner of the building are several. How much is the rental per square foot? How do you calculate the square footage and the usable footage? What kind of a lease is it? Does the rental include upkeep, are the walls sound, does the roof leak, are there hidden costs? Is this site zoned for the type of business that you want to operate there? Some of these questions can be tricky, and might have a significant impact on your business. You should get help from your lawyer in taking a look at the first lease that you are about to sign. Robert S. Cunningham, vice president of Spaulding and Slye, a Boston-based property management firm, suggests asking these ten questions before signing a lease:

1. How long will the lease run?
2. How much is the rent?
3. How much will the rent go up?
4. Can you sublease?
5. Can you renew?
6. What happens if your landlord goes broke?
7. Who is responsible for insurance?
8. What building services are provided?
9. Who else can move in?
10. Who pays for improvements?[8]

These are important, but really form just the tip of the iceberg. Make sure that you bring your lawyer into these issues. Don't sign a thing without letting him or her run through the lease. Recently, an acquaintance set up a retail business with community support in an industrial park. He discovered too late that local rules precluded the kind of sign he needed to operate traffic. He's out.

[8]Robert S. Cunningham, "Ten Questions to ask before you sign a lease," *Inc. Magazine's Guide to Small Business Success* reprints, 1984.

A completely different approach you might consider, which could dramatically reduce your start-up costs and limit the capital you require, can be found in an "executive office suite."

A good business friend, Ray Markman, who started Heritage Home Video, a videocassette marketing company, about three years ago, needed a place in downtown Chicago where he could do business easily and get into and out of O'Hare Airport. The last thing he wanted to invest in was expensive furniture, telephones, carpets, and supplies, but he did need a high image atmosphere for his corporate clients. He found his answer in an executive office suite. This is basically a business support service that can offer real cost reductions in the form of reduced operating costs, trained employees who are shared with other executives, space, furniture, computers, phone systems and, in many cases, the handling of personnel records.

Estimates vary, but to hire an employee and open an office requires a commitment of at least $2,500 per month according to Michael C. Thomasetti.[9] Reporting the results of a national survey, Thomasetti suggested that the largest start-up expense is salaries. "The average cost of a single employee is $1,300 per month—more if you add in payroll taxes and insurance, not to mention the time it takes to keep personnel records, file payroll tax returns, and comply with every law and regulation concerning employer and employee relations." Rent is an extremely high secondary cost, and trying to plan your growth precisely is very difficult; so you may find yourself having to move a couple of times in the first five years of business. Those moves, if only local, can cost anywhere from $1,000 to $10,000. Some of these problems can be overcome by starting up in a business support operation as described. Check it out.

During the two-year period of our rent/buy option, interest rates dropped from approximately 12 percent to around 8 percent. We were able to buy our facility, and then lease it back to the company with tremendous tax advantages, after living with the building a couple of years and finding out all of its strengths and weaknesses.

When you are ready to buy, get expert advice. Fred Steingold, a lawyer from Ann Arbor, Michigan, provides good basic rules for

[9]Michael C. Thomasetti, "Options to overcoming high overhead," *Kiwanis Magazine*, June/July 1986, pp. 21–23.

buying business real estate. He suggests asking yourself the following questions:

1. What is the purchase price?
2. When is it due?
3. What property (real estate and personal property) is being bought or sold?
4. What type of deed and title evidence will you receive?
5. Under what conditions can you withdraw from the purchase and get back your deposit?
6. To what extent does the seller guarantee the condition of the building?
7. When can you take possession?
8. How will taxes and utility bills be allocated between you and the seller?[10]

This suggests only top line considerations. Don't purchase a single thing before you sit down with your lawyer to understand what you are getting into. The purchase of a building is an important, long-term investment consideration, and must be done from both the point of view of business appropriateness and return on your personal investment. Retailers and service companies will have to look at it from the point of view of the traffic that is going to pass by their permanent site, and the likely development of the area. Will it become a business district, a shopping center? Right in our own neighborhood there is a restaurant on Route 7 that is packed every night, while a snack bar that is located 100 yards back from the road is empty. No coincidence.

Check the latest census statistics available to determine expected population growth for the region. Market research firms will even provide latest demographic profiles showing age, income, and household makeup of area populations.

Retailers must be concerned about parking availability. Wholesalers and manufacturers, on the other hand, will be primarily concerned about cheap space, which is more important than a central lo-

---

[10]Fred S. Steingold, "Ten rules for buying real estate," *Inc. Magazine's Guide to Small Business Success* reprints, 1984.

cation. They'll also have to ask themselves whether the labor force is in place and will be able to get to them, and what the interstate transportation patterns look like. Troy, New York was great, Burlington, Vermont was okay, North Adams, Massachusetts is difficult. One trucker trying to deliver a carload of books to us called from the famous hairpin turn in North Adams, Massachusetts, unable to get his 18-wheeler around the corner. He called and asked, "What would you like me to do with your books?" While the hairpin turn is great as a local attraction, it doesn't do much for the speedy shipment of books.

If, on the other hand, you are a mail-order marketer, you probably have already asked yourself whether you can work out of your home. Richard Cabela, who formed Cabela's Catalog in Sidney, Nebraska, 135 miles south of Cody, Nebraska, developed a business starting with fishing lures, on his kitchen table, from which a $70 million a year business has emerged. The address served as no impediment to the building of that business. He has, on the other hand, nearly outgrown the labor force.

Robert Townsend, author of *Up The Organization*, which was popular a decade ago, put it this way. "Work out of your own home as long as you can . . . then move to the garage."[11] Millions of people have been doing just that—operating within their homes during the last several years, putting pressure on residential neighborhoods and zoning restrictions.

The 1980 census showed that more than 2 million people, or 2-½ percent of the nonfarm work force, said that they worked at home for money, according to the *New York Times* News Service.[12] Experts say that figure is extremely low. The U.S. Chamber of Commerce and the American Telephone and Telegraph Company jointly estimate that more than 10 million Americans do all of their paid work there. So you are not exactly starting a new trend if you've considered using your home as a place for business.

As you consider doing this, ask yourself: Can you establish a work space which is separate from your living space? Can you avoid interruptions? When I first got going, I converted a portion of our base-

---

[11]Robert Townsend, *Up the Organization* (New York, Fawcett, 1978).
[12]John Herbers, "Revival of cottage industry ignites debate" (1986 New York Times Wire Service) *Berkshire Eagle*, May 14, 1986, p. 14.

ment into an office space. I was linked with my corporation through a telephone and was really living until we got 3 inches of water in the basement after a particularly strong storm. I moved upstairs. There I found distractions. Ask whether you will you be able to get anything done there. If you plan to have your family working with you in the business, it may be extremely advantageous to start the business where everyone is already located, in your home. A computer tie-in to a central office makes telecommuting possible.

Currently, we have a Fortune Micro Computer system with a multi-user setup in our office. We have a terminal/modem to link the computer to our home which accesses the main system over the telephone lines with a local call. I can bring home a tape which I dictate between 5 and 7 P.M., give it to Jessica who enters it at home, and have it printed out at 7 A.M. in the office the next day. I'll match that against any corporate word-processing department. We will continue to do more "tele-processing" in the future.

While it is important to check zoning to see if you can operate in your home, understand that the zoning rules are being bent and tested these days. In other words, don't be bashful.

FINAL STAFF DECISIONS

The third major area of consideration in your start-up decision making is people: your staff. Start with the simplest possible organization chart. You're the owner/president and if you're lucky enough to have your spouse working, you've got a vice president.

Don't hire a single person until you know exactly what that person is going to do. This will save you money *and* make you smarter about your business. Kiam put it this way, "Make your company 'lean and mean'—no fancy overheads, no frills, fly tourist, no company cars, no executive dining rooms, etc.[13]

Before you hire anyone, understand what you expect your staffing requirements to be in year one, two, and three. You probably won't really know which jobs are most important to fill until you've done each of the tasks yourself. Assessing them properly at the beginning may be a little difficult, but it's awfully important to do. You should

[13]Victor Kiam's keynote presentation and workshop, "Motivation and Direction," at *The Challenge of Growth: The Fourth Annual Conference on Entrepreneurship*, May 18, 1985, Stanford Center for Entrepreneurship, Stanford, California.

be able to explain every job in the company to anybody you hire. Having surplus staff at the outset of your operation is a crime. And you'll experience this sharply the first time you fail to be able to meet the payroll.

Make it clear from the outset that you are the owner and they are employees who are not expected to take the risks, or get the same rewards, that you get. Developing a good working and personal relationship with your staff is important; but remember, you're the one who has stuck your neck out, and you're the one who is going to be most hurt if your start-up venture doesn't work. Make certain that everyone understands your sense of money—which expenditures they can make and which require approval. Every employee should understand what his or her approval capacity is, whether zero or a million dollars. Once you have hired people, get out of the way and let them do the job. As Axel L. Grabowsky recently put it in *Inc.* magazine, "you should let people do what they have been hired for . . . this includes reporting to you especially if there is a discrepancy between projections and results. They should know that that's part of their job. It allows you to stay in control."[14]

Before adding staff, ask yourself whether you really need that extra person. Most entrepreneurial businesses behave very differently from the old corporation and are a one-person show at least initially. Think about it. Do you really need your own secretary or can you do the typing yourself? If you type 80 words a minute that's a good use of your time. If you type 20 it probably isn't.

The advantages of the "lean and mean" approach is that you have no payroll to make except for yourself and you're already prepared to scrape a bit before being comfortable. And second, you'll know every facet of your business firsthand. This will be invaluable especially as you grow.

Ed Stern, publisher of Hilary House, is a great proponent of the no-employee office. "I want my revenue line and profit line to be the same number," he said recently.

Don't expect people to do things happily which you won't do yourself. I talked recently to one of my friends who I had known in college and who had become a lawyer with a prestigious law firm. I

[14]Axel L. Grabowsky, "What to monitor to stay in control," *Inc. Magazine's Guide to Small Business Success* reprints, 1984.

asked him why he had recently left and he said that the owner and managing partner gave all of the new trainees the job of washing his car before he went out on important calls. This kind of ridiculous nonresponsibility causes many firms to lose some of their best young talent.

Understand what you're buying with the "no-staff" decision. If you are not going to hire it means that you're going to put in very long hours. Last week I worked 80 hours and a typical work week might be 60 or 70. You must also be prepared to deal with a problem that comes up at any moment, like the plumbing going bad on a Sunday or the security alarm going off in the middle of the night. Sometimes you'll be tired and lonely. It's part of the territory.

As you do begin to hire people, make sure you don't overhire. It's usually much easier to hire employees than to let people go. Perhaps you've identified an area such as bookkeeping in which you're not skilled and you'd like to cover. Ask yourself first, can you send it outside. Factor the real costs of employment:

Bookkeeper salary	$15,000
Employee benefit plan	4,500
Office overheads	4,000
Total	$23,500

How much outside bookkeeping can you buy for the same price each year? Can you subcontract all of that service? Are there jobs that you just won't have time to do yourself that perhaps don't require your involvement, such as taking inventory? At the same time, avoid thinking that certain jobs are beneath you. I still learn an awful lot about my business by picking up the mail every Saturday morning at the local Post Office and by emptying waste baskets on Friday afternoon.

When you do decide to hire, write a brief but careful and specific description of the job that you need filled, including the duties, hours, experience required, how much you're able to offer in salaries and wages. Also ask yourself how this job will result in cost reductions or revenue creation.

As you enter the personnel area, you're going to need some technical help. I went back to my old corporation and asked a good friend and extremely competent corporate human resources person, Jack Madden, to provide me with good early direction and advice. He did, free of charge, even delegating one of his lieutenants to us when we were getting started. He answered such immediate questions as:

1. Should a salesperson paid on a commission basis be treated like an hourly wage sales clerk with respect to tax withholding? (Yes)

2. Is it mandatory to take out FICA and state and federal withholding tax from a sales representative on straight commission? (Yes if the rep is an employee of the company)

3. How do you handle casual labor and taxes? (If the individual is an employee you must withhold taxes. Exception: if the labor is on an independent contract basis)

4. How do you handle people who live in one state but go to other states to sell goods? (As a business in another state you'd have to collect and remit taxes to the state where the goods are sold)

5. How does the corporation tax stockholders who work as salaried employees who want all profits applied to the liquidation of the original purchase debt? (Salaries of stockholding employees are taxed like other employees. The purchase price of the corporation is not a debt to the corporation but an investment by the stockholders, thus profits can't be used to liquidate this price)

Somebody like Jack, an experienced personnel manager, can be of enormous help to you. If you don't have a person to help you in these areas, ask your lawyer and accountant who they might know and get some assistance. Get your personnel department structured the right way from the beginning. You also have to find out what the going wage rates are in the area. *Inc.* magazine does an annual compensation survey in July and the Bureau of Labor Statistics does area wage surveys that are available to you in order to provide the "going rates."

When you begin to advertise for people in a local newspaper, make certain you use the advertisement to promote your own business at the same time you're looking for help. The ad should have a standard look, with standard corporate logo and description of the company, every time you run the ad. It's an opportunity to further publicize the company.

Don't overlook your existing employees as a low-cost resource in helping you find people who are qualified and interested in working for you. We use this technique regularly and people are happy to bring their contacts and friends in who might "fill the bill."

If you're in a college or university location, consider the college labor pool—students who are working for minimum wage and who might work for less if you are providing training to them in the fields they want to enter. In our case, many students at Bennington and Williams Colleges are interested in publishing and work on a trainee/ internship basis.

These students are good, and frequently free. Once you begin to hire people, make certain you have a simple personnel policy manual for all employees. Make a "contract" in writing that will protect both you and your employees. Get help from your lawyer on this. The policy manual should include both the basic policies of the company and your basic expectations of employees. Edgar S. Ellman pointed out recently in an *Inc.* magazine article that a carefully written handbook for your employees can improve morale, prevent disagreements and keep you out of court. It tells you quite simply what your lawyer will also tell you on subjects such as equal opportunity statements, overtime pay, group insurance benefits, military leaves of absence, bulletin boards, confidentiality, and so on.[15] Check this out. It may save you a lot of grief.

If you want to get much better versed in personnel policies you might pick up a book called *The Personnel Manager's Encyclopedia* by Brady.[16] It's an already-written personnel policy compendium. In it are more than 200 personnel policies from thousands of corporations.[17]

You can get hurt on a surprisingly small issue. A year ago, a brand new corporation was launched in North Adams, Massachusetts, CAPTECH. It was going to buy out the assets of a Sprague Corp. division. But the new owners missed a small detail resulting in a posi-

---

[15]Edgar Ellman, "How to write a personnel manual," *Inc. Magazine's Guide to Small Business Success* reprints, 1984.
[16]John F. Brady, *The Personnel Manager's Encyclopedia* (Stamford, Connecticut: Self Published).
[17]Stephen Simurda, "Going by the book," *Venture*, January 1985, p. 34.

tioning argument as to whether they were a "continuation" corporation or not. This simply meant that when they began to hire people that were not affiliated with the old union, they were hammered by the union and pressured into start-up concessions. The business failed before it even got off the ground. Your lawyer should help you avoid things like this.

Once you have employees on board, keep your communications direct and simple. If you can talk to somebody face-to-face do it, if you can't, talk to them on the telephone. Only as a last resort or as an "employee file" matter would you think of sending a memo to another employee. Get rid of paperwork. Eliminate it and you'll be way ahead of the game.

Have a weekly meeting of your key people. Talk about the objectives, the progress that has been made, the priorities for the week ahead. Bill Yunger, venture capitalist, says:

"As you begin to build your small group and then a management team, you should do the following:"

1. Hire experience.
2. Go for quality people especially when they will be hiring additional people.
3. Try to match their skill with your company's culture.
4. Try to find people you have worked with in the past.
5. Keep the team as small as possible.
6. Focus on money. Profit is the goal.[18]

This advice comes from someone who has watched an extraordinary number of new projects try to get off the ground, and the early lessons learned in them.

So those are your primary start-up decisions: your name and the

---

[18]William H. Younger, Jr., "The Management Team," at *The Challenge of Growth: The Fourth Annual Conference on Entrepreneurship*, May 18, 1985, Stanford Center for Entrepreneurship, Stanford California.

communication of that name and everything you do; your location and facility; the first people you are going to have with you. Make those decisions as carefully as you can, getting assistance from your lawyer or other professional at each step. How they are made will affect the quality and tone of your business from the very start.

In Chapter 7 we'll examine how to get going operationally.

7

Getting Going Operationally: Important Compliance Matters

You've made many of the critical first decisions such as money, a name for your business, a location and facility, and even hired your first staff members. You're ready to open your door for business. Right? Not quite.

Now comes the important step of building a quality foundation. Whether you have one employee, 10, or 50, start right by making the first operational decisions on a sure-footed basis. Save your precious capital and avoid costly "repairs" down the road by doing things right the first time.

I know you're anxious to start selling things, and there's nothing wrong with asking everyone "have we sold anything today?" But there are many details that must be handled before you're ready to serve your first customer. This may not be the most exciting part of starting your own venture, but neglecting any one of these details before you consider yourself "in business" could have negative consequences.

This chapter is designed to help you deal with the first nitty-gritty operational details of your business painlessly and economically, and to help you determine what you need to do for your specific business in order to get off on the right foot. Because different industries and states have different start-up requirements, we'll also include some good places to go for help if you're unsure about what you need to do.

FORMS AND REGULATIONS

I started with Frank Kirkpatrick, a Madison Avenue emigré to Vermont. Frank's seen it all in starting up a country business in Peru, Vermont and a long conversation yielded some incredibly helpful insights.

The federal government and 50 state governments together have more than 250,000 different forms that businesspeople must fill out before they can go into business, practice professions, or work independently at a trade. The regulation of business is itself a huge business operation, employing tens of thousands of people. These men and women are responsible for the credentials, the fees, the exams, and the standards of everyone who supervises your birth, watches over you and your business activities as long as you live, and settles you into the ground when it's all over.

Every level of government employs these business and occupational regulators. From all the employees of the IRS, to someone who spends time worrying about the number of lines on postal reply envelopes, these folks are paid to place barriers in the face of people like you who just want to start a business. If you are in business or if you have an occupation, enforcers of the regulatory laws of the land are behind every door that says "enter" and every sign that tells you to "wait here." The time that business owners must spend waiting in line, waiting in reception rooms, waiting for the mail, waiting for licenses, permits, certificates, registration, can sap your energy and drive.

The taxes, levies, and fees collected by the various governments in the regulation of business help to support our land. As you will see, the nature and number of the requirements that must be met before you can open an office, run a new business, or operate a retail store can be frightening. But for the businesspeople who do not comply, it is even more frightening.

Kirkpatrick tells of a neighbor who leased property not far down the road and had the idea of installing saunas and hot tubs. This made a bit of sense because the business is on the border of a huge ski resort. He bought the equipment, had the water pipes installed, redecorated the building, put up the signs, hired the staff, opened the door—and was promptly closed down. Although he was licensed to practice accountancy by the state and should have been familiar with the laws of this particular town, the owner had not sought a permit from the administrator of the planning commission. This man spent a great deal of money, money he earned advising other business people on their finances, only to watch it go down the drains of the "illegal" soaking facilities.

Another couple bought an inn with the understanding that the sewage situation was adequate. It may have been satisfactory before they bought the property, but it was far below the state's environmental standards at the time of purchase. A simple solution was to build a leach field to meet sanitation requirements, but there was no land on which to build a leach field. There is no possibility that the inn can take guests. Not next week, not next year, not ever. And that's the end of that family's dream. They didn't check with government agencies before buying.

Don't let this happen to you. You can avoid costly, even fatal, mistakes by making certain your first operating steps are taken very carefully. You'll have to grit your teeth. It takes time to fill out the forms, it costs money for the fees. There is nothing to do but bear bravely the ritual of getting the papers you need to make a living.

PERMITS, LICENSES, AND FEES

Just look around you. Every day you do business with plenty of others who've been registered, licensed, and permitted to operate. You deal with professional people. Your needs are serviced by tradespeople. Each of these people at one time or another has filled out forms and said, "Here I am." In one way or another, they've all been through the same thing—satisfying the regulators that they or their machines are competent to carry on whatever it is that they do. If they can go through all of the trouble of getting the right papers, you can too. And you can probably do it much more quickly if you know exactly what you're after and where to go about getting it. But before you look for what you need, here are some tips that may help you, whether you're filing with the federal government, state departments and boards, or right in your own backyard with the local municipalities.

1. Make absolutely sure you comply with the regulations. Don't think. Don't guess. Don't assume. If you're opening a small business, an inn, a store, check your nearest competitor. And check another one just to make sure the first one didn't leave anything out. We want you to avoid problems and this chapter can be very helpful. It is an excellent starting place, but it can't explain every possibility. And regulations change. Make sure you contact every agency that might be involved. Remember that new ownership waves a flag. When you take over another business, regulations may be enforced for the first time.

2. If you're not sure, get legal advice. You don't want a lawyer who has to look up things in books. Get someone who is familiar with the local scene. Check the lawyer out. Avoid someone who is an expert in another field.

3. Make sure you understand all the regulations before you finalize the purchase of business property. This can be difficult, but you can blow an entire life's savings by not being aware of what you're facing. Don't accept anybody's assurance for anything. The best- and worst-meaning people can be wrong.

4. Listen to what the regulators tell you. Don't smile and nod and pretend to know what they're talking about. These people speak different languages. Plead ignorance and they will translate.

5. Be nice to bureaucrats. Remember that these people are doing their jobs. Bite your lip. Don't try to get the upper hand—you can't. Don't try to be superior—you won't win. Don't talk down to them —they won't hear you.

6. Get them on your side. Licenses and permits are renewable. You may see these people every year or so. Get their advice on how to proceed, how to get something fixed to comply with this or that regulation. Encourage their professionalism. They know the system;

they can save you money. These people are experts. Maybe you are, or maybe you're not. Don't be.

7. Avoid conflicts. There may be areas of conflict between state and local authorities, or federal and state, or between two state agencies. Don't get caught in the middle. Don't take sides. Explain the position of one to the other. Keep your fingers crossed.

8. Get it in writing. Everybody says the same thing. But this time it's important. Your living depends on it.

This chapter is not intended to be a complete representation of the legal requirements for going into business. Get the help of the association within your state that represents your kind of business. It can be very useful to find out what other people have been through, how they handled certain situations, personalities, problems. The local Chamber of Commerce can also be of assistance to you. The checklist in Figure 7-1 is a starter.

Licenses and permits are issued for a specific period of time. In New Hampshire, for example, there is an operator's license granted by the state revenue administration to collect a meals and rooms tax if you're running a restaurant or an inn. But you are subject to inspection and control by the Department of Health.

Whenever the health department feels like it, it can turn your place, almost literally, upside down. It can and will happen at the worst possible time. These inspectors are on the lookout for:

Evidence of food contamination

Dishwasher efficiency

Adequate refrigeration

Proper sanitation

If you run a store, you don't need a license to sell gasoline or a permit to weigh cheese. But the Department of Agriculture, Bureau of Weights and Measures, will be there to certify that your pump and your scales are accurate. They'll probably visit at least once a year.

If you own a business that deals in food or human life, you are always subject to inspection by the enforcers; and you are likely to receive anything from a pat on the back to being told you can't operate. Try for a pat.

_____ Register
_____ Get an FIN (federal identification number)
_____ Get a state tax number
_____ Get a state unemployment number
_____ Learn about worker's compensation, wages and hours
_____ Check fire protection, including electrical inspection
_____ Check plumbing, boiler codes and regulations
_____ Check sanitation and health codes and regulations
_____ Check agricultural requirements
_____ Check zoning regulations, building permits, code compliance
_____ Check laws regarding the placement of signs
_____ Check these at state and local levels

Figure 7-1. Checklist.

Try to stay cool. This isn't advice. It's just common sense. Don't lose your sense of humor. Without it, you'll get so mad you won't be able to function. Just keep your cool and you'll get whatever it is that lets you do whatever you want to do. It takes some money, a lot of time, and patience that even Job didn't know about.

FORMS OF BUSINESS

From a tax liability standpoint, it is important to determine which of the various forms of business is best suited for you. They are:

Proprietorship

You are the sole owner of the business, responsible for the profits and the losses. This is the most simple form because no government approval is needed. Profits are taxed as personal income. If your business is to be operated under your own name and will have no employees, you may not have to register. If you are Smith's Laundry Service, you may not have to register with the town or city in which you're doing business. Smith's Laundry is known as "doing business as" (dba) or "trading as" (t/a). Jane Smith dba Smith's Laundry Service.

Partnership

There are two kinds: general and limited. A general partnership is an association of two or more people who share in the proceeds and liabilities of a business. A limited partnership is structured so that liabilities do not exceed a partner's amount of investment. Partnerships must be registered with the town or city. A limited partnership must be registered with the secretary of state for the state in which you're doing business.

Corporation

Setting up a corporation is supposedly the most complicated, but it's not really very complicated at all. A corporation is a business entity with privileges and responsibilities aside from those of its officers. Certain legal requirements and procedures must be met before a corporation can be formed (and fees paid). Subchapter S corporations can be created with 35 or fewer stockholders, and the tax liability is passed directly to the shareholders. The secretary of state in your state is responsible for the incorporation formalities.

Because of the recent tax law changes, it's important that you check with your accountant and lawyer before making any decisions on corporate organization, S or C corporation status. Most experts believe that there will be a general move toward S corporations as a result of federal tax reform.

For the first time in history, corporate rates are higher than individual rates. The business owner now must think very carefully about accumulated earnings, and it's probably that the S corporation form will allow the ultimate liquidation of a company to be accomplished with less tax impact than if you elected a C corporation status.

Currently, if the sale of your business results in a capital gain, you are taxed only individually under S corporation provisions. Under new provisions, you may be taxed both from a corporate point of view and from a personal point of view.

Section 1244 stock is more of a moot point now. Section 1244 allows for losses to be taken as ordinary losses rather than capital losses. Since there are no distinctions now between capital and ordinary losses, the old advantages cease to exist. Because the tax laws will continue to change, with many experts predicting that capital gains will come back, this is an important area to check specifically with your accountant and tax lawyer.

You'll also want to check carefully on the nature of your business loans. Under the old tax law all interest was deductible and many people would borrow money personally and then lend it to their business. Under the new code, there is no point in borrowing personally since none of the interest is deductible. Again, check carefully.

FEDERAL REGULATIONS . . . AND ADVICE

Taxes on the Business Itself

Income and loss of proprietorships, partnerships, corporations, and S corporations are subject to tax reporting on forms 1040, 1065, 1120, and 1120S, respectively. All information for the proper filing of these forms may be obtained from the nearest office of the Internal Revenue Service. They have complete instructions and kits.

Employee Withholding and Payroll

You will be assigned an Employer Identification Number (EIN). If you have one or 100,000 employees, you will be required to: (1) withhold income tax and report on form 941; (2) pay FICA (Social Security) tax and report FICA tax withholding on form 941; (3) pay FUTA (federal unemployment tax) based on taxes paid to state unemployment funds and report on form 940. The taxes due and reported on form 941 will be deposited in an authorized financial institution.

OCCUPATIONAL SAFETY AND HEALTH ADMINISTRATION (OSHA)

The federal government, through the U.S. Department of Labor, enforces the OSHA regulations which pertain to the areas of machine safety, as well as electrical, fire, and construction hazards and health hazards in relation to toxic materials and noise. If you're not sure whether your business is subject to strict control by OSHA, consult the nearest office of this administration.

Federal Minimum Wage and Hour Laws

Questions about these laws should be directed to the nearest Wage and Hour Division office of the Department of Labor.

Child Labor Laws

Sixteen is the minimum age for most employment, except that 18 is the minimum age for manufacturing and mining that has been delcared hazardous by the Secretary of Labor. Employers are required to keep accurate records for employees under 18. Check the Department of Labor for details.

International Trade

The International Trade Division of the U.S. Department of Commerce can help with export and import problems. See the nearest Department of Commerce office.

Small Business Administration

The SBA was established to aid and protect the interests of small businesses. It operates in the areas of:

Helping women in business
Disaster assistance
Minority-owner small business
Small business institutes
Procurement assistance
Financial assistance
Small business investment companies
Management assistance

Small business development centers

Managements, marketing publications

You've taken care of all your permits, licenses, and fees. You've borrowed a huge chunk of money, and recently assumed major accounts receivable. What do you need now?

INSURANCE

I'll never forget the day after all our financing was in place, and I drove home to what I thought would be a pleasant night's sleep after a long day of work. After two hours' sleep, I sat bolt upright in bed realizing I hadn't done anything about my insurance policies. To be sure, I had some personal coverage; but now with nearly $600,000 of new obligations, I was badly underprotected. Why hadn't I thought of this?

The answer has to do with the amount of detail pressure the new entrepreneur is under for several months. The thought of insurance usually comes late, particularly to entrepreneurs who are willing to take some risks. But now, with larger assets to protect, it is time to do something about your insurance.

In my case, I picked up the telephone in the middle of the night and called Dick Salisbury over in Lake George, New York, who wrote up a policy before he got out of his pajamas and met me at the Rensselaer Train Station the next day at 6:45 A.M. so I could sign it. "Thanks for your personal service Dick," I said as I greeted him, bleary-eyed, in the morning. "Don't mention it," he said. "Now that you're covered, I'll just head back to bed!"

Every business has to be insured. Some require considerably more insurance than others, and you should sit down immediately to work with an insurance agent to determine your specific insurance needs. There is what I would call "offensive" insurance to protect your major assets. Obviously, you must cover your receivables, inventory, plant, property, and equipment. You should also cover your employees to one degree or another. Insurance for employees is a benefit to them as well as an asset to you. On the "defensive" side, you've got to think about the unpopular subject of liability—product liability, publisher's liability, and the like.

I remember, specifically, during the early years of the escalation of product liability insurance premiums, sitting with the board of directors at Garden Way Inc., and looking at protection for our key product, the Troy Bilt Rototiller. The premium had risen from $15,000 to $115,000 in a single year. Staggered, we decided not to go along with that increase and began a program of self-insurance.

Less dramatically, but equally hurtful from a percentage increase point of view, was my own publisher's liability policy (slander, libel, etc.) which increased from a premium of $3,000 a year to $11,000 a year in a very short period of time. What can you do about this? What about self-insurance? Let's take a look at it.

Eileen Joseph, writing in *Nation's Business* recently, said, "Liability insurance was getting so expensive for business these days, and for some types of risks it was becoming unavailable, at any price. What does one do?" Joseph pointed out that "Many business people are cancelling all coverage—'going bare'—because they feel premium rates give them no choice." The major problem with this is, of course, is that a single large claim settled successfully for the complainant against a business could result in a business' closing its doors.

Joseph points to the following as possible alternatives to the liability insurance crisis now underway:

1. Reduce or eliminate insurance that costs too much and replace coverage by other means. Reduce costs for necessary insurance by increasing deductibles.

2. Don't waste premium dollars buying more coverage than you need.

3. Invest in items that will control loss by reducing its potential magnitude or preventing it; for instance, a new sprinkler system.

4. Make employees loss-prevention conscious.

5. Hire a risk manager whose full-time job is controlling losses.[1]

---

[1]Eileen Joseph, "Getting past the liability crisis," *Nation's Business*, August 1986, pp. 69–70.

There have been examples recently of companies willing to pay for the insurance they needed, but almost going under because they were denied it at any price. According to Henry W. Nozko, Jr., vice president of Acmat Corp. of Hartford, Connecticut, an asbestos removal firm, "All of our liability insurance was cancelled because of the hazardous nature of our asbestos removal business. Our company, which had revenues of $50 million a year, lost millions in contracts and was unable to bid on any new projects for several months."[2] Fortunately, Acmat was able to put together a syndicate of other corporations that needed the same kind of protection and formed a new business which is now writing insurance for others.

Think about insurance simply as a way of managing the risks that your business faces. Four points can help in making insurance decisions;

1. Identify the various risks that your business could face no matter how obscure they seem (fire, theft, lawsuits, disasters).

2. Evaluate the probability of each occurring, and the cost to you if it does, and the cost of insuring against that risk.

3. Decide whether you would prefer to accept the risk or insure against it.

4. Control the risks by implementing your decision.[3]

In our own case, we carried insurance against business theft and business interruption. As fate would have it, after a full year of operation, our mini-computer system was stolen from our offices. Our insurance coverage guaranteed the replacement cost, which was slightly higher than its original cost. We promptly received a check for $21,000, which allowed us to invest in a brand new and more sophisticated Fortune Micro system, a real windfall to us.

Insurance is complicated. If you don't understand it, ask questions. Maybe you had an entire insurance department in your previous corporation. Now you have—*you*. But in general there are three main types of insurance, although specific policies can be written to insure almost anything you want:

---

[2]*Ibid.*, p. 69.
[3]William A. Cohen, *The Entrepreneur and Small Business Problem Solver: An encyclopedic reference and guide* (New York: Ronald Press, 1983), p. 67.

1. *Liability Insurance.*

This protects you from possible lawsuits resulting from accidents or other unforeseen events somehow connected to you, your employees, or your business. There are many kinds: (1) general (a wide-reaching policy which covers many different areas of liability); (2) automobile (useful if you have a company car or your staff uses their cars for business); (3) product, which will protect you from lawsuits if your product is faulty; (4) worker's compensation; and (5) all-inclusive, similar to a general policy except that whatever is not specifically excluded is covered.

2. *Life and Health.*

For yourself, get enough term life insurance to cover your accounts receivable and your inventory if for some reason you are out of the picture. This is very important, but like the personal type, this will protect you and your employees from your sickness or death and the effects it might have on your firm. It is especially important if your firm is dependent on a key employee who is not replaceable. This so-called key man employee insurance can be purchased at relatively low cost. With any kind of life or health plan, you can reduce costs by asking employees to pay their fair share of the coverage.

3. *Property Coverage.*

This protects your property from a variety of calamities depending on the policy. If it is called "comprehensive," everything which isn't specifically excluded is covered: crime, fire, flood, and vandalism. Check exclusions carefully.

Many businesses require special kinds of insurance. In our business, publisher's liability covers slander, libel or problems that can occur as a result of the contents of a book causing someone a perceived injury. There are ways to avoid this, including printing disclaimers in the front of books. But be sure that you have the kind of liability coverage that covers any peculiarities of your business.

Choosing an insurance agent is an important task. Shop around. Interview a number of people. Make sure the agent understands your kind of business and is interested in it, wants to become closer to it.

Ask several agents for quotes on the kind of coverage you need. Shop around, make sure you're getting the best rate. You can work with either a direct writer—someone who works directly for a particular insurance company—or an independent agent—who is not employed by any one company, and who usually represents a variety of large insurance companies.

The direct writers often can write policies at lower cost than independents, and may specialize in a particular area of insurance. Conversely, because they handle only one product line their policies may not suit your exact needs. An independent agent offers greater flexibility but also possibly higher costs.

A third option is a broker who covers the local area. This individual attempts to pool companies together and procure lower rates through a number of small companies participating. At Storey Communications, our insurance sales for employee health, disability, and life are lower since we began working through a regional broker.

The criteria you should use for choosing your insurer include: (1) cost, (2) types of insurance offered, (3) flexibility and coverage, (4) financial stability of the firm, and (5) amount of the deductible.

Make absolutely certain you don't overlook your insurance. Get umbrella or disaster insurance to cover the unforeseen. Avoid the potential for your dream to be eliminated by an unforeseen surprise. How many times have you read in the newspaper about a small business that was eaten up by flames or by some other business interruption. Don't let this happen to you. Be prepared.

HOW TO MAKE SURE YOU GET PAID

Another area of critical importance, as you begin to get organized for business, is credit and collection. The absolute need for credit in a business economy is well known. Practically all of the goods and services which comprise the $1 trillion-plus American gross national product moved through the channels of distribution on credit.

While it's true that some people can operate their businesses on a pure cash basis, you will find that sales increases will be limited unless you see your way clear to offer credit to your customers. Several years ago, when I was selling Troy-Bilt Rototillers, we had achieved a sales level of 60,000 units a year. We were happy with this but had been stuck on a plateau for three years and couldn't get beyond a 60,000-unit level. We carefully tested and then implemented a Troy-Bilt credit program that was no different from the kind of credit any of these customers could get at their local banks, but which was viewed as an important customer service feature. It increased our sales from 60,000 to nearly 100,000 units a year. While it is true we had to write off some bad debt as a result of expanding our business, there is no question that our profitability was considerably greater at the new higher level of operation.

You'll be tempted, as have we been, even as a small company, to provide trade credit terms of 30 days, 60 days and even beyond. Our sales manager came in one day and proposed a dating program to achieve the level of sales he wanted in the first quarter of the following year. Dating allows the customers to receive shipment of goods and pay for them 60, or even 90 days later. So as you can see, whether large or small, credit plays a critical role in lubricating the wheels of business.

As you decide to increase your sales with the least possible losses, you'll have to implement a credit management program which will include the following:

1. Establishing a credit policy and practice.
2. Administering credit operations with the objective of increasing profits, increasing customer stability, and protecting your company's investment and account receivable.

In establishing a credit policy, you will necessarily be influenced by many things. Ask your credit manager to be aware of the sales and marketing objectives of the company, as well as diligent on following up past-due accounts. Accounts should be evaluated as top, medium or low level. The top accounts should be placed on a preferred list for automatic approval within certain dollar limits. The medium accounts should require closer checking, and the weaker accounts, which represent real risk, should be watched closely.

In conducting a credit investigation, there are a number of factors that come into play:

1. The size of the order
2. The length of the time the customer has been in business

3. The status of the present account
4. Whether the present product is seasonal and how it relates to the products offered by the competition
5. The extent of delivery time
6. The relationship of the order to the total credit exposure of the customer
7. Whether the credit risk falls within the firm's credit policy.
8. If it is a special order, whether deposit should be required or it should be sent C.O.D.

Fortunately, you have some outside sources of help. Mentioned earlier, D&B is a prime resource, and you should explore signing up to their reporting system. There is also a credit association within the industry in which you operate, and credit interchange reports. Check them all out.

Pay careful attention to your collection procedures. Look at your accounts receivable turn-over period, which is normally expressed as days that sales are outstanding, and is computed as follows: average accounts receivable balance over the last three months times 90, divided by the sales for the last three months. When you compute this monthly, along with aging data, the "days sales outstanding" proves an excellent means for watching collection trends. The aged trial balance and percentage of past due accounts also provides a measure of effectiveness.

Many entrepreneurs, understandably, are so excited about building up a large revenue base, and deathly afraid of losing a customer, that they'll continue to do business with a debtor.

Shepherd recommends establishing credit maximums, taking a careful look at your follow-up invoicing and statement periods, and going to a collection agency or to your lawyer for collection efforts if absolutely necessary. In the latter case you will pay as much as 50 percent of what is collected to the collection agent.[4]

Once you begin to establish controls like credit and collection, your business will get tighter. Small things may show up. Are checks missing? Is there the possibility of embezzlement? Are there petty

---

[4]William G. Shepherd, Jr., "Collecting bad receivables," *Venture*, January 1986, p. 28.

cash imbalances? Are there shortages on company accounts? Has anyone been falsifying checks? Who has co-signatory powers?

Axel L. Grabowski, executive vice president of Harte and Company, a New York Manufacturer, described what to monitor to stay in control. His checklist is a classic, and is included on page 186.[5]

Sometimes losses detected through monitoring can lead to enormously profitable changes. Robert W. Cook, president of Sleep Country Inc., was described in an article in the September 1985 issue of *Venture* magazine. Cook began his company in 1967 with $60,000 of his own money and a $250,000 SBA-guaranteed loan. His biggest problem was employee theft resulting in a loss of several hundred thousand dollars in the first year. To remedy this, he opened separate Sofa Country Stores under the same roof and gave a 5 percent share to each partner. He also implemented a computerized system of inventory control and careful control of sales and delivery staffs. Last year, Cook enjoyed $1.1 million pretax earnings on sales of $26.3 million, turns his inventory over eight times a year versus a national average of three-and-a-half, and has been seriously considering franchising Sleep Country and perhaps going public in the near future.[6]

One of the very best checks on yourself and your company is to call yourself when you leave your office. Everytime you are on the road, try calling your "800" number, try calling your corporate switchboard, and see what kind of a response you get to questions that you pose as a customer, supplier, and so on. You'll be amazed at what you learn about your company!

Now you are under way operationally. In the next chapter we'll take a hard look at 50 different imaginative marketing approaches that can increase your revenues and reduce your costs, and that anybody can do.

---

[5]Axel L. Grabowski, "What to monitor to stay in control," *Inc.*, Boston, March, 1981. Reprinted with permission, Inc. Magazine, March 1981. Copyright © 1981, by Inc Publishing Company, 38 Commercial Wharf, Boston, MA. 02110.
[6]"Sleep country," *Venture*, September 1985, p. 16.

KEEPING THE BUSINESS UNDER CONTROL

Below is a summary of the operating information that CEO Grabowsky tracks:

	Daily	Weekly	Monthly
Total company sales	●		
Sales by convenient product groupings		●	
Sales by major product category, territory, and major customer			●
Average sales prices of major products or product groups			●
Gross profit margin for company, large product groupings, and major products		●	
Production costs of major products			●
Direct expenses, with particular attention to large or discretionary items			●
Other income and expenses	●		●
Net profit			●
Cash flow		●	
Accounts receivable			●
Inventory	●		●
R&D status and expenses			●

And once every quarter Grabowsky monitors what he monitors by asking himself: "Am I limiting myself to just the essentials I need to keep track of our day-to-day business?"

8

Low Cost Marketing: How To Get Maximum Marketing Bang for Your Buck

You've completed a sales and marketing plan as part of your overall business plan. It gives good direction for the sales aspect of your business. Now what?

Put a master marketing *strategy* together, and through your own savvy, spend less than your competitor.

Like every other part of your business, you want to begin to build "sweat-equity." Remember sweat-equity—when you bought your first house, rather than hiring an expensive cabinetmaker or painter to come in and redo your kitchen, you and your spouse did it yourself? It's the same thing here. You're trying to convert every dollar invested to an asset, and if you can cut down on the cost of your marketing efforts by paying yourself rather than paying outside professionals, you'll be way ahead of the game.

Remember the most famous line from the Broadway musical, *Music Man*. "You've gotta know the territory!" In your start-up business, you've got to know your market territory. Also your competition.

GUERRILLA MARKETING

What you are trying to do is get the edge over your competition. Much of your competition is considerably larger than you are, but do you have advantages? Think about it. What's your edge? First, you'll be thinking about it all the time, while your competition is not. Second, you can operate with speed. Third, you're going to have to be more willing to follow your instincts rather than waiting for massive market research reports to come back to you, something corporations rarely do. Sandy Clark, president of Clark Associates in New York, said "There's a niche for us as long as corporations strive for 'risk averse' marketing!"

In short, you must become a nontraditional marketer, what I refer to as a "guerrilla marketer." This doesn't mean you can throw caution to the winds, but it does mean that you won't look to traditional ways of getting things done. What you're looking for is the largest possible return on the fewest possible marketing dollars invested.

When I talk about marketing, I'm thinking about perhaps a dozen specific tasks:

1. Business positioning
2. Product
3. Packaging
4. New product development
5. Competition
6. Promotion: your unique selling proposition
7. Market size and potential, sales
8. Advertising
9. Testing
10. Media
11. An advertising agency
12. Customer service

You can read any number of textbooks or you can take courses on marketing, and "marketing" will be explained to you in a variety of ways. To me, marketing is at once the ultimate function and the consummate discipline. Marketers are those people who make things happen. They plan strategically, they identify products, channels of distribution, packaging, shipping, warehousing and how to get it all done. We'll take a look, briefly, at each of these dozen points, and then, perhaps more importantly, outline at least 50 different types of low-cost guerrilla marketing that you can begin to use in your business tomorrow.

What makes an entrepreneur is far more the customer than the revolutionary idea. Effective marketing of that idea without breaking the bank is the difference between success and failure for you and your new entrepreneurial venture.

DON'T OVERSPEND

This chapter is aimed at gauging maximum mileage from your limited marketing dollars available. Too much money can also be a real problem.

In its last year of ownership by Garden Way Inc., the small Garden Way Publishing division suffered from "over-marketing." How can that happen? Simply, a business spends more than can be supported by the size of the business operation.

The hope was that the publishing division could reach out, and through the use of multiple media, bring in lots of new potential customers or inquiries. After investing nearly $1 million in that media campaign, the business, which generated only approximately $3 million per year in sales, lost $1 million.

I looked at another business that managed to lose $750,000 on a marketing investment of nearly $1 million. This was a business that was doing only about $1 million at the time. So beware—one of your worst dangers is having *too much money* to spend.

Perhaps equally critical is the knowledge of your industry—the "territory"—and exactly how you're going to establish a position in it. This is not only vital in securing initial funding, but now that your doors are open, it is crucial to your survival.

SALES: YOUR LIFE BLOOD

Sales, in short, are *everything* in the first year of your venture. Sales happen because of marketing, which is nothing more than knowing your product and how it is going to be distributed.

L. L. Bean decided early in the Ninteenth Century that a unique product, rubberized boots, could be salable directly to the customer. L. L. Bean has more than $300 million in annual sales. Steven Jobs decided that a personal computer called an Apple could be part of everybody's daily routine. Apple Computer is now a billion-dollar corporation. Harry Sherman decided in 1928 that books could be distributed like magazines on a subscription basis and started the Book-of-the-Month Club. Book-of-the-Month does well over $100 million annually.

What all of these people had in common was a marketing vision, and then a strategy, which came from the markets they were in, an awareness of their product line, competitors, channels of distribution, volume levels, pricing trends and geographical biases.

You must decide early on what will set you apart from other businesses which supply a similar product or service. Will you offer higher quality? Lower Price? Faster service?

Then you must ask yourself if it will allow you to carry enough of the market to meet break-even production levels and obtain projected sales? All of these marketing issues are driven by financial considerations. The simpler and bolder your marketing program the better. Federal Express had a very simple marketing concept—overnight delivery. The strategy behind their concept was a lower-cost hub concept, located in Memphis, that would insure overnight delivery.

Teleflower 800 came out of nowhere. It was based on the simple concept that millions of Americans would wire flowers and gifts to people if they had an accessible way to do it. It has grown into a billion dollar industry.

"Avon Calling" grew into a dramatically profitable door-to-door sales business during the 1960s and 1970s. Now, alas, when the Avon Lady calls, no one is home (they're all working). Now Avon is searching for new strategic marketing. All of these were great marketing concepts backed by sound financial logic.

But let's back off for a minute. Where do you begin to do your homework? Presumably, you have already worked in the industry that you are launching your business in, and you may be familiar with the type of data available to help you make informed decisions. Don't overlook the many free sources available to you. Trade associations, such as the Direct Marketing Association or the American

SMALL MANUFACTURER WANTS TO TEST DIRECT MAIL

Include our insert in your mailing, delivery, or invoice on a "per sale" basis.
Excellent products, should have a good response. Percentage negotiable.
Write G.B.P.C. Co., RD 1, Rural Valley, PA 16249.

Figure 8-1. Typical "cheap" space ad. (*Source: DM News*, June 15, 1986.)

Booksellers Association, often publish data for their industry; competitors have annual reports which give sales information, and U.S. Census reports break down the population so that you can establish a target audience. Your local library will carry many of the trade journals of your industry. All publications, by the way, are happy to send you a free media kit and sample publication. When we began, we mailed 100 postcards at a total cost of $14, and received 85 media kits and samples back. You can also get a great deal of information about your competitors simply by calling them up on their own 800 number.

Remind yourself, constantly, that you are a guerrilla marketer. You're going to have to act very differently from large companies and advertising agencies where mail order and television ad space is bought routinely at "card rate" rather than on a cheaper basis—per inquiry or per order. Figure 8-1 is an ad typical of the kind of opportunities for "cheap" space. Always ask for remnant or house space when you are looking to advertise your product and services in outside media.

THE MARKETER'S DOZEN

Now let's take a look at the 12 basic platforms of any marketing program.

1. *Positioning.* What business are you in? Sounds like a silly question, but have you tried to sit down and specifically write the answer to that question in one paragraph? Do it now. Lyman Wood used to say, "Pretend you are on the stage and grab the center of it." Ever notice contending stars on stage and how they go for the center? That's the position you want. Differentiate yourself from your competition and from anybody else that would like to move onto the stage. Let your customers know how you differ, specifically, and why they ought to do business with you. This part of positioning.

2. *Products*. What about yours? Are they hot? Or are they dated and sagging? In the publishing business you have to have hot products. There are too many other titles competing and contending for that center of the stage. With 50,000 new titles each year, how do you possibly grab your fair share? By understanding the markets that you are going into, what's hot and what's not. Workman created the *Preppy Handbook* at just the right time. Mainstreet Press came out with *The Old House Catalog* at just the right time. Our current best seller is something called *The Cat Lover's Cookbook*, launched at a time when the cat has become America's number one domestic pet. There are 50 million of them out there! One way to spread your bets on new product development is to buy options on product being developed by other people. This is a relatively inexpensive way for you to secure a foothold while watching how to spend the marketing dollars.

3. *Packaging*. How do your products look? Are they current, and timely, or are they dated? The major consumer goods corporations spend nearly 3 percent of their total budget on their packaging. How much do you spend? Is it colorful, bright, attractive, inviting? When you walk through the supermarket do you realize why you're buying the products you're buying. How would your products compare on the supermarket shelf? Pay tremendous attention to your packaging, and also to the merchandising that supports your packaging efforts.

4. *New product development*. Do you have a new product program? What percentage of your business comes from new product and what from old? Can you move your business into adjacent areas? Can you edge out? Don't underestimate the need for new products and new titles.

5. *Competitors*. Who are yours? How well are they serving the needs of your consumers? How can you check them out? Sheila Eby, in an article called, "Psst! Do you want to know a secret?" She said that it is perfectly legal to check out your competition in the following ways: (1) buy their products and study them; (2) stalk their territory; (3) read the publications that they advertise in; and (4) purchase one share of stock in their company so you receive their prospectus.[1]

---

[1]*Sheila M. Eby*, "Psst? Do You Want to Know a Secret?," *Inc. Magazine's Guide To Small Business Success* reprints, 1984.

6. *Promotion*: The unique selling proposition (USP). You have probably heard of the USP, and it has everything to do with your promotional plans. It's not enough to find a niche that you are hoping to fill. You then have to put together a "proposition" that will make your potential customers unable to avoid your product or service. Looking for a different way to sell books, in 1960 Time, Inc. created a unique selling proposition in the form of a new "continuity" concept, where books would be shipped to you automatically on a "till forbid" basis. They launched a business that has now grown to $500 million a year.

Chrysler launched a five-year-warranty program that was unique in the business. It sold a lot of cars. Think about how you are going to dramatize your product and service with an absolutely unique promotional approach. It could be price, it could be delivery, it could be packaging, it could be pricing, it could be any of a number of things. But you must have it. Perhaps it is location, quality, or service; but remember, if there is nothing that sets your marketing apart from others, customers probably won't seek you out.

7. *Sales, market potential.* Here you have to ask yourself What's the market looking for? How much do you know about your industry and market? What you invest in product, packaging and distribution is going to be based on how big you can get your business, and how quickly. If it is a growing product in an expanding industry, terrific. If it is shrinking, look out. RCA launched videodiscs at a time when the rest of the world was launching videocassettes. It became a multi-million dollar mistake.

8. *Advertising.* This is important for increasing your sales. Ideally, money spent on effective and well placed ads will generate sales far in excess of the cost of the ads. But beware. Advertising can be *very* expensive, and it is important to start with square inches before you move out to full pages. You must be able to develop a system of monitoring the results of your advertising. I wouldn't spend a dollar unless I had a way of measuring how it was doing for me.

Some people don't advertise at all. A local Italian restaurant, La Veranda, doesn't need to. Word of mouth and superior pasta do it all. Most businesses don't have that luxury.

But before you launch your advertising program, ask yourself what you want it to do, What's your strategy? A few one-shot ads are likely to be ineffective; the more random, the less effective. Defining the intent of your advertising, and establishing priorities, is very important. Do you want to establish a brand or a product image? This could cost you well over a million dollars.

My advice would be to do nothing for awhile. Check what the leaders are doing. Who's advertising what? Who's marketing what? Who's mailing what? Services are available to help you track this.

What are *you* trying to do? Announce your arrival in the industry? You can do this with publicity. Use the David and Goliath approach. Highlight a special product or service? Figure out how you can do this with the least money invested. Develop general goodwill or image advertising? Forget it. You can't afford it. I made the mistake of hiring a Madison Avenue professional at the time when I had to make the cash registers jingle. He didn't. Are you announcing sales or specials? This can give you a very good return on the advertising dollar invested. Act like the local butcher who is having a pork chop special. Trying to cause immediate or direct response? Trying to develop a mailing list?

Each of these kinds of advertising has a different strategy, and therefore a different means of effecting results. Be certain of what you want to try to achieve before you begin to advertise.

9. *Testing.* This is one of the most important, least expensive, and most misunderstood areas. Your business is changing constantly, and you should be testing constantly, to find better pricing, better copy, better design, better packaging, unique selling propositions. The best way to do this inexpensively is through split testing. This can be accomplished easily in advertising or mailings by sending half the circulation one offer, and half another. In a medium like *TV Guide*, you can ultimately split, 12, 24, 48 and more, and you can test your copy and your offer simultaneously. You must work to analyze the results of this testing carefully, and to do more of what works, and less of what doesn't.

10. *Media.* Be familiar with the media available to you, including newspapers, radio, magazines, trade journals, direct marketing, and find out the cost of all of these things through asking the cost per thousand. How many people will I reach? What's my likely response? After you receive all of that, start with the smallest amount of space and work your way upward.

At Garden Way Inc., we had a media department which we called the "brain surgery" and "intensive care" department. We would run one inch of copy for perhaps $22 in a local tabloid, and see what the results were. On the basis of positive results, we would expand the space. Negative results, we would lose $22. Be tight with your advertising dollars.

11. *The advertising agency.* Who will prepare your advertising? My very strong recommendation would be to avoid an agency initially and do it on your own. No one should know better than you what you want to try to achieve with your product. It is a simple and logical matter of sitting down and saying, okay, here's what I want to sell. If you need copy and design help, buy that on an hourly basis. By creating your own in-house advertising agency, you can cut the costs of your advertising budget substantially, between 15 to 18 percent, and produce high quality advertising which suits your needs exactly.[2] Beware, however, of the "naked king" syndrome. Have others around you who are willing to tell you that you forgot to put your clothes on, and that your advertising copy stinks. Get help, if you need it, from local college students who are doing art and design work and who would love to have a chance to lay out a "real" ad. Ask for suggestions. This is important.

Just because you are doing your own advertising doesn't mean that it won't be professional. Keep your standards high and don't skimp on quality. What you are eliminating here is the high commissions charged by professional agencies. Once your in-house agency gets going, you may be able to bring in small jobs for other firms. We've done this for the last several years, and saved approximately 15 percent of the total cost of operating our business this way.

If you have a very specialized advertising need, do hire someone else. But don't make the mistake of hiring the wrong kind of person for the job. Some catalog companies have, and wound up investing a million dollars in a catalog that didn't work. Choose a firm with experience with the type of advertising you're interested in (radio, direct marketing, etc.). Hire the pros and keep a hand in the process. If you don't like what they are producing for you, tell them; and if they don't seem flexible, fire them.

Don't let any agency or consultant talk you into more advertising

---

[2]An excellent reference is: Bert Holtje, *How To Be Your Own Advertising Agency*, (New York: McGraw Hill, 1981).

than you want. Remember, advertisers usually work on commissions, so they are likely to push for expensive, repeated space. Make certain you are getting a return of at least three times on your advertising dollars invested. Create very specific performance criteria. It's your time and your money.

Ron Hume will tell you he nearly went out of business twice through making mistakes in his advertising campaigns. Too much spent on the wrong kind of media at the wrong time of the year. Don't let it happen to you.

12. *Customer service.* Once you have a customer, know how to keep him or her happy. Stan Fenvessey, perhaps the leading consultant on customer service in the direct marketing industry, will tell you, "Keep your customers happy. Smother them with service. Give the customers more than they expect."

Guarantees in customer satisfaction policies have been critical to the building of some of America's most successful catalog companies today: L. L. Bean, Land's End, Cabela's, Lillian Vernon, and others.

Nontraditional Marketing

Those are the dozen planks in a marketer's platform. The entrepreneur must be a marketer all of the time, willing to act on instinct, willing to move faster than larger corporate competitors. Every dollar invested should yield a return, so attempt to maximize your return on every dollar invested. As importantly, react quickly, don't wait for weeks to see whether a program is going to work or not. In short, beat his corporate competitors by building a nontraditional marketing system. My nontraditional marketing system consists of the following 50 points. I hope that each one will yield a money-saving, revenue-generating, and cost-reducing idea for you.

1. *An unusual business card.* This is practically a no-additional-cost marketing innovation. A friend of mine who works for Polaroid has a Polaroid picture of himself on his business card. It works. Another friend in the magazine business has a mini-magazine as a business card. People don't forget that.

2. *A pop-top Rolodex card* (see Figure 8-2). Measure the size of the average Rolodex card, create one that has a "hat" on it that goes

Figure 8-2. Rolodex card.

just a little bit above the balance of the standard Rolodex card. Print these for under $100, send them out to all of your best customers and your potential customers.

3. *"Thanks for your order" postcard.* When an old customer sends you an order, send him or her back a thank you on a preprinted postcard that you can personalize with a quick postscript. Depending on your scope of business, you might outgrow this, but it is a very unusual effort that people aren't used to and enjoy.

4. *Welcome package.* To all new customers, send out a "welcome to the clan" mailing which describes to them briefly the benefits that you can provide to them, the product features that you have, and how to maintain the best possible communication on future business. Give them your 800 number for any problems and welcome them to the family.

5. *Member-get-a-member mailing.* The best source of additional customers are the friends of the customers you already have. This can be simple or elaborate. John Deere did a new business mailing to every household on the adjacent sides of existing customers they could identify. It was most successful.

6. *Bind-in/blow-in cards.* Make sure no product is shipped without a card in it soliciting additional business or soliciting customer reaction. We bind-in a "we love your thoughts" postcard. It costs us very little and we get thousands back every year.

7. *Dramatic advertising.* Avis built an honesty campaign with "We Try Harder." Bartles and Jaymes is dramatically outstripping its competition now with two average looking country-type guys.

8. *Per-inquiry, per-order advertising.* Don't buy at card rate. Buy at remnant and house base rate. If you receive an objection from the sales rep, say you'll buy at 50 percent of card rate with a per-inquiry above that.

9. *In-house agency.* Create one. Save 15 to 18 percent in agency commission a year. Don't pay for expensive professional outsiders at the beginning.

10. *Barter.* You have something that's worth something to someone else. At Garden Way we created the "Joy of Gardening" television program and bartered it, in some cases for three to six minutes of advertising space. We did the same with radio. You can too. If you sell products or services that newspaper or radio offices can use, you can get space and time in return for your production costs alone.

11. *Customer premiums.* Build a dividend or additional discount program for those people that are already doing business with you.

12. *Two step marketing.* Rather than asking people for the order, ask them for their interest in your product. Follow up quickly on those people with a more elaborate conversion package, and turn the inquiry into an order.

13. *Dramatize your offer and proposition.* AMC Jeep went from the Wagoneer, to the Grand Wagoneer, to the Wagoneer Limited, always offering their customers good, better and best. Chrysler launched its five-year, no-quibble warranty. These are dramatic re-positionings of that which already exist.

14. *Computerized personalized mailing.* Make sure that you have the current name and address of your customers on your own data base. Send them a regular first class mailing and always personalize it with your own P.S.

15. *"Hot potatoes".* Send your customers a reason to act now. Make the cash registers jingle with a coupon that is good for only a certain period of time.

16. *Time cut-offs.* Make certain your offers are good only until the 15th of the next month. It gives people reason to act speedily.

17. *Threatened price increases.* Sell hard against the fact that prices will be going up. You can also maneuver with price roll-backs and price holds.

18. *Off-season discount programs.* Explain the logic of your business that you are busiest in the summer, and least busy in the winter. Troy Bilt sold at 20 percent discount in the winter. Toro Snow Blowers should have learned their lesson.

19. *List work and analysis.* Instead of spending lots of money on market research, ask a list broker to provide you with a regular report on the growth of lists by area.

20. *Focus groups.* Don't hire a professional for $10,000 when you can get 10 of your friends to come over for nothing. We did this in Texas with 10 friends of my parents-in-law, provided a Texas barbecue cookout for $57, and picked up copy points and good market research that would have cost us $10,000 through a professional firm.

21. *No price increase.* Keep your prices as low as possible to create a barrier to entry to others who have noticed what you are doing.

22. *Competitive analysis.* Read through media kits, free magazines that are sent to you and free magazines at the library. Discern *who* is advertising *what* in those media.

23. *Customer communiques.* Launch a customer newspaper where recipes and tips can get exchanged. We launched the Troy Bilt Owner News. There is also the Orvis News, and the Vermont Castings annual party that draws 10,000 to Randolph, Vermont.

24. *The headquarters mecca.* People want to go see and kiss the Blarney Stone. Orvis created the Fly Fishing Museum. L. L. Bean is open 24 hours a day, and gives factory tours. You can do the same yourself.

25. *Dramatic customer service.* After L. L. Bean shipped me a hat I phoned to say it didn't fit my head. They said "keep it and we'll send you another one." That's dramatic customer service.

26. *Shows and conventions.* Don't spend $25,000 when you can spend $25. Harper and Row might afford a $25,000 cocktail party in San Francisco to kick off a new title. We can't, so we offered free coffee at our booth when the convention lines were long for coffee at $1

a cup. This year we're going to step up, and offer Bloody Marys at lunch time. I've budgeted $100.

27. *Christmas presents.* Identify your most helpful customers, and suppliers, and send them a thoughtful gift which reflects the kind of business that you're in. When we bought our publishing assets, they included 100 author/publisher agreements, but the authors were edgy. We sent them all a $6 can of maple syrup, and have yet to lose one.

28. *Mailings.* Make sure they are all measurable. Count the number you send out and calculate the cost-per-thousand. Count the number of responses you received in order to come up with a cost per order. Through name acquisition, create a spin-off profit center by making your mailing lists available for rental.

29. *Publicity.* Do it yourself. Don't hire an expensive agent. Fred Kline, a good friend, would have done for me for $3,000 a month in Los Angeles what I figured out how to do for myself. Ruth Owades, who launched *Gardener's Eden*, a catalog, credits her turnaround to a national magazine article that brought "Gucci gardeners to her door."[3] Have a clipping service clip all of your articles for you and send them back to you.

30. *Cross merchandising.* If you have a product, tell the customer how to use it. If you have a publication, offer a merchandise item with it. *Better Homes & Gardens* took our *Cat Lover's Cookbook* and is offering it with a cat bowl. This is excellent cross merchandising.

31. *Newsletters.* Do a "What's New At" newsletter on your corporation and send it to your best customers. The emphasis of the piece should be what change means in terms of benefits and product features for the customer (not for you) and what you can do for them.

32. *Bill enclosures.* Never send out a bill or an invoice without a promotional piece that tells your accounts what's new.

33. *List rentals, swaps and exchanges.* After you've developed a mailing list, use this as barter for other products and services that you need and that are exchangeable.

[3]Ruth M. Owades, "Wooing the green thumb crowd-by mail," *New York Times*, March 25, 1984, Section 3.

34. *Testimonial.* Keep every favorable piece of publicity or customer comment that you get. Get their name and picture and ask them to sign a release. Use it heavily in your advertising.

35. *Giveaways and sweepstakes.* This is a wonderful way to increase response to programs you are offering. Get free merchandise from other people for the publicity value, and increase your own responsiveness through the use of giveaways.

36. *On carton advertising.* With no additional expense, other than the creation of an initial printing plate, all of your shipments can carry marketing-oriented corporate and product information.

37. *Sell directly to catalogs.* There are nearly 7,000 catalogs in this country. Create a mailing program that goes out to them regularly offering your latest products for sale through their catalog. Cecil Hoge, a master marketer, says this is the best kind of free mail-order test that you can do. "By selling Sunset House, Edmunds Scientific, or another catalog, you are getting a mail order test for free. You're not gambling anything for promotion. If it works in catalogs, submit it to department stores for featuring in their catalogs or in cooperative newspaper ads. Your success with a catalog house may influence them favorably."[4]

38. *Be a spokesperson.* Victor Kiam does it. Colonel Sanders did it. Accept any speaking invitation, TV, radio or industry request, and be an excellent spokesperson for your product. Regis McKenna, chairman of his own company in Palo Alto, California, said at the Stanford University 1985 Conference on Entrepreneurship: "The best PR people are not PR people. A CEO or chairman of the board has a much higher credibility with the public than a PR person." And it's free publicity.

39. *Volunteer in your industry.* Teach a course. Give a speech. Do a workshop or seminar. Ron Gerwin, who left American Express in 1985, became a leader of a council within the Direct Marketing Association. Ron Hume spoke on entrepreneurship at a New York industry get-together recently. Cecil Hoge speaks at the Direct Marketing Idea Exchange, an influential New York City lunch group. These are all effective ways to build your authority.

[4]Cecil Hoge, *Mail Order Moonlighting* (Berkeley, California: Ten Speed Press, 1978).

40. *Go to meetings.* If you are in the retail business, go to your Rotary meetings. Dave Schaefer built most of his contacts in Burlington, Vermont through Rotary meeting attendance.

41. *Contacts.* The "old boy" and now the "old girl" network. Don't overlook your alumni contacts from previous institutions, academic and professional. Increasing numbers of corporations have alumni societies. I'm a member of two. (Time-Life and Garden Way)

42. *Delivery.* If you can't call on somebody in person, at a cost of $100, send them a dramatic package for $10. Use Federal Express, instead of calling.

43. *Account leveraging.* If there are important clients that could help you in the long term, quote then at a break-even price. We did this with American Express, and it helped us get a number of other accounts in the bag.

44. *Multi-tier marketing.* Don't rely on one channel of distribution. In our case, we use trade, special, mail-order, book-packaging, and remaindering (deep discounting) to make certain that our books work their way through a full cycle.

45. *An 800 number.* Always use another company's 800 number rather than paying for the call, but install your own carefully, control it, and develop telemarketing that will allow you to replace sales calls at $100 apiece with telemarketing calls at $10 apiece.

46. *Packaging.* Be consistent. Be very sure when you use four color. Look at your interior packaging, your exterior packaging. Test the importance to and response of your customers to high-class and low-class packaging.

47. *Copy.* Make it tough and competitive. Frank Lewis wrote "the fluke of nature" ad and launched his "ruby red grapefruit" into the U.S. consumer consciousness. Bob Jones wrote a 10-page letter on the difficulty of a trip to the South Pole and signed up 100 people at $10,000 each. Point out the outstanding benefits and the most unique features of your product.

48. *Equity.* Remember that every ad and promotion piece should build up equity in your name. Recently, I stood next to a person whose corporation is a thousand times the size of mine. We were both greeted by a new potential customer. I said I was from Storey Communications, and he said, "Oh yes. Storey Communications in

Vermont." My friend from the larger company didn't register recognition, even though his company was more "established."

49. *Overprints*. Do overprints on everything. It is relatively inexpensive to overprint a catalog. It is very expensive to reprint. Send out your overprints to everyone.

And Some More . . .

50. "You, you, you." Point out customer benefits constantly. You will discover, you will learn, you will be shown how.

51. *Consult*. Provide free consultation. A gimmick? It works. We mailed out 300 pieces and received 30 responses in 7 days, a 10 percent response, on the basis of a free consultation.

52. *Free editorial space*. There is a new product development section of every trade magazine. Send your new product information to them and you'll get free publicity.

53. *Customer deposits*. Work on the basis of "reserving a place in line." Ask for a customer advance. Do prepublication selling and advance selling.

54. *Service*. Provide speedy service to your customer. It costs no more than slow service.

55. *Franchising*. Once you have made your formula work, consider building your business growth through franchising. David E. House and wife Dorothy Decarlo launched Mama Mia, a pasta restaurant in Chicago, with $100,000 in savings and loans. Now doing $1.8 million, they're launching a franchising operation that will require a $280,000 initial investment from each franchisee.

So much for low cost marketing. Remember, always, that you can't stop spending on marketing, ever. During the heart of a cash crunch in the weakest time of our year, the summer, we spent money to go to the hardware show in Chicago. Out of that came a lead from the Eckerd Drug Corporation. We spent another $79 on a night flight to their headquarters in Tampa. We came out of the meeting with a $150,000 order.

One of my oldest friends in the mail-order business used to say to me when I would ask him every morning "How's the Mail?" "Ya gotta mail to get mail." So don't underspend. Just spend wisely.

In Chapter 9 we are going to take a look at how to keep your costs absolutely rock bottom.

9

Rock Bottom Costs

You worked extremely hard to get your financing. Whether you arranged it with one source or many, the $100,000, $250,000 or $1 million that you've accumulated is a major piece of work.

Now the question is, how do you hold on to it? By spending it wisely on investments that build equity, and don't represent pure "expense." That's what this chapter is about—how to keep your costs at absolute rock bottom.

I've been accused of being tight, and it's true. I do remove paper clips from old memos and spot things being thrown out that are worth keeping. I also know the difference in cost between staples and paper clips. Hopefully, rather than making me a tyrant, this puts me in a better position to be able to advise other people in the office as to how we should be spending our money.

For starters, it is important for every person that works in the organization to know your attitude about money, and to know what their authorization levels and spending limits are. If they don't, it will eventually cost you money when they make a wrong (uninformed) decision or fail to take action at a time when a decision is necessary. Nor do you want to be ridiculous about it. The time that it would take you to go through all of your old files and peel off paper clips would be far less productive than putting that same time into a new product launch or a new marketing strategy. Don't be absurd about expense elimination.

When Time, Inc. was having earnings problems, a group VP sent out a memo suggesting "brown bag lunches." The *Wall Street Journal* ran the memo and Time's stock dropped further!

DOWNWARD MULTIPLIERS

Start by letting everyone know how the business is going to operate in terms of money and the financial side. At a staff meeting, get out a flip chart and draw a pie showing where the money comes from and where it goes. In our case, of the 100% of revenue, we show people we want to spend 40 percent on cost of goods sold, 40 percent on sales, marketing and general expenses, 10 percent on administration, and 10 percent for profit. This is not an atypical revenue and expense breakdown.

Someone should be identified specifically as being responsible for keeping the cost of goods sold below 40 percent, keeping the selling, general, and administrative expenses below 40 percent, and that person or persons should be rewarded on their effectiveness. Everyone else then participates in the process of trying to eliminate, defer, or avoid costs so that the company can hang on to what it has.

The effects of cost elimination can be dramatic. When we started our business, there were 66 employees and a payroll of $750,000. On the first day of our new operation, we had four people and a payroll of $100,000. After the first month we had a profit of $37 turning the tide of what had been 10 years of losses.

Was it magic? Not really. Every dollar of cost needs perhaps five dollars of sales to support it. What you're really doing is creating a kind of reverse leverage. By eliminating one dollar of expense, you're eliminating the need for five dollars in sales. If you eliminate the expense and still get the five dollars in sales, you're way ahead of the game.

Your objective is to find the break-even point in your business as quickly as possible, and then to do everything possible to build on that solid base. Without determining what that break-even cost is, you'll never know which cost should be absorbed and which should be eliminated. At the outset of a new venture, the general expectation is that it's going to be a lean, mean, and low-cost operation. It's a great time to get everybody behind the effort of spending no money, and simply trying to create revenues.

A good rule of thumb: Don't buy anything unless and until it's absolutely, positively necessary for your new operation. Even then, lease rather than buy. The reason for this is the critical nature of cash flow in the early days of your business. Do everything possible to eliminate large commitments while developing supplier credit and deferring expenses that aren't necessary.

The old rule of 2 times comes back again . . . where everything takes twice as long, is twice as expensive, and half as profitable as you thought it was going to be. This can be frustrating, but this is a critical time for you to exercise your leadership.

Chairman Mao Tse Tung served the troops their soup before he had his own. This is not a bad approach, albeit for a dramatically different system. Make certain there aren't gaps in the early days between what you're doing, the way you're behaving, and the way you expect your troops to behave. You won't get away with a system for very long where everyone else suffers while you're driving in a limousine or staying at a fancy hotel.

Gordon Baty, author and entrepreneur, suggests 10 quick things to do in terms of cost elimination

1. Share office space with others
2. Do fix-it work yourself
3. Rent capital equipment from someone else during their off hours
4. Buy used office and plant equipment
5. Use part-time specialists such as engineers, artists, and so forth on a straight fee/no-benefits basis
6. Use sales representatives who are agents rather than a full time sales force
7. Have your product manufactured outside your company
8. Utilize free public relations rather than paid advertisements
9. Buy materials from a large user to get volume discounts
10. Push customers for prompt payment.[1]

[1]Gordon B. Baty, *Entrepreneurship: Playing to win* (Reston, Virginia: Reston, 1974), pp. 89–91.

EQUIPMENT

Let's take a look now at the major areas of initial expense. Most firms cannot do business without some basic form of equipment, whether typewriters, word processors, or postal machines. Equipment costs therefore are unavoidable. However you can do much to reduce or eliminate the expense of new equipment purchase.

Michael Meehan, a local warehouser and packager, attends business auctions virtually every month and, in effect, gets bank financing for office equipment at deep discount. Meehan buys equipment at perhaps 20 percent of its original value and can then, if he chooses, turn around to a local banker and say "I should be able to get 100 percent financing on these desks, scales, mailing machines, racks, and other equipment because I've just paid a rock bottom discount price on them." Most bankers agree.

Can you rent or use someone else's equipment on a time-sharing basis? Often large companies are willing to rent time on their equipment during off-peak hours. In our case, we buy much of our typesetting from a local larger magazine publisher who is happy to provide a discount rate during off-peak hours simply to give them some return on a major investment they've already made in typesetting equipment. Benefit from the sunk costs of others.

If you must buy, look for bankruptcy sales or existing firms which are expanding and which may be happy to get rid of their smaller scale equipment at a good price. A good source for deeply discounted merchandise and equipment is the Federal Government Services Administration, sells millions of items a year at deep discount. (Perhaps 5 cents on the original purchase dollar.) They publish a supply list regularly. *Venture* magazine recently noted that Associated Aircraft of Fort Lauderdale, Florida, bought over $600,000 in aircraft parts for $20,000; while another company, Magnacheck in Warren, Michigan, bought a $60,000 magnet inspection unit for only $1,000.[2] Property sales are held at over 200 locations annually.

What office equipment will you choose? Do you really need it? Remember, you're not trying to impress anybody, just to get your business up and going successfully. The latest fancy typewriters, copy

---

[2]R. J. Duhse, "Bargains from Uncle Sam," *Venture*, February 1985, pp. 33–34.

machines, telephones, furniture, and carpets are probably unnecessary luxuries at this early point in your business development.

If you're buying a business from a larger corporation, you're going to save enormously from day one. In our case, we went from an IBM 370 Main Frame to an IBM PC XT at a savings of $250,000 a year. We worked hard to see how many hours a day we could use the IBM PC XT, and at one point had it up to 16 hours. This gave us a great return on a relatively small investment. The same can happen on a phone system. In the larger corporation you'll be allocated a huge share of a centralized, state-of-the art system. We went from a $250,000 AT&T Dimension System down to a $12,000 Executone system and saved enormously.

INVENTORY

A second major area of expense is your inventory. Controls on the planning and use of that inventory are critical.

Start with informing everyone of *your* expectations in terms of inventory turnover each year. If you're in the retail business, it should turn at least four times a year. In the publishing business, we aim for a twice-a-year turn, unimpressive by other industry standards, but acceptable given the large number of new products and relatively high margin on paper products. We try to buy six-month supplies to gain economies of scale in printing.

A good inventory model can be a simple one as well. It has four primary components:

1. Forecasting.

Can you get good, solid estimates from your sales staff?

2. Turnaround time for printing or procuring.

How fast can you resupply if demand builds?

3. Order points.

At what minimal level must you produce something to get a decent cost-per-unit?

4. A system.

To track carefully what's in stock, what's out of stock, and what the demands are.

By the way, it's not the worst thing imaginable to have a product out of stock. Any company that is 100 percent in stock is probably carrying half again as much inventory at high carrying costs than its competition. We aim for an out-of-stock rate of below 5 percent and are pretty much on track.

We've already talked about the importance of getting trade credit from your supplier, which allows you to sell something in many cases before you pay for it. The trade book system works on the basis of advances to the book trade (Waldenbooks, B. Dalton, etc.) which in turn allows us to create a significant advance order or backlog. This "advance" becomes yet another asset that is collateral for the bank, and all of this takes place before the books arrive in the warehouse. This advance allows us to keep overhead and fixed costs at a minimum.

Make sure you thin your inventory regularly. Don't let weeds grow in the warehouse. Basically, after one of our books has run its course, it makes sense to remainder it or to contribute it to some worthy group.

Don't own your own warehouse/storage space. There is too much space available at low cost for you to invest heavily in a warehouse building. We're currently paying slightly over $1 per square foot for warehouse space in Massachusetts.

PEOPLE

Obviously, one of the largest costs of staying in business, especially for a small firm, is the payroll. We've discussed this earlier and advocated keeping the payroll down as much as possible. Remember the earlier estimate that adding a secretary and the equipment that he or she will need costs an average of $2,500 per month. Keep your costs low in the personnel area.

John Williams, president of Spence Corp. in Milwaukee, reported at Stanford University that he was able to increase his business from

$25,000 in industrial fittings distribution, to nine times that with only minimal personnel increases. Not bad.[3]

Again, leadership from the top is important. I would advocate not having any secretaries. Rather, make everyone that you hire self-starters and operationally independent. Give them a word processor and expect them to do all of their work by themselves. Keep salaries low. Start with yourself first. Cut your salary dramatically from what you've been used to earning. If your family can swing it, don't plan on taking any salary for the early period. Why?

Remember that you're trying to build value—asset value—so that you have something really significant to continue to borrow against. If you must take a salary, however, keep it as modest as possible. It will allow you to tell everyone else in the organization honestly that you're not taking very much out of this business and you don't expect them to either. Realistically, employees will require competitive salaries for the area in which they are living; but if your firm has potential for growth, you may be able to pay a portion of their total compensation in bonuses and eventually profit-sharing or stock ownership in the firm. This will obviously make them part owners of the business, a fact you'll want to consider carefully before you begin doling out stock. Also, they should know that the stock may be almost worthless when you begin; but that it has a real chance for appreciation, and they'll be in on the ground floor. Try to do as much as you possibly can yourself. Not only will you be eliminating costs, you'll be learning the business very well in the process.

Assets, whether staff or inventory, need controls. Little things can crop up, such as personal phone calls, personal use of the mailing machine, taking intra-office business lunches. Believe in your people deeply, and be honest and direct with them; but build some controls into your system as well so they know exactly what your expectations are and that there are controls in place to keep track of what is going on in the business.

SPACE

Don't pay for a fancy or expensive location at this point in the game. Find yourself a good, clean, low-cost work place and try to pay as lit-

[3]John Williams, "Stanford Conference on Entrepreneurship," Stanford University, 1985.

tle as you possibly can for it. Garden Way Inc. tried to run a brand new sunroom/solar greenhouse business out of $15-per-square-foot space. It made no money. After shifting it to $2-per-square-foot warehouse space, it began to make money. IBM had the famous "PC skunkworks" down in Florida, which not only saved money but also set a decided tone for how new business development was going to take place at IBM. So what do you really need? Lot's of space? An impressive address? An active retail district? Look for the best deal that you can find and don't worry about the frills. They won't do you any good if you go out of business. Keep things clean, safe, functional, but low frill.

TRAVEL AND ENTERTAINMENT

This is an area that can balloon before you know it. Again, set the tone for the organization yourself. Know what the airline fares are and when the deals occur. Get a good travel agent. Pick up the schedules and make your own reservations from time to time to make sure your agent is on his or her toes.

Consider staying with friends. They're surprised and happy that you call, once. Don't do it a number of times.

Group your trips. It's a lot less expensive to go to Montreal on Monday, Tampa on Tuesday, Washington, DC on Wednesday, and New York on Thursday, than it is to make each of those trips independently on week one, two, three, and four.

Unlearn your corporate habits. The year before we started our business, I stayed in a corporate suite at the Royal Orleans Hotel in New Orleans. Last year I stayed at a $49-a-night Holiday Inn. When I went to New York in the old days it was the Park Lane Hotel, today it's the Williams Club.

Keeping your costs as low as possible is a vital aspect of a healthy, growing business. Even if you have a good profit margin, the lower your costs the more your company can grow. Whenever you run across a brand new cost, be it a piece of machinery, a computer, a convention, a telephone bill, ask yourself: "Is there any way of avoiding this cost? Can it be eliminated? Deferred?"

Be creative but frugal. Keep records of every penny that you spend and analyze where your money is going. Is it following what you've predicted in your business plan? Is your cash flow plan on track? Are you getting something for the money that you spend? If not, can you readjust?

When you see losses or abuses, cut quickly. Close a bad location. Don't hook yourself into a long-term way of doing business by buying mold dies, and printing presses. Anything that represents inflexible, locked-in overhead will limit your future choices. In short, try to avoid significant capital and staff investments.

Once you've achieved positive cash flow, keep it invested. Try to minimize your bank charges and maximize the interest you're receiving. One business writer recently pointed out that most entrepreneurial business fortunes are accomplished "through other investments, not as a direct result of the firm they own or operate."[4] Keep all your assets working all the time. Your mailing list, for example. We earn $50,000 in rental income from ours each year, which partially offsets the cost of renting other lists. The firm that rents our lists for us also does our mailing list update and label generation. We work on a swap basis. Be on the lookout constantly for bartering opportunities, whether for services, lease, rent, or products. Try not to buy anything.

TWENTY-FIVE COST REDUCERS

You would be surprised at the fat you can squeeze out of any business. Remember the reverse-leveraging effect of cost elimination? Put together your own list of cost reductions or eliminations. Here are my favorite 25:

1. *Salaries.* Announce at the beginning of the year what your company-wide increase is going to be. Make it a fraction of a percentage point above the national average, but then stick to it. If it's 5 percent nationally, make it 5.2 percent across the board.

2. *Consultants.* Eliminate them completely. Consultants grow up in organizations, weave their way into the fabric, and then are there forever. When we started our business, we eliminated one fellow in Tennessee who hadn't done a piece of work in five years but was still

---

[4]Baca Smith, *Setting up shop: The do's and don'ts of starting your own small business* (New York: McGraw-Hill, 1982), p. 14.

drawing $20,000 a year. I had to introduce myself to him in order to terminate him.

3. *Postage*. Lease a good combination postal meter/scale in both your offices and your warehouse. Don't leave calculations up to your employees. Pitney Bowes claims you'll see a minimal 10 percent savings through computerized calculations.

4. *Commissions*. Negotiate these annually with your independent sales representatives. Make certain you adjust for customer returns, claims and uncollected payments.

5. *Conventions*. Absolutely no frills. Fly bargain airlines. Insist that every salesperson get a five-time return on their expenses invested. If a convention costs $5,000, require they work from their booth or hotel room and not have fancy lunches and dinners. Set per-day expense limits for meals.

6. *Processing fees*. If you use outside service bureaus, they will probably bill you 10 to 12 percent for order processing, credit, billing, and collection. You can do it for about 6 percent of your net revenues, but this means you will have to invest in facilities, equipment, and a staff of your own. Negotiate hard to bring down the 10 percent, then hold out a savings for yourself for some future time when a 4 percent savings could be timely. Then be sure you're set.

7. *Freight*. Pass as much of your freight expense as possible along to your customers. Look for frequency and volume discounts as well as consolidation opportunities. Find out the best freight companies to service your particular routes.

8. *Bad debt*. Do a credit screen up front. Hire a collection agency. You'll pay 40 to 50 percent of collections, but they'll get some money.

9. *Bank charges*. Negotiate hard on this with your banker. Lump all your small deposits on one slip. Avoid per-item charges.

10. *Casual labor*. Pay the minimum wage. Try to keep your family on board. Keep a pool of low-cost labor available. Pay no benefits, but make sure they have doughnuts.

11. *Dues and subscriptions*. One early year at Time-Life, I was assigned a task by the corporate comptroller's office which involved looking at the dues and subscriptions expense area. I was astonished. It ran into hundreds of thousands of dollars. There were over 100 in-

dividual subscriptions to *Playboy* magazine. This is the kind of thing that crops up in most corporations. Don't let it happen at your shop.

12. *Employee education.* Select courses, seminars, and college credits very carefully. Make sure the professor or lecturer is outstanding, and then insist that the employee provide a report back to you for the benefit of other employees.

13. *Equipment rental and lease.* Don't buy anything. Lease everything with an option to buy. Put in pieces of equipment that facilitate labor, reduce the number of labor hours, and that give people better tools for their trade. Try to improve your cash flow through leasing.

14. *Insurance.* Shop around constantly. Don't buy from friends. Use brokers who will be able to put you in touch with larger pools. Buy term insurance rather than whole life. Take your employee plans and benefits a step at a time, checking local competition. Don't offer orthodontia if you're the only one in the county who does.

15. *Legal and accounting.* Make certain you don't call these pros frivolously, and that you are the only one in your organization who deals with the lawyer and the accountant. One of the fastest ways to escalate your legal bills is to give everybody in the organization a chance to talk. Remember, the meter is always running.

16. *Mileage.* Try to eliminate the number of times you ask employees to use their own cars. Ask your suppliers to drive to you. Remember, you are paying at least 20½ cents a mile, and this adds up quickly, as does employee time "on the road."

17. *Motor vehicles.* Don't have company cars.

18. *Rent.* Avoid fancy overheads.

19. *Repairs and maintenance.* Try to do all of your repairs and maintenance yourself, or have a trusted, local handyman on call who can come quickly. Ditto for rubbish and snow removal.

20. *Subcontractors.* Use them selectively and often. Realize you are paying them no benefits or space costs. Use them instead of hiring additional employees.

21. *Supplies.* Put one person in charge of the supply operation. Insist on three bids for everything you buy. Reuse all of the materials that you have on hand; for instance, cartons. We ship out books in cartons that come to us from other suppliers.

22. *Telephone.* Get as sophisticated a system as you can, but allow it to grow with you. We shifted to a consolidated micro system with long distance access through Call America and saved thousands of dollars over the old corporate system.

23. *Utilities.* Monitor this carefully. Always get two bids. Recently we bought oil at 60 cents a gallon. The highest bid was $1. We saved $400 on the first delivery.

24. *Paper, (raw materials) printing and manufacturing.* Get multiple bids. Have at least 10 suppliers. Ask for terms. Gang your jobs together in order to achieve economies of scale. Consider paper purchases when you have major jobs, and cut out the printer's markup.

25. *Data processing.* Don't invest until you must. When you outgrow your manual systems, move into data processing a step at a time.

That's my list of the major cost-reducing, eliminating, and deferring possibilities. Work hard to stamp out any kinds of unnecessary cost within your company, and make certain that everyone else shares your sense of why it is important to do so.

You've come a long way. You have your business going. You have your financing. You're fighting to get rid of expenses. You should feel proud. There will be many risks and equivalent rewards ahead. One of the nicest ways to get ready for those is to talk with a number of different people who are one, two, and five years ahead of you in their own low-cost entrepreneurship. We'll do this in Chapter 10.

10

Risks and Rewards

No one understands better than yourself the risks you've undertaken. For each of us, they are somewhat different. It can be frightening. There's a possibility that you'll lose all the financial resources you've accumulated over the years. You could also be out of a job. But there are also the wonderful potential rewards—the privacy and your name on the sign, the exhilarating feeling of being in charge, the joy of your first profitable month, quarter, and year. A large part of the reward is in the process itself. You will be a different person than you were in your old corporate life. Your self development and appreciation of your own assets will be much greater.

You will have a wonderful feeling of having made something work, after others have tried and failed.

You'll have the great feeling of reaching new plateaus. Entrepreneur Gordon Baty commented that the entrepreneur has "won" when he or she succeeds in bringing his firm to a position where, in order to continue the growth of sales and earnings, a substantial infusion of new capital is required.[1]

You'll enjoy the experience of independent growth. E. Joseph Cossman, who started his firm with a minimal payroll and parlayed

[1]Gordon Baty, *Entrepreneurship: Playing to Win* (Reston, Virginia: Reston, 1974), p. xi.

217

it into a $25 million enterprise, said "you're better off making $30,000 in your own business than $50,000 in corporate salary."[2]

You also may be able ultimately to cash in your equity chips at some particularly right time for a large amount of money. Droves of entrepreneurs did that at the end of 1986, just before the capital gain rate increased from 20 percent to 28 percent. Whenever you do it, you'll have a wonderful feeling of having built a house, put good value into it, and getting more back for it.

While the risks are great, your survival chances improve dramatically after the first year. At that time, go back to your banker, as I did, and tell him or her it's time to get rid of the personal guarantee. You'll feel enormously different in year two without the personal guarantee from how you felt in year one. Your banker, impressed by the growth that you've shown, will go along with you. A way to further reduce that risk is simply not to leave your present job until you're confident you have something to replace it with.

And remember, if your business fails, there are alternatives. There's always the corporate world to go back to. Perhaps, if you're of continuing entrepreneurial persuasion, you'll launch something else. Certainly Nolan Bushnell at Atari was not slowed down by his first failure. But you can also enter the job market again. It's extremely likely that the skills you've developed at entrepreneurship will make you a far better corporate manager. Many of my good friends, including Dick Leventer, director of circulation promotion at Hearst, have enjoyed entrepreneurial experiences and will say they're happy to be back at the corporation.

Another friend, Kurt Medina, started an entrepreneurial business called "Wine of the Month" in California, which worked well on a pilot basis then ran into the 1974 recession and, undercapitalized, it folded. Was it a success? As Medina says, "by every tangible measuring stick absolutely not. However from the standpoint of my own personal gain and experience, fun, maturity, business sense, and ability to run with things, it was a howling success. Even knowing the end I'd do it all over again."

Then on the other hand, things might work, and if they do, by far the biggest reward of being a successful entrepreneur is the personal

[2]Albert J. Lowry, *How To Become Financially Successful by Owning Your Own Business* (New York: Simon & Schuster, 1981), p. 22.

reward of knowing you took an idea and turned it into a profitable business over which you have control. For many entrepreneurs this feeling makes it all worth while.

Along the way you'll learn humility, the value of money, the value of failure, and the value of those precious hours of leisure time that you find.

But I'm assuming you're going to be successful.

You have your new corporation. You are up and running on your own.

Be prepared for changes. Early in our experience, I drove up to my new Storey Communications worldwide headquarters one hot summer morning, and rather than working on strategic planning, I started the day by replacing screens that flies were buzzing into and out of in our reception area.

But it's worth it. Your start up will create some exciting changes in your life. The highs will be higher, and the lows will be lower. You will always remember the agony and the ecstasy of your first 90 days. We asked other entrepreneurs about their feelings of risk and reward, and whether it was all worth it.

"I think everyone in the organization takes more pride," said Victor Kiam. "They are in a stand-alone outfit now. They are making their own way. They know they've got problems, but, by God, they're doing it on their own. They don't have big daddy down the street calling the shots.

"If more than one manager is participating, there is a feeling of togetherness and ownership that extends downward into the organization.

"You'd be surprised how the hours worked per day go up when somebody has a piece of the action."

"I think it brought out the best in all of us," Vermont State Senator Douglas J. Baker said of his family partnership that bought the Sugarhouse Motor Inn & Restaurant.

"My own personal feelings about myself, my own self-worth, went up five hundred percent," Baker said. "I found I had abilities I didn't even know existed."

"I tend to sleep a whole lot better. I'm running my own show and am master of my own destiny," said Richard E. Hug of Environmental Elements. "I don't have to worry about going to this meeting and that meeting and reporting to somebody in Pittsburgh. I feel a hell of a lot better."

When John T. Mahoney finished signing and exchanging documents at the closing of his 1983 purchase of TransLogic Corp., attorneys cheered and champagne was opened in celebration. Mahoney sipped one glass—then rushed back to the factory. "Suddenly it was our buildings, machinery, and payroll," Mahoney explained.[3]

Jerry Gura, of CWT Specialty Stores, put it this way: "I have not really changed my intensive work routine, but I have enjoyed three great psychological benefits: (1) the enjoyment of being an entrepreneur; (2) a growth in personal net worth; and (3) a measurable feeling of security."

What surprises and problems should managers-turned-owners expect and prepare for? Lots, said several managers we interviewed:

"Market downside," answered Vaughn L. Beals, chairman/CEO of Harley-Davidson Motor Co.

"Self-complacency," answered the chairman/CEO of another firm employing 2,300, who asked to remain unidentified.

"A danger of going it alone is that, exclusive of your lender, you're really not answerable to anyone," said Jerry Gura.

Freedom and independence in your new business will have their costs. You will be faced with new responsibilities and risks. There will be fewer controls on you, your life, and business.

But you will have fewer controls you can use in areas outside of your business. Starting something new will require that you replace your traditional information sources and early-warning systems. Immediately. You will need to create new communications and management systems for following your decisions and policies through to implementation.

You will find new ways to interact continuously with outsiders such as consultants, customers, suppliers, your peers in the industry, and, of course, your counselors and members of your board of directors.

Gura said, "We know some people who tend to let their guard down. They are reveling in their glory. But our business, retailing, is

[3]Robert Johnson, "Going it alone," *Wall Street Journal*, February 6, 1985.

very unforgiving. Once you goof, you goof, and it is very costly. We need to keep each other sharp."

We faced an early crisis with one of our key printers after our buyout of Garden Way Publishing. The printer said the terms we were expecting only applied to the parent company. He told us we would have to work with a reduced credit limit (and we were already well beyond that) before they could be comfortable with our new company and give us the old terms. This news meant we had to instantly develop alternative suppliers who were happy to work with us. Significantly, we are better balanced today in terms of printing and paper suppliers than we've ever been.

You will be faced with similar surprises every day. Some will be good, some bad. If you buy an existing business, the response to your purchase by employees will be a surprise—not exactly what you anticipated. The inventory you inherit will include some slow-moving surprises. The accounts receivable will contain some slow-paying surprises.

If you have bought a company and plan to move it right away, as we did, mail clerks at the parent company or your old post office may be returning mail orders not addressed to their satisfaction. A long-time customer may use the occasion of the change in ownership to desert you for a competitor. A key manager who seemed to share your vision of an independent company decides to remain with the old corporation.

My advice: Don't take any of those changes personally. Remember, there's always another supplier, customer, and employee. Fight like hell to keep the good ones you have, but don't cry over those you lose.

In your new independent business, you will miss those old corporate cushions you had, such as the corporate "deep pockets." To yourself, you can blame unexpected business problems on the recession, on the election, or on the weather, but you will have to pay for their costs out of your own pocket.

Even the timing of your start-up, which may have been perfect for you and the lender, may turn out to be all wrong for your employees or customers.

Your role as an entrepreneur will be to expect and welcome the surprises as a continuing flow of opportunities to learn, correct, and improve. There will be no more running to a corporation for shelter.

Larry Munini said he faced unexpected hazards in the marketplace after his purchase of Genesys Software Systems. Instead of two major competitors, Munini found four.

Tom Madsen, who led a Key Technology acquisition from Applied Magnetics, told a similar story of more scrutiny from both suppliers and customers.

"Our customers range from large to small food processors, but we do business with all the large food companies—Campbell's Soups, General Foods—and these companies sometimes feel one way about doing business with a company that is backed by an Applied Magnetics and they feel another way when all of a sudden there is a new ownership or a start-up situation."

"You have to convince them. In a couple of cases we had to demonstrate to our customers that we had staying ability, because we are talking big-ticket items.

"Luckily, we had a long track record on a personal basis with these customers. There was credibility there. Had we been with the company only two years before we bought it, I think that could have been a much tougher problem."

Executives-turned-entrepreneurs are also surprised, according to the *Harvard Business Review* (*HBR*), by "a pervading sense of loneliness."

In a survey of 300 small-business CEOs, *HBR* reported a high correlation between loneliness and stress in 109 respondents who complained of frequent loneliness: "Among respondents to our survey, 68 percent reported they had no confidant with whom they could share their deep concerns."

The truth of the matter is that you frequently look over your shoulder and find there is no one there for support anymore. I remedy this by making phone calls every day to sales reps, distributors, potential customers, and suppliers. You'll wonder where the time went.

After doing its survey of loneliness among small-business owners, the *Harvard Business Review* presented several recommendations for curing this. Among them:

Participate in organizations of business leaders.

Be attentive to family, friends, customers, and suppliers, and seek their counsel.

Look for recreational and social activities that balance job-related isolation such as team sports and other group activities.[4]

Your most important source of support and outside information, of course, will be your outside professional counselors. That's what they're getting paid for.

Think of your counselors as your silent business partners, and keep them as well informed as the insiders. Continually ask your counselors questions—all the right questions. Listen carefully to their answers.

Perhaps previously, in a management career, you were sheltered from certain economic realities by the parent corporation. Now you need to learn how to make your own forecasts and cope with business uncertainties.

Keep notes of conversations with your counselors and advisors. Then make a rough copy of those notes and send it back to them for their hand-written observations. You may find you missed some hints and offhand remarks that were intended to be danger signals.

Retain only the counselors and advisors who share your enthusiasm and will tell you what you can do as well as what you cannot do. Seek alternatives with them through a continuing dialogue.

If you've completed your start-up with an advisor who continues to remain withdrawn and uncommunicative, arrange for a timely switch to a more responsive professional.

Start-up managers frequently reported they were surprised how much they missed corporate supports such as accounting and computer services.

"We thought it would be great to get rid of the corporate charge on our profit-and-loss statements for which we didn't think we really got much," Tom Madsen said with a laugh. "But we found out there are a lot of other charges that crop up to replace the missing corporate services."

Visit your advisors at their offices and ask for a full inventory of all available services. Establish a line of communications with all of their assistants.

[4]David E. Gumpert and David P. Boyd, "Growing concerns: The loneliness of the small business owner," *Harvard Business Review*, Cambridge, Massachusetts, November/December 1984.

Devise a process for keeping your lenders informed and protected from your surprises. Talk with them about new products, new customers, and new problems. Include them in your discussions of long-range financial planning. Ask them to keep you posted on available industry and government marketing research.

In my own case, I found myself, the entrepreneur, taking 50 trips in the first year of business. In my last year as a senior executive at Garden Way Inc., I made half that number.

Be sure your outside accountants understand that their work for you must go beyond tax returns and financial reviews. Keep them involved in overall reviews of your inside financial operations, from petty cash to raising capital. Ask them to help with planning for employee benefits, insurance, profit centers, and internal controls.

Setting up your own shop is like starting a new family in a new home. How your business grows and develops, just as your family does, will include some surprises.

"Some of the surprises are the way you're viewed by employees and fellow workers," according to Lou Auletta of Bauer/Electro.

"My true role is not that much different. I have retained my role as general manager. But, all of a sudden, as an owner, people looked at me differently. You are tested a lot more."[5]

Auletta said the changes in business relationships, although exhilarating, can be inhibiting "to a degree."

Larry Munini of Genesys Software said he was first uneasy with his high visibility as company president. He said he sometimes still feels uncomfortable when his salespeople portray him publicly as a "bigger than life" problem-solver and force him to go out and live up to that image.

Tom Madsen said his Key Technology employees at first felt some apprehension about his acquisition with three other top managers from Applied Magnetics.

"This is not malicious. The same thing happened when the firm was first acquired by Applied Magnetics in 1968. Up to that time, the company had been privately owned. The employees became apprehensive and formed a union. This was voted out three years later.

"Being aware of that previous experience, we did our very best job

---

[5]Lou Auletta quoted in Donald Dubendorf and M. John Storey, *The Insider Buyout* (Pownal, Vermont: Storey Communications, 1986), p. 207.

at communications," Madsen said. "We have about 140 people in our company, and I can get them all in one room and talk. We did that. We also had small group meetings about changes in benefit plans—how the new plans were going to be structured. We basically kept the plans just the way they had been.

"We wanted the employees to view it as much as possible as a continuation of business as usual," Madsen said.

"There are seven people on the management staff. Four of them became owners. . . . The people who got involved had all expressed an interest in wanting to do this. But it was tough trying to decide. We operate pretty much as a group. All of them are still here."

In talking about his own new business venture, Dick Hug of Environmental Elements said, "The attitude and productivity change is amazing.

"We did it through a lot of sessions. . . . Big sessions, small group sessions. One-on-one sessions. I involved myself personally in almost all of the sessions to explain what we had done, why we had done it, what effect it would have on our people, and what kind of rewards they could expect if we were successful.

"Basically, we told them how good the company is, the kind of reputation we have in the marketplace, and the kind of pride that they could have in the company," Hug said.

"We have to work on it continually. We share our financials with almost everybody in the company. We don't have any secrets to speak of, but we expect them to keep that information confidential and not to be talking to their friends, neighbors, or the newspapers. . . . They have a sense of involvement in knowing what's going on. I think that's important, to bring people into the fold.

"We have 511 employees. They understand what we are doing and are better motivated with a better sense of purpose.

"It becomes infectious. We literally have 511 people in this company who are cheerleaders."

Hug said that since the sale, relations between Environmental Elements and the previous owner, Koppers, have remained good. "I have been with the company Koppers for a long time, and I have a lot of friends with the company. Most everyone in the company was really for me. Although there are always some jealousies that develop in a thing of this nature—someone wonders, 'Why didn't I do it?' —for the most part the relationships have been good."

At Storey Communications, we instituted a weekly meeting for all 10 employees, then a monthly meeting when we reached 20. Now, at 30, we meet on a staffwide basis each quarter, and communications are considered good.

Regarding relationship changes with customers, Lou Auletta of Bauer/Electro said, "I felt comfortable in taking over the business because I had a good rapport with the customers and good understanding of what they were looking for.

"The customers realize they are dealing with the president and the owner of the company, and I think that is very positive. They know that you will back up any commitment you make. This is very important."

Regarding his business relationship with his partner, Doug Baker, restaurant and motor inn owner, said, "While I was a virtual optimist, my partner was a bit more conservative. We balance ourselves very well, I have the drive. He has the reins.

"I admit to myself I could have overstepped on several occasions, but he knew when to pull in."

Your buyout could also mean profound changes in your family relationships. In many of the new business we spoke with, spouses, sons, and daughters are now working in the business and making the buyout a family affair.

Dick Hug's son joined him at Environmental Elements. Lou Auletta's son is with him at Bauer/Electro.

Dick Snyder of the Snyder General Corp. has been married 26 years and has three grown children in or recently graduated from college. "By wife is very actively involved in the business now in advertising and sales promotions," Snyder said. "It has really brought the family close together," he said of his buyout. "The business is a huge part of our life. All the kids want to know what's going on."

In researching start-ups, we called a Connecticut firm and asked to speak to the CEO. Let's call him Mr. Oliver. He was out of the office and his secretary was away from his desk, the telephone operator said. She asked, "May I help you?"

We took a chance and explained our hope of interviewing Mr. Oliver. We were well aware that many "telephone operators" are in reality management assistants skilled at shielding the boss from sales reps, local politicians, news reporters, book authors, and other interruptions.

"Mr. Oliver is usually very interested and cooperative with this type of thing. I'll tell him you called, and he will probably be glad to meet with you. . . . This is Mrs. Oliver."

Or take our own case. During the summer, our 20-year-old daughter sells advertising space in the *Gardeners' Marketplace*. Our 17-year-old does word processing, and our 12-year-old photocopies and empties the wastebaskets. Martha Storey, a company officer and full-time operations manager, handles everything from paper purchases to conference-room clean ups. As she stopped in our meeting room recently to say goodbye, she reminded, "Don't forget to take out the trash, John."

It's difficult to find families more involved in the business than at Doug Baker's restaurant and motor inn business in Vermont. Baker's partnership is with his wife's brother, Jim Kendall, and their two wives. The two families and their parents have homes adjacent to the business and their children have all worked in the business.

"Try to maintain a balance between your family life and your business life," Baker said. "The family is going to have to learn to give up a little. But you've got to learn when to leave the business at the office and go home and be with your family.

"Too often, when you shift gears going into a start-up, you let the business dominate you, and soon you have a family situation which can overlap into the business. Then you've got a real problem."

Baker said working closely and intently with a spouse in the business is a matter of having the right attitude. "Each of you is intelligent and brings something that the other doesn't have. Each of you has an instinct for a certain portion of the business. She knows certain areas. You know certain areas. And you have to accommodate each other in that way.

"It takes some adjustment. It doesn't come overnight. It comes over a period of time. It's a learned experience.

"It's a partnership. . . . Many businesses have failed where the husband and wife tried to work together and failed simply because one or both have been unbending. And you both get burned . . . I would call that an inbred inability to accept the other as a partner."

Do you believe effective corporate management is accomplished only under tension applied from above?

Or are you more comfortable relaxing the rules and fostering a team effort in an entrepreneurial environment?

The style in which you organize and manage your new firm is too important to be left to charisma, chance, or management systems carried over from the parent corporation.

Keep yourself sensitive to the reasons you decided to embark on your start up. Don't assume your employees will be as enthusiastic about the deal as you are. A frightened and insecure work force could cause you trouble while you are busy launching your new firm.

In the absence of old corporate support systems, you will need to stop and think carefully. Who is supposed to do what, when, where, to whom, and how much will it cost?

You will need to foster an environment for developing your own new business culture. And, as your business grows, you will need to encourage adjustments to suit, not stunt, your dynamic new situation.

Our own goals are simple: to build supportive, communicative relationships with our employees, and long-standing relationships with our customers.

Employees will follow the rules, use the controls, and meet the goals you ask them to help you write. Fit the organization to the expertise of your employees, not the other way around.

Dick Hug said, "Our biggest challenge was changing the mentality of the work force. They are no longer working for a large company where a few extra dollars here and a few extra dollars there don't count. They no longer spend money quite as freely and as loosely as they did in the past. Not that the business was managed loosely before, but it's just a different mentality. We had to reinforce that among our people.

"We cut our salaried employment about 20 percent. Most of those people took early retirement. Many had lost their drive and mission in life. We worked out a good severance plan with Koppers as part of our acquisition. Then we renegotiated the pension and health-medical plans to effect phenomenal savings."

Your first step in a dynamic business reorganization is to establish interactive, as proposed to hierarchical, systems for communications and meetings.

This process will permit a gradual evolution of your management systems, systems you will design and implement as you progress together with those employees involved.

Put your best efforts into teaching, leading, and encouraging your employees as opposed to directing, supervising, and controlling them. Teach them to be self-starting and self-managing. Instill pride through recognition and rewards for their commitment and innovation.

We made a lot of changes in our first month, moving corporate offices 125 miles, moving 300,000 books to Harper & Row in Scranton, Pennsylvania, hiring 10 new employees, and reducing overhead by $750,000. We could not have done it without a committed new staff who shared our vision.

CAPITAL

After your start-up, you will be managing more than people. You will also be managing capital. Managing capital means projecting your capital needs, organizing and securing the financing, appropriating the funds, directing and controlling the spending, and accounting for all of these activities.

If you worked for a corporation, you were held accountable for the profitability of your division, but you also had the parent company behind you to share the blame and losses during poor years.

As a manager—owner, you will not have this backup. You need to follow even more closely your costs of sales and production down to the bottom line. You cannot avoid the fact that you as an individual are totally responsible for the payroll.

New business owner Lou Auletta of Bauer/Electric said, "Before, I always did a good job at making the company profitable for the owners. But I was amazed at how differently you look at things as the owner. You have a different set of eyes when you become the owner. You are much more conscious of things that you took for granted before, such as employee benefits. I have looked at this as an opportunity to do better for the employees as well as management," Auletta said.

Look for mistakes and misjudgments in your deal and don't be afraid to admit you made your share. Make your corrections immediately. You will need to revise continuously your plans and goals, especially from your changing perspectives as a new owner—manager.

The company organization that will follow your start-up will be the time for you to stop doing what you were doing and start heading where you want to go. Organize your new company into profit centers, each with its own budget and performance goals. Establish at the beginning a divestment policy that will weed out the losers. Study each of your new policies and decisions for the impact on your employees and resources.

Seize this opportunity to apply new productivity measurements to goals, not to activities. Fine tune your systems for estimating costs, sales, and production.

Institute new reporting systems for your sales, production, financials, and most important, cash flow. Implement controls for cash, expenses, accounts receivable, inventory, and, most of all, payroll.

"You try to go faster and further than your cash flow and your ability to earn will take you," Doug Baker said.

John W. Jordan of the Jordan Company said, "We always find the asset management companies improve dramatically. Once the guy's got his own money on the line he really doesn't need that extra half a million in inventory. And he's not about to let the customers take 40 or 50 days to pay. And instead of paying his suppliers in 15 days, he starts paying them in 35 days.

"You start to get a whole new dynamic and culture. This is, 'Save the buck. Start putting in the screws.' That is always good. It creates dollars on the bottom line. It's a dynamic resulting from a whole multitude of things," Jordan said.

If you worked for a corporation, you could ignore tax consequences and trust that the corporate staff counsel and accountants would solve the problems. Now you have to hire, educate, and supervise your own tax and accounting assistance, no matter whether this is in-house or not.

Speaking of lenders, Tom Madsen said, "I heard this story before, and it is typical of what happened to us. After you buy a company, your bankers are your friends until you need them. During the first year or so of our operations, we were generating a fair amount of cash and the bankers were asking us, 'When are you going to borrow some money?'

"Then we went through about six months that were quite lean, with an order rate that was very low, and this drained our cash. We finally got to the point where we needed working capital, and, of course, at that point our receivables were quite low.

"Our business tends to be a seasonal business. This is not as much of a concern to us as it is to someone looking at the current P&L (profit and loss). When we went to the bank we found the cupboard rather bare. . . . Our account is handled mainly through the Portland office.

"The local banker was very instrumental in helping us with the corporate bankers. He knew our business better, even though we had never had any previous banking relationships with him. . . . He went to bat for us on the corporate level in Portland, and we were finally successful in extending our line of credit.

"And since that time they have traveled out here and now understand our business a lot better. I don't envision any further problems.

"You need to nurture those relationships, even when you don't need them. We don't need them now, but we're continuing to nurture them and educate the bankers as to where our company is going and where the industry is going. We have invited them to our trade shows and that sort of thing, so they really understand our business. Make them a partner with you so when you need them, they will be there."

For example, ask your lenders and other counselors to review and comment on your insurance coverage and your contingency plans. Plan ahead for quick financing response to technological and environmental demands.

Ask your lenders to keep you alerted to the latest problems and opportunities of the money markets and the national economy as they relate to your company financing.

Most important, in a start-up, focus on your cash flow, capital accounts, and reducing your debt. Less important now are profit-and-loss statements and quarterly earnings reports.

"Profits are for public companies," said Robert E. Lee, a partner in Maul Technology Corp.

"As far as I'm concerned," Lee said, "profits are a cash drain because you pay half to Uncle Sam. Cash flow is the lifeblood of any privately owned business."

In my case, I stopped looking for a monthly P&L statement and began looking at daily receipts and disbursements. What a difference a day makes.

You have started the company that you have dreamed of. You have discovered how to get control of your business life. You have learned that freedom and independence are the thrills of a lifetime.

Now you need to be sure that in the rush to establish your new independent business, you are continuously making the right business decisions.

"You've got to face the fact that the buck stops here," Victor Kiam said. "The manager in a large corporation can bluster and bluff, 'If I were making the decisions, this is what I'd do.'

"But when he runs his own ship and it is his decision, the confidence he gained by presenting his ideas to a corporate group who then made the decision is shaken because he doesn't have that corporate group to go to.

"He sits in a little mental cubbyhole of his own, and he has to come up with the solution. Maybe he has some good people around him who will suggest what has to be done. But ultimately it is his decision."

Kiam was talking about the loneliness of being both boss and owner, the difficulty of a corporate manager making the transformation from a player in the middle to the star at the top. "Sometimes you cannot come up with a decision based on your intellect, and you have to come up with a decision based on your feelings, or emotion. Your gut is what's going to tell you what's right or wrong.

"And once you've done it, you cannot let on that you may have misgivings. You have a whole group of people who are dependent on you and your decision. You've got to bull it through. You've got to keep going. You cannot show your doubts."

As a corporate manager, you were trained to make decisions. But as an owner—manager, Kiam said, you must go beyond the mere making of decisions into an expanded role of championing your decisions.

"You've got to exude confidence that you're sure of your decisions. Don't sit on a decision for three months. Make the decisions and make them decisively.

"I've always felt that making no decision is worse than making a poor decision. Be decisive once you get in there."

Kiam is not suggesting that owner—managers make their decisions decisively in lonely isolation after consulting only their gut reactions. Kiam believes you should beef up your board of directors with strong personalities who will ride herd on you.

"When I went into my first business deal, about 1967, I tried to get people around me that other people would respect, so that I would be known by the company that I kept. I didn't get personal friends I could maneuver. . . . A lot of public companies have rubber stamp boards. I went out and got the most difficult, the most honorable people who were proven successes so that no one could say Kiam had a mamby-pamby group that was a rubber stamp."

A strong board of directors as recommended by Kiam is not a threat to your life's goals of business control and personal independence. A strong board of directors is a challenge to your intellect, and it can strengthen your business and ensure that you reach your life's goals.

In reality, your board of directors does not hire you, you hire its members. The relationship is similar to the one you have with your lawyer and accountant. If you ignore their advice, you don't get fired. They withdraw and go spend their efforts and expertise where they are better utilized and respected.

At Storey Communications, we're blessed with a strong board of directors. Professionals from New York, Boston, and Westport, Connecticut, they travel quarterly for no compensation. The fact is, we couldn't have afforded their advice, and they weren't asking to get paid.

The people you need on your board are your outside peers or mentors. They are people with expertise that balances or exceeds your experience, people who can serve as your confidants and counselors in a close professional and personal relationship.

Select board members for professional reasons, not as a payoff for services rendered or anticipated, and certainly not for any perceived public-relations benefits.

"Board of directors" is the accepted term, but if you are worried about losing control of your business before you've had time to enjoy it, think of your board of directors as an advisory board or council of advisors.

"I'm the sole owner (of Remington Products) and the company is very successful," Kiam said. "But if you attended our board meetings, you'd think these guys each had an equivalent stake in the business and that the company is . . . about to go bankrupt. It's that kind of a knock-down, drag-out meeting.

"On my board, when we started out, I had a financial guy, a former managing partner of a major accounting firm, and my personal lawyer.

"When we went into the retail business with a chain of special retail stores, I added a very astute retailer because I didn't know retailing. My retail operating manager would come to me, and I couldn't really help him when he needed help. So we asked this gentleman to go on our board, and they (the veteran retailer and the operating manager) now have a one-on-one relationship.

"And I have just added a senior marketing chap because I was the only marketing guy on the board. So when I talked about a marketing idea . . . they said that was a lousy idea because of the legal, tax, or accounting implications. But they didn't look at it from the marketing point of view. I added a guy for marketing so they would have the benefit of someone else's input . . . so if I came up with something they thought was a hairbrainer . . . there was another voice.

"You want people who are going to argue with you," Kiam went on. "If you try to get a mirror image of yourself, a yes man, so that you can live a happy, contented life with no discussions and arguments, you're going to be a failure. You want people who have strong opinions, who are able, who are going to argue like hell with you so that you have to prove your point.

"It's very key," Kiam said. "When you're out on a limb, you've got to get the best brains you can get."

At Unitog, Bob Hagans said 29 employees are shareholders, and there is a "great desire to have every employee" a part-owner. "It has changed the attitude. These are not sophisticated investors. Now they have second mortgages on their homes. Our good managers have become great managers. Everything we've got, we've got in it. All our physical and monetary resources. And our first year has been super."

"It was more than worth the gamble," Jerry Gura said. "I had nothing to lose. I could have always stepped back to a corporate job."

"If something did not work out," Tom Madsen said, "well, we

just never thought about what would happen if things did not work out. Except that we are all young enough so that we could go out again and do our own things."

Dick Hug said, "A lot of people ask, after 26 years of working for a major company, going up through the ranks, and doing relatively well, 'Why would you think of becoming an entrepreneur?'

"I think it's a tremendous way to go. There are some tremendous opportunities out there for those who are willing to take a little bit of risk."

Hug said he was inspired to do his start-up by entrepreneurial friends in the 4,000-member Young Presidents' Organization, an association of CEOs under the age of 50 who attained their positions before the age of 40.

"I got to thinking, 'If they can do it, by golly, I can do it.' I gave a talk with my partner to a group of persons on what we had done, and they were all amazed at how we had leveraged and structured it. I ended that talk by saying, 'If I can get one of you to do a leveraged buyout over the next 12 months, I'll feel the time was well spent."

Victor Kiam said the rules for performing a small acquisition are the same as those for doing the bigger deals. "All the points we have touched upon existed in my situation as well.

"Whether you do a $1 million, a $10 million, a $200 million, or even a $200,000 deal, you still need all the basic guidelines we have discussed. And you certainly need the support and guidance of other people who are much more steeped in certain other areas than you are."

"It's something that we're proud of," Lou Auletta said of his start-up. "Anyone who's faced with a similar situation, I'm sure a few tips wouldn't hurt. This is an opportunity to share some of our experiences, having gone through it."

"There are going to be continuing (insider) acquisitons going on," Jerry Gura said. "Maybe to a greater degree than what we've witnessed—and we've certainly gone through some halcyon (sic) years. The most important thing from my perspective is SOS—the self-ownership-syndrome. That's where it's at."

When we completed our acquisition of Garden Way Publishing, I was determined to rest, to savor the moment of success, to share that good feeling with my family and friends. I wanted to go over with my lawyer, Don Dubendorf, the many negotiating sessions, the days and nights of planning, our little victories and our defeats, much as athletes go over the big game.

Where was the best place to do this? The Virgin Islands? South Carolina? And I planned to do this. I counted on it. But first there was the matter of finding a new home for the business, moving a huge inventory of books. I had to put off the victory celebration—just until next month.

And then there were the accounts receivable to handle, the new books to be created, the need to hold fast to old customers and to find new ones. And more months slipped quickly past.

Now four years have gone by, busy years, years of growth. And it's certainly too late to think of a victory celebration.

Maybe we've had that celebration already, in odd moments, on the phone with Don, at breakfast with Martha, in quick conversations with many others who, like us, tried start-ups and found it one of the most satisfying experiences of their business careers.

And just perhaps the writing of this book has been part of that celebration. For this book has given me the opportunity to share with you and other readers the thrills of starting your own business, with no money down.

I hope that it gives you the push you need to try a start-up of your own.

If you're the entrepreneurial type, wanting to try it on your own in the business world, I can assure you that you'll never work harder in your life, never get so scared about business matters, or feel more adrenalin, never put yourself to a sterner test—and never feel more sure of yourself, more elated than when you do your own business start-up and it works.

How To Prepare Yourself for Your Loan Request

I. Types of banks and lending officers
  A. Types of banks
    1. Thrifts—Savings and loans, co-ops, savings, mutuals, "people banks"
    2. Commercial—Can be either state or federally chartered like the thrifts. Use of National or N.A. "business banks"
    3. New era of expanded services—banks moving into each other's niche—commercials in mortgages and savings banks in commercial lending
    4. Recent mergers, name changes, expanded services
  B. Banks are not all the same
    1. Loan policy
    2. Lending area(CRA)
    3. Loan limits
    4. Participation loans
    5. Local decisions
    6. Types of loans offered

    C. Loan officers are not all the same
      1. People with different personalities, loan experience, loan approval authority, the specialist
    D. Country versus city banker
    E. Talk to more than one bank, ask questions, where do you feel comfortable

II. Types of loans available—the right loan for the right purpose. (Rates and terms quoted will vary from bank to bank so general ranges will be used.)
    A. Two basic loan types: Cash cycle and cash flow loans
    B. Cash cycle loans deal with current assets and their cyclical short-term movements: cash → inventory → sales → accounts receivable → cash. The bank places emphasis on the balance sheet for these types of loans due to their asset conversion repayment basis.
      1. Types: Revolving lines of credit, nonrevolving lines— primarily to support seasonal inventory/accounts receivable needs—secured by inventory or accounts receivable—maybe unsecured—fees—compensating balances—yearly or more frequent review—annual or biannual payout. Used to obtain discounts, that is, 1 percent 10 Net 30 = 18%/year 360 days/20 day cycle = 18 periods/year at 1 percent each
      2. Time loans—one-time specific cash cycle purpose. For example, large manufacturing job, substantial up-front material purchases—15 days for materials, 45 days to construct, 30-day billing terms—request a 90-day note. Due to short-term, fixed rates are often quoted; usually doesn't exceed 120 days and sometimes are renewable; loan can be unsecured or secured
      3. Accounts receivable financing (asset-based lending) —typically higher rates—prime + 3 to 4 percent— fees—labor intensive, direct accounts receivable verification; accounts receivable are aged (current, 30, 60, 90 +) then qualified. Those under 60 days—bank advances 60 to 80 percent of qualified accounts receivable; accounts receivable payments directed to bank-controlled lock box for daily processing; normally

performed by a larger bank with an asset-based lending dept.

4. Inventory financing (asset-based lending); also higher rates charged—fees; either outside warehouse firm or an employee bonded by the warehousing firm verifies daily the flow of inventory in and out (raw, in-process, and finished); advances made on agreed percent of manufacturing cost, 40% to 60 percent; many times used in conjunction with accounts receivable financing

5. Floor plan—type of inventory financing, that is, autos, appliances—invoice financed—unannounced floor plan checks—bank holds trust receipts; automated drafting (electronic) system from manufacturers— result of their desire to speed up cash cycle.

C. Cash flow loans—long-term loans. Cash flow is net profit after tax + depreciation + amortization. Cash flow is made up of many cash cycle components. Cash flow determines the ability to support long term assets with long-term debt service. The bank places most of the repayment analysis on the operating statement for these loans.

1. Real estate loans—term 15 years for commercial property, sometimes 20 years. Variable rate or short-term fixed rate but adjustable every 1 to 3 years. Range from 1 to 2.50% over prime (prime versus base). Commitment fees. Requirements may include plot plans or surveys, title insurance and engineering soil sampling; note may have demand features or call options, and prepayment penalties. Bank will advance 70% to 80 percent of appraised value as determined by independent appraisal firm. Advance is less if single purpose building, that is, greenhouse

2. Other fixed assets—machinery and equipment; term is normally five years or less—financed over the useful or depreciable life. The variable rate range is 1.5% to 3.5% over the index; banks will finance 70% to 80 percent of cost

3. Working capital loans—permanent working capital should cover business seasonal low point; if not, additional capital is needed; working capital is the difference

between current assets and current liabilities; the lack of an adequate working capital base is one of the primary reasons for business failure. The right amount of capital varies according to each business. Working capital is a function of sales volume, the percent of cash versus credit sales, the rate of inventory turn and the rate of accounts receivable turn as well as the terms and amount of credit supplied by banks and trade creditors (trade credit is the largest single source of credit in the world); the term is normally three years or less

4. Term loan agreements—accompany the normal loan documents and recite certain positive or negative covenants in consideration of the bank approving the loan, that is, minimum financial ratios, type and frequency of financial statements, salary restrictions, dividend restrictions, life insurance requirements, management and/or owner change restrictions, and negative borrowing or pledging restrictions are most common

III. Internal cash sources—no loan needed
   A. Improve accounts receivable collection
      1. Frequency of statements
      2. Good follow-up system—letter and phone contact
      3. Discounts don't work—taken anyway
   B. Improve inventory turn
      1. Dispose of slow-moving items
      2. FIFO (first-in, first-out) to LIFO (last-in, first-out) inventory valuation change with accountant—LIFO increases cost of goods sold, decreases gross profit and therefore reduces taxes during inflationary periods.
      3. Remember to increase all inventory when your price increases, if goal is to retain the same margin
      4. Make use of significant discounts
      5. Evaluate seasonal inventory—wait until next year?
      6. Evaluate inventory composition and turn of each component
   C. Fixed assets—dispose of seldom-used equipment—proceeds to working capital—rent the machine if seldom

used—decide what/where your market is— perhaps you pass up some business
  D. Accounts payable—pay on time, not before or after they are due. Always maintain cash for the unexpected
  E. As an exception, ask trade creditors for extended terms— compare to bank financing
  F. Progress payments—if the market will allow; a progress payment can enable you to discount the material purchase

IV. How to apply for a bank loan
  A. Small business association material explanation
  B. Business plan
  C. Local help is available

 V. How the bank processes the loan request
  A. 5 "C's" of credit: character, credit, capacity, collateral, and capital
    1. Credit—research industry, obtain background and trends
      a. Check trade, bank and personal references
      b. Check D&B and credit bureau
    2. Character—call personal references
      a. call attorney and accountant
      b. Management experience and education—prove it!
      c. Management team and adequacy of management succession—need for life policy
      d. Entity—sole proprietorship, corporation, or partnership (2 types), partnership agreements, corporate by-laws, resolutions, and buy-out agreements
    3. Collateral—banks like as much as possible
      a. Determine value—cost, replacement, or market value?
      b. Use of expert appraisers, some done by bank, some done by independent bank-approved, outside appraisers, for example use of real estate expert who may approach the value from cost/replacement, market, or income-capitalization methods, or any applicable combination
      c. Insurance limits check against value
      d. Title checked—Search for personal property or title

search requested of borrower's attorney if real property

4. Capacity—analysis of the financial statements and/or
    projections

    a. Internal comparison—spread several years—trend
        analysis

    b. Ratios and general rules of thumb: current 2:1;
        quick (acid test) 1:1; sales/receivables: 12 times; cost
        of goods sold/inventory—by industry; accounts
        payable turn—match to trade credit offered; sales/
        working capital—by industry; inventory reliance
        percent—trends; officer compensation/sales— by
        industry; term loan repayment ability—1.5:1—
        built in cushion for unknown and unfavorable
        events; debt/worth—normal comfort level is 4 or
        5:1; many other ratios depending on industry

    c. Pro forma—projections using assumed information
        and/or new request blended into existing financial
        information for both the P&L statement and balance
        sheet; cash flow statement is projected inflow and
        outflow of cash (i.e., check book) over a period of
        time normally shown on a monthly or quarterly ba-
        sis; be realistic and use the commonsense approach.
        "Dream Sheets" (e.g. research industry margins
        and key financial ratios), research expenses, obtain
        quotes of backup for projected expenses, build in a
        cushion, figure expenses high (do you have a contin-
        gency for the varying cost of money), and be conser-
        vative with income projections. Offer your back up
        plans if projections are wrong; *banks recommend
        that borrowers make use of financial advisors and/or
        an accountant and attorney especially with a new
        business*

    d. Bank looks for primary and secondary repayment
        sources, that is, term loan repayment: primary—the
        business cash flow; secondary—independent in-
        come stream of the principal or cash reserve or asset
        liquidation. Know the bank looks for both. Offer
        your plans for both!

5. Capital—equity contribution from 10 to 30 percent of total needs is required; banks don't finance intangibles, i.e. goodwill, covenant not to compete; covered by borrower's capital and/or seller financing (benefits of seller financing: Taxes on capital gains and lower borrowing costs); banks want 25 to 30 percent equity—bank may not include all seller financing toward required equity.

VI. The cost of money
   A. The interest rate for the loan is a function of risk, either real or as perceived by the banker, through the loan presentation and/or business plan
   B. Generally—fixed rates (if available) cost more than floating rates, long-term money costs more than short-term money, start-up situations are more expensive to finance than established businesses, and secured loan rates are lower than unsecured loan rates
   C. Credit is given for overall bank relationships and, specifically, interest-free balances (business checking accounts)
   D. Banks utilize loan-grading and rating systems as a component—competition is another
   E. Rates may be negotiated or at least an attempt may be made
   F. The loan rate should change as the business changes, either higher or lower. Ask about the rate at the annual review of business statements. It may take several years to change a rate.

VII. How long does the decision take?
   A. Response is quicker with existing customers because of the bank's experience with the company and current financial information should be on file—immediate to two weeks
   B. Start-up businesses take longer due to bank's desire to become familiar with all aspects of the business; banks will normally undertake start-up situations only with assistance of small business association (SBA) or similar programs; banks are not in the venture capital business; without the reduction in risk as provided by an agency like SBA, start-up situations offer too many unknowns and variables and the repayment of the loan depends solely upon the pro-

jected success of the business. This is a venture capital risk, not a conventional bank loan risk. Two weeks to several months depending upon complexity and number of agencies involved

C. SBA Certified Lender Program (CLP)—three-day turn-around once bank submits loan to SBA. Rates: 7 years or less, maximum rate lowest New York prime + 2.25 percent, more than 7 years lowest New York prime + 2.75 percent, SBA will also consider 7-year term financing for working capital and equipment and will assume a greater risk than a bank

D. Read and understand the commitment letter—don't be afraid to ask questions

VIII. Conclusion

A. Keep your banker informed, both good and bad; bankers don't like surprises

B. Ask the opinion of your financial advisors before you act; two or three heads are better than one

C. You must take the next step; ask for assistance

D. Business is not for everyone; however, you'll never know unless you explore your business plans with the human resources available to you; *this will be your business—no one will do the work for you—the plan of action is ultimately yours!*

INFORMATION FOR THE LENDER

Although there are a number of ways to prepare a presentation to accompany a loan application, here are some points that should be considered in preparing such a presentation:

Summary of Highlights

1. Purpose for which funds are to be used and information to substantiate the need

2. Security or collateral/original cost and present market value

3. Nature of the business

4. Total capital need and amount of loan request
5. How and when funds will be repaid (cash flow, liquidation of assets, cash cycle)

History of the Business

1. Type of organization, date organized, and names of principles
2. Background of each of the principals and personal financial statements

Management

1. Chart of organization and manner in which management is functioning
2. Ages of key managers and ability to provide management continuity
3. Information on insurance held including officer's life, key man, stock redemption, and disability insurance

Business Activities

1. Products or services sold
2. Credit terms, sales policies, and distribution methods
3. Territories covered and important customers
4. Competitive situation and new product information
5. Number of employees
6. Trade and bank references

Physical Facilities

1. Description of plant and equipment and whether they are owned or leased, including original cost and present market value
2. Adequacy of plant and equipment
3. Availability of sources of supply of materials and labor
4. Future needs for plant and equipment

Professionally Prepared Financial Statements

1. Current balance sheet including an aging of accounts receivable and accounts payable, and statement of profit and loss including accountant's opinion

2. Cash flow statement

3. Comparative balance sheets and operating statements for previous three year-ends

4. Projected statement of profit and loss cash flow projections for period of the loan amortization

5. List of professional advisors

B

Sources of Help

Donald J. Dubendorf	Attorney	Williamstown, MA
Thomas Gajda	CPA/Accountant	Williamstown, MA
Daniel O'Brien	Berkshire Bank	North Adams, MA
Gail King	Northern Berkshire Development Corp.	Adams, MA
Lee Schwartz	SCORE	Menlo Park, CA
Knute Westerland	First Vermont Bank	Bennington, VT
Joe Dolan	Coakley, Pierpan, Dolan, and Collins	North Adams, MA
Victor Kiam	Remington Products	Fairfield, CT
Andrew Hunter	Consultant	Wellesley, MA
Ed Stern	Hilary House Publishers	New York, NY
Prescot Kelley	Gold Collection	Redding, CT
Jim Edgar	Edgar, Dunn, and Company	San Francisco, CA
Martin Greif	Main Street Press	Pittstown, NJ

John Suhler	Veronis, Suhler Assoc.	New York, NY
Tom Frenz, President	List Advisor	Massapequa, NY
Frank Kirkpatrick	J. H. Hapgood's	Peru, VT
Cecil Hoge	Huber, Hoge Assoc.	St. James, NY
Ron Hume	Hume Associates	Toronto, Canada
John Ladd	Ladd Associates	San Francisco, CA
Dick Benson	Consultant	Savannah, GA
Al Goodloe	Intl. Direct Marketing	New York, NY
Gene Cowell	Gene Cowell Assoc.	Woodstock, VT
Sandy Clark	Clark Direct	New York, NY
Robert A. Sawyer	Sawyer Direct	Rye, NY
Bill Black	The McNamee Consulting Company, Inc.	New York, NY
Stan Fenvessey	Fenvessey Assoc.	New York, NY
Jack Beardsley	Fulfillment Production Systems	Middlesex, NJ
Richard King	The McCall Publishing Co.	New York, NY
Richard Leventer	Hearst Magazines	New York, NY
M. Lee Vander Waal	JC Penney	New York, NY
Robert E. Overton	Overton Direct Marketing Services	Houston, TX
Kurt Medina	National Liberty	Philadelphia, PA
Walter Marshall	CMS	New York, NY
Bernice Bush	List Management	Huntington Beach, CA

Richard Jordan	Richard Jordan Creative Services	Bronxville, NY
Lillian Katz	Lillian Vernon's	Mt. Vernon, NY
Sally Reich	Reich Associates	New York, NY
Robert M. Sabloff	Consultant	Springfield, VT

C

SBA Regional Offices

ALABAMA

908 S. 20th St., Rm. 202
Birmingham, AL 35256
(205) 254-1344

ALASKA

701 C St.
Anchorage, AK 99513
(907) 271-4022

101 12th Ave.
Fairbanks, AK 99701
(907) 452-1951

ARIZONA

3030 N. Central Ave., Rm. 1201
Phoenix, AZ 85012
(602) 241-2200

301 W. Congress St., Rm. 3V
Tucson, AZ 85701
(602) 762-6715

ARKANSAS

320 W. Capitol Ave.
Little Rock, AR 72201
(501) 378-5871

CALIFORNIA

2202 Monterey St.
Fresno, CA 93721
(209) 487-5189

1515 Clay St., Rm. 215
Oakland, CA 94612
(415) 273-7790

350 S. Figueroa St., 6th Fl.
Los Angeles, CA 90071
(213) 688-2956

660 J St., Rm. 215
Sacramento, CA 95814
(916) 440-2956

880 Front St., Rm. 4-S-29
San Diego, CA 92118
(714) 293-5540

450 Golden Gate Ave.
San Francisco, CA 94102
(415) 556-7487

211 Main St., 4th Fl.
San Francisco, CA 94105
(415) 556-7490

2700 N. Main St.
Santa Ana, CA 92701
(714) 547-5089

COLORADO

721 19th St., Rm. 407
Denver, CO 80202
(303) 837-2607

1405 Curtis St., 22nd Fl.
Denver, CO 80202
(303) 837-5763

CONNECTICUT

One Hartford Square West
Hartford, CT 06106
(203) 244-3600

DELAWARE

844 King St., Rm. 5207
Wilmington, DE 19801
(302) 573-6294

DISTRICT OF COLUMBIA

1111 18th St. N.W., 6th Fl.
Washington, DC 20417
(202) 653-6963

FLORIDA

400 W. Bay St., Rm. 261
Jacksonville, FL 32202
(904) 791-3782

2222 Ponce de Leon Blvd.,
5th Fl.
Miami, FL 33134
(305) 350-5521

700 Twiggs St., Rm. 607
Tampa, FL 33602
(813) 228-2594

100 S. Narcissus St.
West Palm Beach, FL 33401
(305) 659-7533

GEORGIA

1375 Peachtree St., N.E., 5th Fl.
Atlanta, GA 30367
(404) 881-4999

1720 Peachtree Rd., N.W.,
6th Fl.
Atlanta, GA 30309
(404) 881-4749

52 N. Main St.
Stateboro, GA 30458
(912) 489-8719

GUAM

Pacific Daily News Bldg.,
Rm. 508
Agana, GU 96910
(671) 477-8420

HAWAII

200 Ala Mona, Rm. 2213
Honolulu, HI 96850
(808) 546-8950

IDAHO

1005 Main St., 2nd Fl.
Boise, ID 83102
(208) 334-1696

ILLINOIS

219 S. Dearborn St., Rm. 838
Chicago, IL 60604
(312) 353-0355

219 S. Dearborn St., Rm. 438
Chicago, IL 60604
(312) 353-4528

Four North, Old State
Capital Plaza
Springfield, IL 62701
(217) 492-4416

INDIANA

575 N. Pennsylvania St.,
Rm. 552
Indianapolis, IN 46204
(317) 269-7000

501 East Monroe St., Rm. 120
South Bend, IN 46601
(219) 232-8163

IOWA

373 Collins Rd., N.E.
Cedar Rapids, IA 52402
(319) 399-2571

210 Walnut St., Rm. 749
Des Moines, IA 50309
(515) 284-4422

KANSAS

110 E. Waterman St.
Wichita, KS 67202
(316) 269-6571

KENTUCKY

600 Federal Pl., Rm. 188
Louisville, KY 40201
(502) 582-5971

LOUISIANA

1001 Howard Ave., 17th Fl.
New Orleans, LA 70113
(504) 589-6685

500 Fannin St., Rm. 5B06
Shreveport, LA 70113
(318) 226-5196

MAINE

40 Western Ave., Rm. 512
Augusta, ME 04330
(207) 622-6171

MARYLAND

8600 La Salle Rd., Rm. 630
Towson, MD 21204
(301) 962-4392

MASSACHUSETTS

60 Batterymarch St., 10th Fl.
Boston, MA 02110
(617) 223-3204

150 Causeway St., 10th Fl.
Boston, MA 02114
(617) 223-3224

302 High St., 4th Fl.
Holyoke, MA 01040
(413) 536-8770

MICHIGAN

477 Michigan Ave.
Detroit, MI 48226
(313) 226-6000

200 W. Washington St., Rm. 310
Marquette, MI 49885
(906) 225-1108

MINNESOTA

100 N. 6th St.
Minneapolis, MN 55403
(612) 725-2358

MISSISSIPPI

111 Fred Haise Blvd., 2nd Fl.
Biloxi, MS 39530
(601) 435-3676

100 W. Capitol St., Ste. 322
Jackson, MS 30201
(601) 960-4378

MISSOURI

911 Walnut St., 23rd Fl.
Kansas City, MO 64106
(816) 374-5288

1150 Grande Ave., 5th Fl.
Kansas City, MO 64106
(816) 374-3416

One Mercantile Tower,
Rm. 2500
St. Louis, MO 63101
(314) 425-6600

731-A N. Main St.
Sikeston, MO 63801
(314) 471-0223

309 N. Jefferson, Rm. 150
Springfield, MO 65083
(417) 864-7670

MONTANA

301 S. Park Ave., Rm. 528
Helena, MT 59601
(406) 449-5381

NEBRASKA

19th & Farnum St., 2nd Fl.
Omaha, NE 68102
(402) 221-4691

NEVADA

301 E. Stewart
Las Vegas, NV 89101
(702) 385-6611

50 S. Virginia St., Rm. 114
Reno, NV 89505
(702) 784-5268

NEW HAMPSHIRE

55 Pleasant St., Rm. 211
Concord, NH 03301
(603) 224-4041

NEW JERSEY

1800 E. Daves St.
Camden, NJ 08104
(609) 757-5183

970 Broad St., Rm. 1635
Newark, NJ 07102
(201) 645-2434

NEW MEXICO

5000 Marble Ave., N.E.,
Rm. 320
Albuquerque, NM 87100
(505) 766-3430

NEW YORK

445 Broadway, Rm. 236-A
Albany, NY 12207
(518) 472-6300

111 W. Huron St., Rm. 1311
Buffalo, NY 14202
(716) 846-4301

180 Clemens Center Prkwy,
Rm. 412
Elmira, NY 14901
(607) 733-4686

35 Pinelawn Rd., Rm. 102E
Melville, NY 11747
(516) 454-0750

26 Federal Plaza, Rm. 3100
New York, NY 10278
(212) 264-4355

26 Federal Plaza, Rm. 29-118
New York, NY 10278
(212) 264-7772

100 State St., Rm. 601
Rochester, NY 14614
(716) 263-6700

100 S. Clinton St., Rm. 1071
Syracuse, NY 13260
(315) 423-5383

NORTH CAROLINA

230 S. Wryon St., Rm. 700
Charlotte, NC 28202
(704) 371-6563

215 S. Evans St., Rm. 206
Greenville, NC 27834
(919) 752-3798

NORTH DAKOTA

657 2nd Ave., N., Rm. 218
Fargo, ND 58108
(701) 237-5771

Оню

550 Main St., Rm. 5028
Cincinnati, OH 45202
(513) 684-2814

1240 E. 9th St., Rm. 317
Cleveland, OH 44199
(216) 552-4194

85 Marconi Blvd.
Columbus, OH 43215
(614) 469-6860

OKLAHOMA

200 N.W. 5th St., Rm. 670
Oklahoma City, OK 73102
(405) 231-4301

333 W. 4th St., Rm. 3104
Tulsa, OK 74103
(918) 581-7495

OREGON

1220 S.W. 3rd Ave., Rm. 676
Portland, OR 97204
(503) 294-2682

PENNSYLVANIA

231 St. Asaphs Rd., Ste. 400
Bala Cynwyd, PA 19004
(215) 596-5889

100 Chestnut St., Ste. 309
Harrisburg, PA 17101
(717) 782-3840

960 Pennsylvania Ave., 5th Fl.
Pittsburgh, PA 15222
(412) 644-2780

20 N. Pennsylvania Ave.
Wilkes-Barre, PA 18702
(717) 826-6497

PUERTO RICO

Carlos Chardon Ave., Rm. 691
Hato Rey, PR 00919
(809) 753-4572

RHODE ISLAND

40 Fountain St.
Providence, RI 02903
(401) 528-4580

SOUTH CAROLINA

1835 Assembly, 3rd Fl.
Columbia, SC 29202
(803) 765-5376

SOUTH DAKOTA

515 9th St., Rm. 246
Rapid City, SD 57701
(605) 343-5074

125 S. State St., Rm. 2237
Sioux Falls, SD 57102
(605) 336-2980

TENNESSEE

502 S. Gay St., Rm. 307
Knoxville, TN 37902
(615) 637-9300

167 N. Main St., Rm. 211
Memphis, TN 38103
(901) 521-3588

404 James Robertson Prky.,
Rm. 1012
Nashville, TN 37219
(615) 251-5881

TEXAS

300 E. 8th St.
Austin, TX 78701
(512) 397-5288

3105 Leopard St.
Corpus Christi, TX 78408
(512) 888-3331

1100 Commerce St., Rm. 3C36
Dallas, TX 75242
(214) 767-0605

1720 Regal Row, Rm. 230
Dallas, TX 75235
(214) 767-7643

4100 Rio Bravo, Rm. 300
El Paso, TX 79902
(915) 543-7586

501 W. 10th St., Rm. 527
Ft. Worth, TX 76102
(817) 334-3971

222 E. Van Buren St.
Harlingen, TX 78550
(512) 423-8934

2525 Murworth, Rm. 112
Houston, TX 77054
(713) 226-4341

1205 Texas Ave., Rm. 712
Lubbock, TX 79401
(806) 762-7466

100 S. Washington St.,
Rm. G-12
Marshall, TX 75670
(214) 935-5257

727 E. Durango St., Rm. A-513
San Antonio, TX 78206
(512) 229-6250

U.S. VIRGIN ISLANDS

Veterans Dr., Rm. 283
St. Thomas, USVI 00801
(809) 774-8530

UTAH

125 S. State St., Rm. 2237
Salt Lake City, UT 84138
(801) 524-5800

VERMONT

87 State St., Rm. 204
Montpelier, VT 05602
(802) 229-0538

VIRGINIA

400 N. 8th St., Rm. 3015
Richmond, VA 23240
(804) 771-2617

WASHINGTON

710 2nd Ave., 5th Fl.
Seattle, WA 98104
(206) 442-5676

915 2nd Ave., Rm. 1744
Seattle, WA 98174
(206) 442-5534

W. 920 Riverside Ave., Rm. 651
Spokane, WA 99210
(509) 456-5310

WEST VIRGINIA

Charleston National Plaza,
Ste. 628
Charleston, WV 25301
(304) 343-6181

109 N. 3rd St., Rm. 302
Clarksburg, WV 26301
(304) 623-5631

WISCONSIN

500 S. Barstow St., Rm. B9AA
Eau Claire, WI 54701
(715) 834-9012

212 E. Washington Ave.,
Rm. 213
Madison, WI 53703
(608) 264-5205

517 E. Wisconsin Ave., Rm. 252
Milwaukee, WI 53202
(414) 291-3941

WYOMING

100 E. B St., Rm. 4001
Casper, WY 82601
(307) 265-5550

Bibliography

Baty, Gordon. *Entrepreneurship for the Eighties*. Reston, VA: Reston Publishing, 1981.

The Challenge of Growth: The Fourth Annual Conference on Entrepreneurship. May 18, 1985, Stanford Center for Entrepreneurship, Stanford, California.

Cohen, William A. *The Entrepreneur and Small Business Problem Solver: An Encyclopedic Reference and Guide*. New York: Ronald Press, 1983.

Kiam, Victor. *Going For It!: How to Succeed as an Entrepreneur*. New York: Morrow, 1986.

Lowry, Albert J. *How to Become Financially Successful by Owning Your Own Business*. New York: Simon & Schuster, 1982.

Nierenberg, Gerard. *The Art of Negotiating: Psychological Strategies for Gaining Advantageous Bargains*. New York: Hawthorn Books, 1969.

Osgood, William R. *Basics of Successful Business Planning*. AMACOM, 1980.

Smith, Randy Baca. *Setting Up Shop: The Dos and Don'ts of Starting a Small Business*. New York: McGraw-Hill, 1982.

Steingold, Fred S. *Practical Legal Guide for Small Business*. Englewood Cliffs, NJ: Prentice-Hall, 1982.

Index